IRRIGATING DESERTS

D1564433

Water will gush forth in the wilderness and streams in the desert. Isaiah 35:6

IRRIGATING DESERTS

C. S. LEWIS ON EDUCATION

JOEL D. HECK

CONCORDIA PUBLISHING HOUSE · SAINT LOUIS

ACADEMIC PRESS

*This book is dedicated to my wife, Cheryl, my sons, Peter and Alan,
and my daughter, Brenda, all of whom have taught me much
(this book is about education!) during our years together, especially
in the living out of our common faith in Jesus Christ.*

*This book was completed with the generous assistance
of the 2004 Clyde S. Kilby Research Grant from the Marion E. Wade Center,
Wheaton College, Wheaton, Illinois*

Published by Concordia Academic Press, a division of Concordia Publishing House
3558 S. Jefferson Avenue, St. Louis, MO 63118-3968
1-800-325-3040 • www.cph.org

Manufactured in the United States of America

Library of Congress Cataloging-in-Publication Data
Heck, Joel D., 1948–
Irrigating deserts : C. S. Lewis on education / Joel D. Heck.
p. cm.
Includes bibliographical references (p.   ).
ISBN 0-7586-0044-5
1. Lewis, C. S. (Clive Staples), 1898–1963. 2. Education—Philosophy.
3. College teaching—England—History—20th century. I. Title.
LB775.L423H43 2006
370'.1—dc22
2005032168

1 2 3 4 5 6 7 8 9 10   15 14 13 12 11 10 09 08 07 06

CONTENTS

Part III: C. S. Lewis as a Teacher

PERMISSIONS AND ACKNOWLEDGMENTS

right © 1992, 1979 by James T. Como, reprinted by permission of Harcourt, Inc.

Excerpts from *An Experiment in Criticism* by C. S. Lewis reprinted with the permission of Cambridge University Press.

Excerpts from *A History of Magdalene College Cambridge, 1428–1988* by Peter Cunich, David Hoyle, Eamon Duffy, and Ronald Hyam. Cambridge: Magdalene College Publications, 1994. By kind permission of the master and Fellows, Magdalene College, Cambridge.

Excerpts from *The Letters of C. S. Lewis*, by C. S. Lewis, copyright © 1966 by W. H. Lewis and the Executors of C. S. Lewis and renewed 1994 by C. S. Lewis PTE Ltd., reprinted by permission of Harcourt, Inc.

Excerpts from *A Preface to Paradise Lost* by C. S. Lewis (1942) used with permission of Oxford University Press.

Excerpts from *In Search of C. S. Lewis*, edited by Stephen Schofield, used with the kind permission of Bridge-Logos Publishing.

Excerpts from *Jack: A Life of C. S. Lewis* by George Sayer. Reproduced by permission of Hodder and Stoughton Limited, copyright 1988. US rights used by permission of Crossway Books, a division of Good News Publishers, Wheaton, Illinois 60187, www.crosswaybooks.org.

Excerpt from *K. B. McFarlane: Letters to Friends, 1940–1966*. Magdalen College, Oxford, copyright 1997. Edited by Gerald Harriss. Reproduced by permission of Magdalen College, Oxford.

C. S. Lewis, *Letters to an American Lady*, copyright 1967 William B. Eerdmans Publishing Company. Reprinted by permission of William B. Eerdmans Publishing Company.

Excerpts from James Patrick, *The Magdalen Metaphysicals: Idealism and Orthodoxy at Oxford, 1901–1945*, reprinted by permission of Mercer University Press.

Excerpt from "No Glory, Please, I'm Cringing," by John Leyerle in *The Canadian C. S. Lewis Journal*, No. 3 (January 1979): 12.

C. S. Lewis, *The Pilgrim's Regress*, copyright 1958 William B. Eerdmans Publishing Company. Reprinted by permission of William B. Eerdmans Publishing Company.

Excerpts from *Present Concerns*, copyright © 1986 by C. S. Lewis Pte. Ltd., reprinted by permission of Harcourt, Inc.

Excerpts from *Recollections of a Tour Made in Scotland* by Dorothy Wordsworth. Reprinted by permission of Yale University Press, copyright 1997.

Excerpts from the unpublished diary of J. O. Reed, Manchester, England. Reprinted by permission of J. O. Reed.

Excerpts from *Studies in Medieval and Renaissance Literature* by C. S. Lewis, copyright 1966, 1998, reprinted with the permission of Cambridge University Press.

ACKNOWLEDGMENTS

Thanks to several people who read portions of the manuscript and made helpful suggestions: Steve Beebe, Michael Butterworth, Beryl Dunsmoir, Johnny Humphreys, Margaret Humphreys, Dorothy Kramer, Angus J. L. Menuge, James and Pollyanna West, and especially Paul Piehler (Magdalen College, Oxford, 1949–1952), Gene Edward Veith, Michael Ward, and my editor, Dawn Weinstock. Thanks are also owed to several Englishmen who allowed me to interview them at Magdalene College and St. John's College, Cambridge: Dr. Ronald Hyam, Bishop Simon Barrington-Ward, Dr. Richard Luckett, and Dr. George Watson. I would like to thank Dr. Robin Darwall-Smith, the archivist at Magdalen College, Oxford, whose kind assistance was indispensable, and Marjorie Lamp Mead, Christopher Mitchell, and their colleagues at the Marion E. Wade Center at Wheaton College, Wheaton, Illinois, for the use of their research library to learn more about Oxford and Cambridge during the Lewis years. The week I spent with my daughter in Wheaton was thereby made even more enjoyable. The center also awarded me the 2004 Clyde S. Kilby Research Grant, which allowed me to complete this book.

In addition, I must thank several Oxford alumni who responded to my plea in the *Magdalen Newsletter* and *Oxford Today* for reminiscences of C. S. Lewis: Charles Arnold-Baker (Magdalen College, 1939–1940), A. E. F. Davis (Magdalen College, 1947–1950), Edward L. Edmonds (University College, 1934–1937), Pamela Egan (Somerville College, 1952–1955), Ursula K. Everest (Somerville College, 1941–1944), Michael Figgis (Queen's College, 1946–1948), F. L. Hunt (Ruskin College, 1951–1952; Magdalen College, 1953–1954), D. M. Lewis (St. Hilda's College, 1941–1944), Hugh Whitney Morrison (Merton College, 1930–1934), J. O. Reed (Magdalen College, 1949–1952), D. J. Ritchie (Magdalen College, 1940–1942), Geoffrey Stone (Magdalen College, 1949–1952), Donald Whittle (Magdalen College, 1943, 1947–1949), and Charles Wrong (Magdalen College, 1935–1938). They have graciously allowed me to incorporate their recollections of C. S. Lewis the educator into this book.

INTRODUCTION

This book has grown out of a practice which was at first my necessity and later my hobby; whether at last it has attained the dignity of a study, others must decide. —C. S. Lewis, *Studies in Words*[1]

In one of the best-known quotations in the writings of C. S. Lewis, Professor Kirke asked no one in particular, "I wonder what they *do* teach them at these schools."[2] Earlier in *The Lion, the Witch, and the Wardrobe*, Kirke asked, "Why don't they teach logic at these schools?"[3] That certain subjects are worth studying we learn from Cor (also known as Shasta), who gave Bree a list of subjects he would be studying: reading, writing, heraldry, dancing, history, and music.[4] But we learn relatively little about Lewis's educational views by reading the Chronicles of Narnia except that he had questions about the quality of some schools, about the type of history that is taught, and some thoughts about shaping a curriculum.

Well-known from *Surprised by Joy* are Lewis's fond reminiscences of his time with W. T. Kirkpatrick and his bad memories of Wynyard School and Malvern College. The more than casual reader of Lewis knows of the alternate title to *The Abolition of Man*, namely, *Reflections on Education with Special Reference to the Teaching of English in the Upper Forms of Schools*. In that book Lewis explained some of the major problems with modern education. Less well-known is the fact that the hero of the Space Trilogy was an educator, a philologist, and a Fellow (see Glossary) from one of the colleges of Cambridge.[5]

But what else do people know about Lewis's views on education? We know Lewis as the creator of Narnia, the Christian apologist, a poet, a novelist, a literary critic, and the subject of the film *Shadowlands*. However, Lewis was first and foremost an educator, an Oxford don (see Glossary), a tutor of Magdalen (pronounced *maudlin*) College, Oxford, and later a professor of Magdalene College, Cambridge. In this book, therefore, I intend to look more closely and more systematically at the views of Lewis on education as they are expressed in various places in his writings and in the reminiscences of people who knew him. I will also summarize the education Lewis received, the educational environment in which he worked, and the way in which he taught, including information about his colleagues and the intellectual climate of Oxford and Cambridge. Such an exploration will help us to understand better the reasons for Lewis's own views on education. I intend, furthermore, to ask what we can learn from Lewis for the educational endeavor today.

For the frequent reader of C. S. Lewis, we will traverse rather familiar territory, though only the territory that has relevance for Lewis's educational views. We will gain insights into the Oxbridge system of education. We will see various references to education gathered widely from the Lewis corpus into one place. We will begin to see a Lewis whom most have seen only in glimpses.

As to the title of this book, *Irrigating Deserts*, the phrase appears in *The Abolition of Man*, where Lewis wrote: "The task of the modern educator is not to cut down jungles but to irrigate deserts."[6] He contended that education was not so much a matter of pulling out the weeds of false knowledge and ways of thinking but a matter of encouraging learners, stimulating their thinking, helping them to add to their knowledge and to broaden their ways of thinking. Education is far more a positive venture than a negative one. No wonder that John Wain, in reviewing Lewis's *English Literature in the Sixteenth Century* for the *Spectator*, would say that Lewis wrote "now as always, as if inviting us to a feast."[7]

The task of the educator is to irrigate the deserts of the mind, to make the deserts bloom with the blessings of wisdom and knowledge, as the prophet Isaiah wrote of the coming of the Messiah: "Water will gush forth in the wilderness and streams in the desert" (Isaiah 35:6). If anything shines forth from the writings of C. S. Lewis, it is his commitment to truth, especially the transcendent truth found in the Christian faith.

Chapter 1 will give us insight into the brilliant mind of Lewis, demonstrating the God-given intellectual ability that made his career possible.

Chapters 2 and 3 form the heart of this book, spelling out Lewis's educational philosophy and how he saw that philosophy expressed in the curriculum. In Chapter 4, we see one of the separate but fundamental issues for Lewis's educational philosophy: how we read a printed text. Chapter 5 will look at the education Lewis received while growing up, excluding his education at Oxford. Chapter 6 shows the undergraduate education of Lewis at University College (known as Univ.), Oxford University. We will see how Lewis performed in the Oxford setting, also explaining the preparation he underwent for the university, much of it an irrigating of his own mind. Chapter 7 will introduce C. S. Lewis, the fellow and tutor of Magdalen College. Chapter 8 will highlight Lewis's career at Cambridge, while Chapter 9 will focus on the two chief functions of the Fellow: tutoring and lecturing. Finally, in Chapter 10, we draw some lessons from the life of C. S. Lewis the educator for our lives today.

ONE

THE MIND OF C. S. LEWIS

"[Adam's] mental powers," says St. Augustine, "surpassed those
of the most brilliant philosopher as much as the speed of a bird
surpasses that of a tortoise."—C. S. Lewis, *Preface to Paradise Lost*[1]

Only a truly brilliant mind could have written as deeply and as per-
ceptively and with the same emotional power in each field, and in as
many fields, as did C. S. Lewis. Only a person with a powerful memory, a
clear understanding of different fields of knowledge, and an ability to
integrate those fields of knowledge could have captured the minds and
imaginations of so many people to the point that his books still sell mil-
lions each year, though decades have passed since his death. And the sales
of the Lewis corpus are on the increase!

The brilliance of the mind of C. S. Lewis has been amply emphasized
by virtually everyone who has written about him. The growing size of
the literature about Lewis testifies further to the most widely read man of
his day. Sheldon Vanauken wrote: "His was perhaps the most brilliant
and certainly the most lucid mind we ever knew."[2] George Sayer wrote:
"Everyone recognized the breadth of his knowledge. He was widely read
and had a remarkable memory that enabled him to quote at length from
any author who interested him and even from some who did not."[3]
Richard Ladborough wrote: "It is now common knowledge that his memory was prodigious and that he seemed to have read everything."[4] A
glimpse at Appendix I will show the many volumes Lewis read during the

last years of his undergraduate experience and his first years as an Oxford don. Following Lewis's rise in prominence, stories about the brilliance of this man have been shared, some of them undoubtedly true and some of them perhaps hyperbole.

Portions of Lewis's diary demonstrate a rather detailed memory of conversations he had with various individuals. For example, Lewis recorded a three-page summary of a conversation he had on February 14, 1923, with a fellow undergraduate named Rink.[5] Other excerpts from Lewis's diary illustrate some of the activities that contributed to the development of his mind, for example, his commitment of large segments of notes to memory. In fact, it seems that Lewis routinely memorized large masses of material.[6] Derek Brewer, a former student of Lewis, told this story:

> Once, in the middle of my essay, his phone rang. I stopped, and he answered it in the other room. When he returned after a five-minute interruption, he repeated *verbatim* my last sentence as far as it had got. He had an astonishing verbatim memory and could repeat whole passages of prose to illustrate a point arising in discussion. Given any line in *Paradise Lost*, he could continue with the following lines.[7]

Concerning Lewis's ability to use quotations, Owen Barfield once stated: "It would take too long, and would be too difficult, to illustrate properly the illuminating and enlivening use he made of quotation in general, for which he had a phenomenal memory."[8] And Robert E. Havard, the personal physician of the Lewis brothers and a member of the Inklings (see Glossary), stated: "Lewis, who had read everything and who seemed to remember everything he had read, supported his thesis with inexhaustible quotations."[9]

The most remarkable story about Lewis's ability to retain the contents of virtually any book in his library was told by Kenneth Tynan.

> He had the most astonishing memory of any man I have ever known. In conversation I might have said to him, 'I read a marvelous medieval poem this morning, and I particularly liked this line.' I would then quote the line. Lewis would usually be able to go on to quote the rest of the page. It was astonishing.
>
> Once when I was invited to his rooms after dinner for a glass of beer, he played a game. He directed, 'Give me a number from one to forty.'
>
> I said, 'Thirty.'

He acknowledged, 'Right. Go to the thirtieth shelf in my library.' Then he said, 'Give me another number from one to twenty.'

I answered, 'Fourteen.'

He continued, 'Right. Get the fourteenth book off the shelf. Now let's have a number from one to a hundred.'

I said, 'Forty-six.'

'Now turn to page forty-six! Pick a number from one to twenty-five for the line of the page.'

I said, 'Six.'

'So,' he would say, 'read me that line.' He would always identify it—not only by identifying the book, but he was also usually able to quote the rest of the page.[10]

It would be easier to dismiss this story if it were not for a similar tale that relates events that occurred on Friday, December 3, 1954, the day Lewis gave his last tutorial at Oxford. The English Fellows gave a farewell party that evening for Lewis. In addition to faculty, the event was attended by students of the Florio Society, an undergraduate society at Magdalen College. When asked the nature of his current writing project, Lewis did not say. However, he did say that he was having trouble with writing because he tended to end his paragraphs in iambic pentameter.

"If you *will* end your paragraphs in iambic pentameter," commented Richard Selig, a Rhodes scholar who had also taken tutorials from Lewis, "why do you grumble about it?"

"As usual, Selig, you missed the point," said Lewis. "The difficulty is that I remember everything I ever read, and bits of it pop up uninvited."

"Surely not *everything* you've ever read, Mr. Lewis?"

"Yes, everything, Selig, even the most boring texts."

"What about Lydgate's 'Siege of Thebes,' Mr. Lewis?"

"Give me a line," said Lewis. "You'll have to start me."

Selig went to the college library, returning with a copy of the volume. He opened it at random and began to read.

"Stop!" shouted Lewis. He raised his eyes to the ceiling and continued the passage from memory.[11]

Lewis demonstrated not so much rote memorization, though he had this ability, but what could be called locational reference, the ability to recall the substance and structure of a literary work and the place of an important text within that structure.[12] This would explain J. O. Reed's favorable comment about Lewis's response to a presentation at a meeting of the Socratic Club during the 1951 Trinity term (see Glossary). The Russian professor Nikolas Zernov had presented on Dostoevsky, and Reed later wrote in his diary: "Lewis displays what appears to be a minutely detailed familiarity with Dostoevsky's novels."[13]

The Rev. Dr. Austin Farrer, chaplain of Trinity College, Oxford, in the 1940s, called Lewis's powers of memory and applied knowledge perhaps the greatest and most amazing of his generation.[14] As to his ability in foreign languages, Lewis knew Norse, Old and Middle English, Latin, Greek, French, German, Italian, and Old Welsh.[15] John Walsh, a historian of Magdalene College, Cambridge, wrote: "Lewis seemed not only to have read everything but to have remembered it as well; if one quoted—say—an obscure bit of Calvin, as likely as not he would continue or complete the quotation. He was the best-read man I have ever met, almost too well read."[16]

The nature of Lewis's research in *English Literature in the Sixteenth Century excluding Drama* shows another side of his wide reading. He read everything on which he wrote and is said to have read everything published in English in the sixteenth century and still extant in preparation for writing the book. This volume remains the best-selling book in the Oxford History of English Literature series.

Ronald Hyam, one of Lewis's colleagues at Cambridge during the final three years of his life, remembered a conversation one evening over coffee in the Combination Room. Hyam, who described Lewis as "the most formidably and entertainingly learned don I have ever met,"[17] was worried about a lecture he was to give the following morning because he was not well prepared.

> In desperation I asked him about colour-prejudice in eighteenth-century literature—not expecting much of an answer, since the subject was obviously way outside his normal range of interests. And there was indeed a long and awkward silence. Then, "Of course, you've read Captain Cook's *Journals*?" I hadn't, of course. And he proceeded with gusto to regale me with every possible bit of evidence which could be distilled from this volu-

minous source. I subsequently discovered that his recall had been flawless, omitting nothing which might be relevant to the subject.[18]

To what end did Lewis apply this brilliant mind? Clyde Kilby, who knew Lewis and tried to understand the essence of his brilliance, captured it best. He once wrote that Lewis had two essential qualities: "a deep and vivid imagination" and "a profoundly analytical mind."[19] Lewis himself had written about the two hemispheres of his mind, one "a many-islanded sea of poetry and myth" and the other "a glib and shallow 'rationalism.' "[20] He demonstrated these qualities both in the clear logic of *Mere Christianity* and *The Abolition of Man* and in the soaring imagination of the Chronicles of Narnia and the Space Trilogy. Lewis combined both hemispheres, perhaps preeminently, in *The Pilgrim's Regress*, *The Screwtape Letters*, and *The Great Divorce*, works of great imagination and insightful theology. In these works, Lewis demonstrated the classical education he received at home from W. T. Kirkpatrick and at Oxford University. In his inaugural lecture at Cambridge, in which Lewis claimed to be a dinosaur, able to read as native texts those documents that others had to read as foreigners, he was summarizing a type of education that was becoming exceedingly rare, except under his tutelage, wherein heart and mind were steeped in both poetry and myth, as well as reason and logic. The liberal arts education of the Middle Ages would become far less common as, for example, the concern for the criticism of secondary literature replaced contact with the primary texts and as subjects such as Greek and Latin became less common in the curriculum.

Couple the qualities of imagination and analytical skill with Lewis's prodigious memory, his wide reading, his ability in languages, his training in logic, as well as many other characteristics mentioned elsewhere in this volume, and you have a brilliant mind. Such a mind became a brilliant tool in a life dedicated to the service of God. What did that brilliant mind think about education? To that topic we turn in the next chapters.

PART I

C. S. Lewis on Education

TWO

C. S. Lewis on the Purpose and Practice of Education

The task of the modern educator is not to cut down jungles
but to irrigate deserts.—C. S. Lewis, *Abolition of Man*[1]

In a university setting where learning was a way of life and where great
learning was admired, exalted, and rewarded, how did C. S. Lewis view
education? If we were to extract from his writings both a philosophy and
a practice of education, what would these look like?

For Lewis, extensive discussion of literary theory meant that one had
done too little reading *of* literature and too much reading *about* literature.
For Lewis, literature was a field that did something to you rather than one
in which you did something to or with literature. Lewis's essay "Meditation in a Toolshed" argued that those who have looked *at* things, that is,
those who have analyzed and criticized and moralized, have had it their
way, while those who looked *along* things, that is, who have allowed literature to enable them to see various aspects of life, have received too little
attention. In this conviction Lewis was expressing a part of his educational philosophy, a philosophy for which the primary experience of literature was essential.

In the pages that follow, we will glean from Lewis's writings the philosophy behind his educational practice, a philosophy that made him one
of the most effective speakers, teachers, tutors, and writers of the twenti-

eth century. Although many works will be explored, the primary focus will be on "Our English Syllabus," the single most important piece of Lewis's writing on education.

An important part of Lewis's approach to education comes from the phrase that serves as the title of this book: "irrigating deserts." The phrase appears in Lewis's brief, philosophical work *The Abolition of Man*: "The task of the modern educator is not to cut down jungles but to irrigate deserts."[2] In *An Experiment in Criticism*, Lewis said much the same when he wrote: "The real way of mending a man's taste is not to denigrate his present favorites but to teach him how to enjoy something better."[3] Lewis believed that the task of education was not a matter of cutting down the jungles of false ways of thinking but a matter of stimulating the thinking of learners, helping them to add to their knowledge and improve their method of thinking, assisting them in developing creativity by bringing their imaginations to bear on the task of writing, and raising their sights to appreciate art, literature, music, drama, and other subjects.

"But my mind is no desert! My mind is fertile, capable, and imaginative. Don't insult me with a comparison to a wasteland!" someone might say. To that Lewis would respond that we are all far less than what we could be. Lewis himself once went through a desert before he became a Christian. He wrote of his conversion: "[T]he long inhibition was over, the dry desert lay behind . . . . There was nothing whatever to do about it; no question of returning to the desert."[4]

Lewis tells us that the fundamental problem is not our wrong thinking but our lack of thinking: "[I]t would seem that Our Lord finds our desires, not too strong, but too weak. We are half-hearted creatures, fooling about with drink and sex and ambition when infinite joy is offered us, like an ignorant child who wants to go on making mud pies in a slum because he cannot imagine what is meant by the offer of a holiday at the sea. We are far too easily pleased."[5] Therefore Lewis would have us irrigate the deserts of our minds.

Lewis is simply advocating what thousands have championed for years in a liberal education. This type of education liberates the mind from ignorance, filling it not only with facts and figures but also with critical thinking skills and the ability to communicate, with the appreciation of beauty and a moral sensibility, with problem-solving skills and an understanding of the foundations of Western culture. But irrigating minds is not an easy task. Anyone who has attempted to draw college students out as they study a poem, a text of Scripture, or a mathematical problem knows that students often lack self-confidence. They hesitate to speak and must be encouraged. The same is true at virtually all levels of education. When we fail in the educational task, the learner remains trapped in a thirsty desert, much as the Dwarfs in *The Last Battle*. They would not be taken in; the Dwarfs were for the Dwarfs. Aslan said of the Dwarfs: "Their prison is only in their own minds, yet they are in that prison; and so afraid of being taken in that they cannot be taken out."[6] Dwarf-like students must be challenged, encouraged, shaped, and molded.

Edward Edmonds summarized Lewis's thoughts on education and illustrated his disputative style and high standards when Edmonds cited William Johnson Cory, a master (see Glossary) at Eton in 1875:

> In school you are not engaged so much in acquiring knowledge as in making mental efforts under criticism. A certain amount of knowledge you can indeed, with average facilities, acquire so as to retain, nor need you regret the hours you spend on much that is forgotten, for the shadow of lost knowledge at least protects you from many illusions. But you go to a great school not so much for knowledge as for arts and habits; for the habit of attention, for the art of expression, for the art of assuming at a moment's notice a new intellectual position, for the habit of submitting to censure and refutation, for the art of indicating assent or dissent in graduated terms, for the art of working out what is possible in a given time, for discrimination, for mental courage and mental sobriety.[7]

According to Lewis, too much stock is put in literary criticism (i.e., cutting down jungles), especially of the F. R. Leavis type,[8] when compared with the actual reading of literature (i.e., irrigating deserts). We have too many axes to grind when we teach history, so Lewis spoke out against historicism. We have too many personal red herrings when we teach science, so Lewis spoke out against scientism. According to Lewis, educators have too many personal positions that are not always matched by the facts that they seek to inculcate in the minds of their students. Many of these facts are the result of chronological snobbery rather than a product of transcendent, timeless, and objective truth. In short, to use Lewis's phrase, we have too many "amateur philosophers" masquerading as literary critics, historians, and scientists.

From the 1930s until the 1960s, F. R. Leavis commanded a great following at Cambridge. His graduates and their followers staffed many positions within the British graduate school system and wrote the enormously popular and influential Penguin History of Literature. Leavis and his followers held that English literature was the post-Christian basis of civilization and individual soul formation and as such required a high standard of discrimination in critical teaching. Condemnation of literature was considered good, whereas appreciation showed gullibility and bad moral character. Leavis and company claimed that the taste of pupils needed correcting (cutting down jungles), while Lewis said that it needed encouraging (irrigating).[9]

Lewis believed that a major shift in education began not at the time of the Renaissance but around the year 1830.[10] He had been persuaded to this position by J. R. R. Tolkien.[11] Lewis's former tutor in English literature, George Stuart Gordon, also held this viewpoint as did H. F. B. Brett-Smith (see Appendix V). According to this position, before 1830 most people had a greater respect for tradition and religion, views expressed in the writings of Jane Austen and Walter Scott, for example, both of whom, for Lewis, concluded that period. The rise of the industrial revolution and its impact upon human thought—whether in the sciences, philosophy, theology, economics, or other areas—caused a major shift in the modern approach to education. Because progress occurred regularly in the fields of science and technology, the *intelligentsia* assumed that progress was also occurring in every other field. Few believed that a new idea might actually cause regression rather than progression. From that point on, "chronological snobbery" carried the day. For Lewis, if one is traveling in the wrong direction, the best solution is to go back, make your correction, then begin in the right direction. It does no good to continue in the wrong direction, even if you are making good progress.

Lewis had a well-developed rational side and an imaginative, or romantic,[12] side—both of which are amply illustrated in *Surprised by Joy* (in which Lewis reviews his early atheism, his course of study in Greats, and Kirk's logical nature, as well as Northernness, poetry, Wagner, and Celtic and Greek mythology[13]) and *The Pilgrim's Regress*.[14] Lewis once described the qualities he most admired about John Gower: "The heart is insular and romantic, the head cool and continental: it is a good combination."[15] For Lewis, both romanticism and reason were supremely compatible with Christianity.

In his teens, Lewis studied with W. T. Kirkpatrick, a man who came close to being pure rational thought, though Lewis did experience glimpses of desire in those years. However, both the youthful Lewis and the adult Lewis, having had his imagination baptized by George MacDonald, saw imagination as one of the keys to communication. Indeed, Lewis once wrote: "The imaginative man in me is older, more continuously operative, and in that sense more basic than either the religious writer or the critic."[16] John Stevens and Raphael Lyne believe that "[h]ere perhaps supremely is the reason for the lasting appeal of all these,"[17] that is, Lewis's literary criticism, apologetic works, and fiction.

We should not be surprised that the imagination held such a high position for Lewis when we realize that the most significant event in Lewis's life—his conversion to Christianity—occurred when his reason and imagination were brought together. In 1931, Hugo Dyson and J. R. R. Tolkien showed Lewis that he greatly appreciated the idea of sacrifice or the idea of the dying and reviving god, provided that he met it anywhere but in the Christian Gospels. Thus Lewis began to see how God had prepared his imagination to find meaning in the truth of the Gospel and, years later, how he might convey that same truth through imaginative stories.[18]

Lewis once wrote: "For me, reason is the natural organ of truth; but imagination is the organ of meaning. Imagination, producing new metaphors or revivifying old, is not the cause of truth, but its condition. It is, I confess, undeniable that such a view indirectly implies a kind of truth or rightness in the imagination itself."[19] It could be stated this way: The intellect especially speaks to the cognitive domain of human learning, while imagination especially speaks to the affective domain of human learning. The former speaks primarily to the head, while the latter speaks primarily (but not exclusively) to the heart.[20] The best in education speaks powerfully to both reason and imagination, and Lewis argued that the story does both.[21] In the ceremony in which Lewis received an honorary Doctor of Divinity from the University of St. Andrews, D. M. Baillie, dean of the Divinity Faculty, described Lewis as a man who reflected "a new kind of marriage between theological reflection and poetic imagination."[22]

Lewis could capture the reader's head with his intellect and the reader's heart with his imagination.

Although imagination is not to be equated with emotion, both imagination and emotion possess a nonrational nature, which is often set alongside reason or intellect. One of Lewis's poems speaks of the interaction between reason and imagination:

> Set on the soul's acropolis the reason stands . . .
> So clear is reason. But how dark, imagining . . .
> Who make in me a concord of the depth and height?
> Who make imagination's dim exploring touch
> Ever report the same as intellectual sight?[23]

In writing against the perspective of *The Green Book*,[24] Lewis stated that the authors felt their job was "to fortify the minds of young people against emotion. My own experience as a teacher tells an opposite tale. For every one pupil who needs to be guarded from a weak excess of sensibility there are three who need to be awakened from the slumber of cold vulgarity. The task of the modern educator is not to cut down jungles but to irrigate deserts."[25] Educators must irrigate deserts, and one of the best ways to do so is to teach an appropriate use of emotion because emotion always aids education, functioning as a servant rather than a master. Elsewhere Lewis quoted Aristotle with approval: "Aristotle says that the aim of education is to make the pupil like and dislike what he ought."[26] Properly trained emotion, whether negative or positive, serves the intellect both by helping the person to avoid that which is bad and to benefit from that which is good. The trained emotion confirms the conclusions of the intellect. Trained emotions are not the same as imagination, of course. However, trained emotions travel in the world of the imagination more easily than in the world of the intellect.

THE PURPOSE OF EDUCATION

Lewis did write about the purpose of education. As we have pointed out previously, Lewis said the *task* of education is to irrigate deserts; however, the *purpose* of education is to produce the good citizen. In support of this, Lewis believed that the purpose of the university is to advocate learning rather than education, knowledge (what Lewis called "the natural food of the human mind"[27]) rather than skills, as the following quotation indicates:

Schoolmasters in our time are fighting hard in defence [*sic*] of education against vocational training; universities, on the other hand, are fighting against education on behalf of learning.

. . . The purpose of education has been described by Milton as that of fitting a man 'to perform justly, skillfully, and magnanimously all the offices both private and public, of peace and war.' . . . [T]he purpose of education is to produce the good man and the good citizen . . . . The 'good man' here means the man of good taste and good feeling, the interesting and interested man . . . . Vocational training, on the other hand, prepares the pupil not for leisure, but for work; it aims at making not a good man but a good banker, a good electrician, a good scavenger, or a good surgeon.[28]

For Lewis, learning, or the pursuit of knowledge (the business of the student), was the top level of the educational hierarchy.[29] Learning is the search for knowledge for its own sake, apart from a utilitarian purpose for gaining knowledge. By itself, learning has no connection with education nor is it to be equated with education.[30] For Lewis, the level below learning is education.[31] Education is one step down from learning because it fits within a system and comes at the initiative of that system, that is, at the initiative of the school. At the lowest level of the hierarchy is training. The banker, the electrician, and the surgeon are trained; the good person is educated, that is, capable of a broad range of activities, because he has learned how to think, how to apply a principle in different settings, and how to integrate various fields of knowledge. Often Lewis does not distinguish between learning and education, but at times he does. Learning takes place both within an educational system and outside of it; therefore learning has the highest value. For Lewis, education takes place within the school and university system, but learning is what we most desire. Education does not guarantee learning, though education should facilitate it.

Lewis wanted students to fall in love with learning, as he had done. He wanted students to enjoy learning for its own sake, for the pleasure of discovery, and for the pleasure of enjoying the aesthetic, the profound, and the good, not for the sake of what learning can do for them. According to Lewis, learning should even be "a kind of madness."[32] Learning will do much for a person, but most important it will teach an individual to think. To be able to think will have many practical results, but the results ought not drive the learning.

In the process of irrigating deserts, the purpose is to produce the good person and the good citizen. Thus Lewis agreed with John Henry Newman, who said that the purpose of the university was to train good members of society.[33] The good person cannot be produced simply by telling the individual what jungles must be cut down. Something positive and solid must be put in place of the jungle so the vacuum is not filled with the spirit of the age.

Those educators who seek to destroy what they perceive to be false concepts, that is, those educators who cut down jungles (such as professors in the secular academy who try to destroy students' allegiance to the Christian faith), are not thereby educating. They are philosophizing. By providing skills for living, educators are not producing good people. Skills for living provide little ability to determine what is good, beautiful, noble, true, and just. The good person and the good citizen are produced by broadening the mind so it can support the state through good citizenship, altruistic concern for the neighbor, and concern for the things of God. Such an individual also supports the arts and sciences through an appreciation of good literature, good theater, good art, and good science. Along with producing graduates who know the higher good must come development of the lower goods, which support the higher good. The higher good is the beautiful piece of art, while the lower good is the ability to appreciate it.[34]

Part of the ability to irrigate deserts comes from an understanding of the tools at the disposal of educators. In his essay "The Parthenon and the Optative," Lewis described two types of education. Lewis quoted a classical scholar who complained that teachers had been teaching the Parthenon (literary appreciation) when they should have been teaching the optative (the basics). Therefore Lewis said that one type of education deals with the "hard, dry things like grammar, and dates, and prosody," that is, the optative.[35] The other type of education, allegedly advocated in the Norwood Report,[36] attempts to teach such things as literary appreciation, that is, the Parthenon. The first is a prerequisite to the second, but the type of education that begins with literary appreciation has failed to provide the basics that make appreciation possible.[37] One cannot appreciate that which one does not first understand on an elemental level. Therefore, wrote Lewis, though both types of education are important, one dare not eliminate or limit the first without endangering the second.[38] Although Lewis incorrectly read the Norwood Report, this comment shows Lewis's commitment to the basics before one approaches some of the higher forms of learning. To borrow the language of the medieval Trivium, one must learn the grammar (the basics) of a subject before one can learn the logic (how everything fits together) and rhetoric (how to present the subject to others) of that same curriculum. One cannot irrigate deserts without the tools of irrigation and the water to flow in the irrigation ditches. The stuff of any given discipline is the water that must flow. The fundamentals of education must consist of grammar and dates and prosody. Those fundamentals provide the underlying structure of a good education, they are the ditches educators dig to allow the water of irrigation to flow.

In "The Parthenon and the Optative," Lewis also argued against the Norwood Report's recommendation that a colleague, even if relatively untrained in literature, do the testing rather than an outsider. Lewis correctly wrote that this will eliminate objectivity, something that is much needed in education.[39] Lewis also disagreed with the Norwood Report's conclusion that any teacher could teach English.[40] He suggested that the authors of the Norwood Report saw little in the way of standards for teaching English, preferring the person who could teach more subjects than English rather than the specialist in English. Lewis argued that the Norwood Report saw the teaching of English literature as only an aid in appreciation because literature is intended only to entertain.[41] He felt that the Norwood Report failed to see the value of English studies.

THE LIBERAL ARTS

Lewis received a strong liberal arts education under the tutelage of W. T. Kirkpatrick and at University College, Oxford. Thus he was better able to provide a liberal arts education to his students. However, the student at Oxford and Cambridge focused on a single area of study, so Lewis did not receive an education founded upon a liberal arts core as we understand it today. However, the subjects Lewis studied are well represented in the offerings of the modern liberal arts college, and the entire Oxford education was based upon the medieval liberal arts curriculum.

The three Firsts that Lewis earned at Oxford were in the liberal arts: Greek and Latin texts (Honour Moderations), ancient history and classical philosophy (Greats), and English language and literature. Consequently, Lewis rated the liberal arts highly. He was what they call in England a polymath, a person well grounded in a wide range of subjects, which is one goal of the liberal arts system of education. In fact, Lewis considered the English faculties at the universities as the primary guardians of the humanities, and he considered English as "the most liberal—and liberating—discipline" among the three schools of history, literae humaniores, and English.[42]

The medieval Trivium, the heart of the modern liberal arts system, consisted of three subjects: grammar, dialectic (or logic), and rhetoric. The medieval Quadrivium focused on four subjects: arithmetic, music, geometry, and astronomy.[43] In the medieval period, the Trivium was the course of study for the bachelor's degree, while the Quadrivium comprised the coursework for the master's degree.[44] According to Lewis, this did not simply mean these seven subjects and no more. History would be included because Isidore included history in the category of grammar.[45] Within the medieval system, grammar meant the building blocks of a subject,[46] dialectic the manner in which they fit together,[47] and rhetoric the manner in which those building blocks were presented.[48] Harry Wakelyn Smith (Smugy) taught Lewis grammar and rhetoric, while Kirkpatrick taught him logic or dialectic.[49] At home, Lewis probably absorbed some rhetoric from his father and some logic from his mother.

The purpose of education, which is, substantially, to develop the character by developing the mind, is accomplished through the liberal arts rather than through vocational training. In *The Discarded Image*, Lewis wrote about the emphasis upon the liberal arts among the medievals, who highly prized it. As a medievalist, therefore, Lewis also emphasized the liberal arts.[50]

Lewis's commitment to the liberal arts, especially literature, was reflected in *An Experiment in Criticism* when he wrote about the importance of accepting an author's writing for its own sake,[51] that is, not for utilitarian purposes or, as Leavis argued, for social criticism. Something that is accepted for its own sake is not accepted, therefore, for its utilitarian value. Later in the same work, Lewis said of poems: "To value them chiefly for reflections which they may suggest to us or morals we may draw from them, is a flagrant instance of 'using' instead of 'receiving.'"[52] Elsewhere Lewis said of his upbringing: "I had been brought up to believe that goodness was goodness only if it were disinterested, and that any hope of reward or fear of punishment contaminated the will . . . . A thing can be revered not for what it can do to us but for what it is in itself."[53] This commitment runs counter not only to the Leavis approach to literature but also to the modern U.S. emphasis upon assessment that is required by regional accrediting bodies, which, in fairness, actually consist of members of the academy. The growing call for the assessment of the liberal arts is not necessarily utilitarian because those who issue the call are asking institutions of higher education only to demonstrate that they are accomplishing what they claim. However, it is a short step from reasonable assessment of the liberal arts to the expectation that the increase in a student's appreciation of a work of art can be measured.

As an undergraduate, Lewis had refined his understanding of the nature of literature. Considering literature that lacks imagination and only tends to vicarious satisfaction as mere pornography, he met opposition from other undergraduates in a discussion class with George Gordon. Lewis conceded the point, which was supported by Gordon, that literature must have both imagination in the writing of it and the ability to allow the reader to enter the world of the writer.[54]

Accepting a piece of literature "for its own sake" also presupposes an emphasis upon primary rather than secondary material. It assumes a grappling with the text itself rather than with what people have said about the text. Lewis once wrote: "Here, plainly, are young people drenched, dizzied, and bedeviled by criticism to a point at which primary literary experience is no longer possible."[55] Criticism even places examinations secondary to student contact with the written word. One acquaintance of Lewis states that he "never seemed concerned about exams, nor about the fashionable currents of opinion on a work, nor about whether one had covered the secondary material sufficiently."[56] Derek Brewer concurs with this perspective: "[R]arely did he [Lewis] suggest any critical books. . . . Neither he nor anyone else ever mentioned to me such names as I. A. Richards or F. R. Leavis."[57] However, Lewis did insist that undergraduates read some criticism before writing their essays on an author. Such reading was not required so students could learn about the author but so students could learn what parts of their reaction were generally accepted—and therefore need not be argued—and what parts of their opinion differed from the critics so their case could be argued more closely.[58]

The arts were one of the areas in which Lewis expressed his concern. In his book *English Literature in the Sixteenth Century*, Lewis included a sixteenth-century lamentation by Thomas Elyot concerning the decay of the arts in England and a plea for aesthetic education.[59] Elyot reminded us that one understands and retains far better the visual. The visual arts have great power in their ability to educate, to motivate, and to shape people's thinking. But the arts in general, especially literature, also have the ability to enable people to enjoy real life.[60] The arts prepare a person for leisure. In discussing Elyot's essay, Lewis claims that Elyot was laying the foundation of classical education by supporting a person who is both learned and skilled in a profession and by encouraging the formation of young minds with the study of great poets and philosophers.[61]

The enjoyment of life and leisure, the appreciation of the arts and the liberal arts for their own sake, is not a mere anti-utilitarian function. The liberal arts educate the mind, enabling the reader of literature, the viewer of art, the listener to music, the student of history to see the sweep of life in the themes expressed, much as the literary reader does. Lewis describes the opposite in the unliterary reader: "As the unmusical listener wants only the Tune, so the unliterary reader wants only the Event. The one ignores nearly all the sounds the orchestra is actually making; he wants to hum the tune. The other ignores nearly all that the words before him are doing; he wants to know what happened next."[62]

Thus, according to Lewis, the liberal arts form the foundation of a good education, providing the Trivium of every subject matter and knowledge for its own sake.

UTILITY AND VOCATIONALISM

Training and conditioning are all that is left when society abandons the development of character through the liberal arts, as Lewis indicated in *The Abolition of Man*.[63] For Lewis, this produces people without chests, that is, without trained emotions.[64] At that point, the culture sees primarily a utilitarian purpose for education, and it settles for training rather than education. Lewis saw the rise of the industrial revolution as a movement that advanced utility at the expense of the liberal arts, especially the classics.

Following the lead of Oxford University,[65] Lewis was not opposed to vocational training in and of itself. Many people in society require training for particular occupations. Lewis advocated training for those for whom it was appropriate, but he opposed the encroachment of vocationalism upon a liberal arts education. Indeed, Lewis put into the mouth of Weston the view opposite to that which he himself held. In his speech shortly after his arrival on Perelandra, the scientist Weston spoke to Ransom about the utilitarian cause to which he was dedicated: "[K]nowledge as an end in itself never appealed to me. I always wanted to know in order to achieve utility."[66]

Clearly, Lewis valued knowledge as an end in itself—knowing for the sake of knowing, learning for the sake of learning, knowledge that as of yet had no practical value was most practical of all. A literary kind of reader who receives a text rather than uses a text will likely be one who values learning for its own sake.[67] This is why Lewis wrote about the higher calling of higher education in "Our English Syllabus." The question that a freshman should ask is not the utilitarian one that many ask today: How can I get a well-paying job after graduation? but What do I most want to know? or What part of reality can I get to know? Self-help or self-improvement ("blackboards and certificates," to use a Lewis phrase) is not the goal of higher education; rather, the goal is understanding life, contributing to society, and adopting an altruistic approach to living.[68]

Closely akin to this utilitarian approach to higher education is the consumer mentality of many students: Because I'm paying lots of money for this education, I have certain expectations. Because of such an approach, the question What part of reality can I get to know? is replaced by the question How can I get the most product for the least price? To carry that second question to an unexpected conclusion, however, we find that "the most product" is actually the most learning.

The Tao

The primary allegiance in the life of C. S. Lewis was to Jesus Christ. Lewis once wrote that most of his books were evangelistic.[69] He also wrote about the centrality of his faith: "I believe in Christianity as I believe that the Sun has risen, not only because I see it, but because by it I see everything else."[70] Lewis's "everything else" includes education.

For Lewis, God was the source of all truth, even in the pagan religions. When an educator teaches truth, he or she is teaching God's truth, and the search for truth must be a portion of that education. In *Mere Christianity* and *The Abolition of Man*, Lewis argued that God had set an objective standard of right and wrong that all peoples of the world recognize. Lewis called this the Tao.[71] If there is an objective morality, it is based upon objective truth. Where there is objective truth, those truths serve as the foundation for all academic disciplines. Other religions can teach some of this truth to the extent that they possess natural knowledge of God or by experience learn, for example, that honesty in business dealings results in better business and, at the same time, leaves one's conscience untainted. The Bible contains the primary record of this objective truth or objective morality, though it appears elsewhere as well, but not in as complete and pure a form.

Medieval people thought of the universe in the opposite way in which modern people look at the universe. For modern people, we are at the center of the world, whereas in medieval thought, God was at the center and human beings were very much subject to God.[72] Therefore medieval people actually had a more accurate picture of the universe in this regard than do modern people. The medieval mind-set, which Lewis portrayed in his fiction, can teach us much about humility, sacrifice, servanthood, and perspective. Furthermore, to support the true purpose of education, namely, to produce the good citizen, we must believe in objective and transcendent truth.

Second, the Tao—"the doctrine of objective value, the belief that certain attitudes are really true, and others really false"[73]—is present in virtually every religion. Throughout *The Abolition of Man*, Lewis argued against subjective values that are based on feelings and in favor of "objective values that differentiate between right and wrong and thus provide the true way to assess attitudes and behavior."[74] He argued that the head must rule the belly through the chest.[75] Lewis based his views fundamentally on Paul's letter to the Romans, wherein Paul argues that the Law is both written on our hearts (Romans 2:15) and evident in nature (Romans 1:18–20), but also on Immanuel Kant's moral law within and the starry heavens without.[76]

The purpose of education according to Milton and Aristotle, as described above, underscores the good, whereas the writers of *The Green Book*[77] prefer to discuss the emotional state of the speaker rather than the values of the speaker, and philosophize against the dangers of emotion. Students learn nothing about English or literature in the process. According to Lewis, in education, "[w]hen all that says 'it is good' has been debunked, what says 'I want' remains."[78] Lewis wrote that "[t]he practical result of education in the spirit of *The Green Book* must be the destruction of the society which accepts it."[79] A result of this sort of education is to despair of the possibility of ever being certain of anything. One could easily conclude that there is no such thing as absolute truth; everything is relative. If the viewing of a waterfall, a piece of art, or a sculpture only tells someone what he or she feels at the time, then there is no basis upon which to judge art or music or drama. Anyone's feeling is as valid as any other person's feeling. Likewise, there is nothing to be gained from a comparison of different viewpoints, for no position is more likely to be true in any objective sense than another.

An appreciation of objective truth appears in Lewis's attack on what he called the personal heresy. Much of what Lewis was reacting to in the publication of *The Personal Heresy* (1939) was prevalent at the time in Oxford. Many literary critics both within Oxford and outside of Oxford, such as E. M. W. Tillyard, argued that a piece of writing reflected the personality of the author more than the actual content of the work. Lewis once argued that all criticism should be criticism of books, not criticism of their authors.[80] The exchange of views between Tillyard and Lewis resulted in increased understanding because both Lewis and Tillyard finally agreed that understanding the personality of the author could be helpful but also that a literary work was primarily not a simple matter of understanding that personality. Ironically, Lewis himself is one of the best examples of the viewpoint he repudiated, thereby demonstrating some value in Tillyard's perspective. Much of Lewis's personality is expressed not only in the autobiographical *Surprised by Joy* but also in occasional comments in the Chronicles of Narnia about the value of religion or the type of history that is taught, in his self-designation as a dinosaur in his inaugural address at Cambridge University, in the Space Trilogy, and in other places in his writings.

Scattered through many of Lewis's books are references to Christianity and the Bible. In *The Silver Chair*, Lewis wrote about the model schools, which discouraged Christianity. He wrote (not in the mouth of any of the characters but in his own): "Bibles were not encouraged at Experiment House."[81] In *The Magician's Nephew*, Lewis wrote: "Things like Do not Steal were, I think, hammered into boys' heads a good deal harder in those days than they are now."[82] Elsewhere Lewis wrote of the value of a clear presentation of the Christian faith, stating that, though Christianity is not presented to schoolboys, in the rare instance when it is, most find it acceptable.[83] Lewis knows, however, that not only will Christianity not be put before most schoolchildren, but Christianity will be discriminated against, something we are seeing more frequently in our day.[84]

Schools should teach morals. In a U.S. educational system in which morals are often equated with religion, this concept will not sit well. Yet for Lewis, who lived in a country in which religious education is a part of the public school system, morals were an integral part of education. Morals will refer to that set of objective truths, which Lewis called the Tao, that virtually all peoples have upheld in every age. The great problem of humanity is not ignorance, and the great cure is not education.[85] The great problem is sin, and the great cure is the Gospel of Jesus Christ.

Boston College philosopher Peter Kreeft has written: "The three major mind-molding establishments in the Western world—formal education, entertainment (i.e., informal education), and journalism—are massively dominated by the subjectivists and secularists."[86] We need Lewis's understanding of objective truth, indeed, God's revelation of Himself, more than ever.

EGALITARIANISM

In his essay "Membership," Lewis considered the difference between the body of Christ—in which there is neither Jew nor Greek, slave nor free, male nor female (Galatians 3:28)—and what he called "the secular collective" or the homogeneous class. Christians could be accused of being hypocritical, or at least muddle-headed, if they opposed egalitarianism on the one hand yet affirmed the oneness and equality of all believers in Jesus Christ on the other hand.

But Lewis clearly saw a difference. Yes, he opposed egalitarianism: "I do not believe that God created an egalitarian world."[87] Yes, he believed in equality, but he saw the equality in God's love rather than in us. Just as a color in a painting, a spice in a dish of food, or a dog in a family is not the same as the other colors, spices, and family members, so also differences exist among people. Equality in our treatment of people is important to avoid evils,[88] but that equality is protective, not a matter of the essence of people. Not everyone is of equal value, though God equally loves everyone.

The mother is both different from the daughter and also a different kind of person.[89] In other words, to say that we should treat people equally is much different than saying that all people are of equal value. Our social structure, which treats different people differently, proclaims this, even as it looks to root out instances of unfairness or discrimination, though usually only in those instances where secular culture determines that such unfairness should be rooted out. Discriminatory action against African Americans is rightly condemned, but discriminatory action against Christians is not. For example, when a decision was made not to consider Ron Brown, an assistant coach at the University of Nebraska, for the position of head football coach at Stanford University, Stanford officials told the *Daily Nebraskan*, the University of Nebraska student newspaper, that Ron Brown's Christian perspectives would not fit at Stanford.[90]

Lewis believed in equality in the treatment of people because he believed in democracy. And he believed in democracy because he believed that no one could be trusted with complete power over other people. Lewis was fully aware of the problem of sin, far more so than the problem of pain, because the problem of sin preceded the problem of pain and caused much of the problem of pain. The equal treatment of people is not something good in itself (a view held by many of Lewis's contemporaries) but something that is in the same category as medicine—it is good because we are ill; it can solve the problem of sickness. Equality is good because the equal treatment of people constrains the few from imposing their will upon the many, at least in a democracy. When equality is not treated like medicine, it creates that mind-set that views the overachiever with jealousy and despises all forms of superiority.[91]

If he supported equality in the treatment of people, what did Lewis oppose? What effects of an egalitarian approach concerned Lewis? He was concerned about the negative effects of the self-esteem movement, the dumbing down of the curriculum (for the sake of not harming the self-esteem of those not gifted), the inappropriate rewarding of the lazy, and the holding back of the gifted (the negative side of egalitarianism) at the elementary school levels, as well as in higher education. Egalitarianism is too often employed as a means to avoid hurting anyone's self-esteem when such esteem should be grounded in the biblical concept of being created in the image of God and being recreated in the image of Christ Jesus (2 Corinthians 5:17). In the attempt to avoid damaging anyone's self-esteem, educators don't want to leave anyone behind, but they also don't want to move anyone ahead. According to Lewis, "[a]ll incentives to learn and all penalties for not learning will vanish"[92] in an egalitarian educational system. Although the concept of teamwork is a good one, life is not like that. Lewis said that many concepts, such as beauty, are not democratic.[93] If they were, we could also imagine wrestling meets with no weight classes, so heavyweights would wrestle against lightweights. If life were truly egalitarian, we could imagine a business in which all employees had an equal say in business decisions. Although this might work on issues such as the implementation of flex time or the length of coffee breaks, it would not work in making the decision about which new markets to enter. Lewis supports equality in our daily treatment of one another, but in situations in which hierarchies must apply, such as in organizations and definitely in education, Lewis opposes egalitarianism.

According to Lewis, "[t]he demand for equality has two sources; one of them is among the noblest, the other is the basest, of human emotions. The noble source is the desire for fair play. But the other source is the hatred of superiority."[94] Lewis sees a democratic, or egalitarian, education coming that endeavors to appease envy, which comes hand in hand with the hatred of superiority. The appeasement of envy will not succeed because envy is insatiable and because it introduces equality where equality is fatal.[95] Lewis writes: "Equality . . . has no place in the world of the mind. Beauty is not democratic . . . . Virtue is not democratic . . . . Truth is not democratic."[96] The true democratic education, that is, the education that will preserve democracy, will be, according to Lewis, "ruthlessly aristocratic."[97] He writes: "In drawing up its curriculum it should always have chiefly in view the interests of the boy who wants to know and who can know."[98]

Lewis faced the problem of removing incentives to learn when he wrote to a schoolgirl in Florida named Joan, congratulating her on her high score on a Latin test. In the letter, he deplored the idea, which she had apparently expressed, of granting credit for time spent in the classroom rather than for what students had learned.[99]

Lewis expressed many of his thoughts about education in a classic statement by Screwtape about the abolition of education:

> The basic principle of the new education is to be that dunces and idlers must not be made to feel inferior to intelligent and industrious pupils . . . .

At universities, examinations must be framed so that nearly all the students get good marks. Entrance examinations must be framed so that all, or nearly all, citizens can go to universities . . . . At schools, the children who are too stupid or lazy to learn languages and mathematics and elementary science can be set to doing the things that children used to do in their spare time . . . . But all the time there must be no faintest hint that they are inferior to the children who are at work. . . . The bright pupil thus remains democratically fettered to his own age group throughout his school career, and a boy who would be capable of tackling Aeschylus or Dante sits listening to his coeval's attempts to spell out A CAT SAT ON A MAT.

In a word, we may reasonably hope for the virtual abolition of education when *I'm as good as you* has fully had its way. All incentives to learn and all penalties for not learning will vanish. The few who might want to learn will be prevented; who are they to overtop their fellows? And anyway the teachers . . . will be far too busy reassuring the dunces and patting them on the back to waste any time on real teaching.[100]

Through the mouth of Screwtape, Lewis attacked the theory of democratic education. He attacked the theory in several places besides *Screwtape Proposes a Toast*,[101] most prominently in his essay "Democratic Education." Lewis reminded us that Aristotle taught that democratic education meant not the education that most democrats like but "the education which will preserve democracy."[102] The sort of education that will preserve democracy is one that allows students to excel. And the truth is that everyone excels at some things, though not at others.

The sort of education that currently is considered democratic does not preserve democracy. Instead, it is democratic only in the sense of being egalitarian—it ignores the differences between the bright students and the others. Lewis saw two ways of succumbing to the lure of democratic education: One abolishes all compulsory subjects that show the differences among students, and the other makes the curriculum so broad that every child will succeed at something. In either method, the objective is to make no child feel inferior.[103] However, "a nation of dunces can be safe only in a world of dunces."[104] In reality, democratic education of this sort undermines democracy, in part because it frustrates the student who has the ability to excel and in part because it denies any objective ground rules for education. Lacking a foundation, modern education can aim only for an idealized version of "all people are created equal."

Egalitarianism would also cause a shift toward vocational training. To level the playing field would require aiming at a low enough level to include all students. Therefore abstract thinking and higher levels of critical thinking and problem-solving would be excluded. Lewis was not opposed to vocational training, and he did not want to eliminate it. However, he opposed vocational training making incursions where it did not belong, particularly at the university level. According to Lewis, we must have electricians and surgeons, but they are trained rather than educated. Only egalitarianism would insist upon providing this sort of training to all students. Lewis wanted to limit training to certain professions (he mentions bookkeeping and commercial French) and education for others (he mentions subjects such as Latin and literature). According to Lewis, replacing education with training would cause the death of civilization, something Lewis feared greatly. Furthermore, an egalitarian society promotes training, whereas the unequal societies of an earlier day promoted education for some and training for others. The more egalitarian a society becomes the more likely education is to be left behind.[105]

In Lewis's time, England was moving toward its current system of comprehensive education. In this modern system, the attempt has been made to remove the social barrier between those who attend grammar schools and those who attend modern schools. This system also aims to eliminate the elitism of those who attend the best schools. At times in the past, those with a weak educational background had to attend a modern school, though they had the ability to succeed in a grammar school. The attempt, though laudable in many ways, had the effect of holding back the better students rather than raising the performance of the low achievers, and it has not thereby removed any social or academic barriers. Perhaps Lewis was prophetic in speaking out against a system that would dim the brightest lights of England's intellectual future.

ATHLETIC COMPETITION

Lewis's disdain for the athletic side of schools is well known, as is the lack of a joint in his thumbs[106] that prevented him from success at sports. He once wrote to his father that his lack of athletic prowess was a disadvantage at school.[107] Today Lewis would undoubtedly champion those who have challenged universities to place education ahead of success on the athletic fields. Although such criticism seems self-serving (as if Lewis opposed athletics because he wasn't good at them), some universities are too interested in athletic success and the financial gain and national prestige it brings.

Lewis would not oppose athletics in the university, if athleticism was combined with learning. He lamented the absence of what he called the sixteenth-century "tradition of gentlemanly philistinism." Writing about Thomas Elyot,[108] Lewis spoke kindly of that sixteenth-century philistine who was also a gentleman, the warrior who also attended Shakespeare and enjoyed other aspects of culture. Until the reinstating of compulsory games or sports in the English schools of the twentieth century, there were no such creatures.

Of necessity, this section on athletics is short when exploring Lewis's views on education. After all, Lewis once classified sports as his least favorite subject on which to write.[109]

DISCIPLINE

Writing to his father in 1929, Lewis summarized his view of education in the public schools[110] and their lack of discipline: "Except for pure classics . . . I really don't know what gifts the public schools bestow on their nurslings, beyond the mere surface of good manners: unless contempt of the things of the intellect, extravagance, insolence, self-sufficiency, and sexual perversion are to be called gifts,"[111] in other words, behavior gone bad. Lewis was not speaking, of course, of university education, but he would have seen university education in England continuing many of the practices of the primary and secondary schools.

Lewis supported the idea of corporal punishment by criticizing model schools for being reflections of progressive ideas in education. The Chronicles of Narnia occasionally mentioned "fat foreign children doing exercises in model schools."[112] Some of the characters in the Chronicles of Narnia went wrong at model schools. The lack of discipline in those schools was one object of Lewis's criticism, a fact suggested by the reference to "fat" children because obesity suggests a lack of discipline. After

Reepicheep swatted Eustace with the side of his rapier, Lewis wrote that Eustace had been at a school that did not have corporal punishment.[113]

At the end of *The Silver Chair*, Aslan returned with Eustace, Jill, and Caspian to Experiment House in England, where Jill and Eustace had been students. After Aslan made the wall of the school fall down, he lay down in the gap in the wall, turning his back to Experiment House and his face to Narnia.[114] The bullies of Experiment House intended to do the children harm, but when they saw Alsan and the others with their swords, they ran for their lives. The bullies were given a beating with the flat side of the sword and ran to get the Head (or principal). When she saw Aslan and the others, she behaved like a lunatic and was no longer able to be Head. These few references to model schools in *The Voyage of the 'Dawn Treader'* and *The Silver Chair* demonstrate Lewis's disapproval of the lack of discipline in many schools.

THE INNER RING

That Lewis opposed the concept of the "inner ring" while he belonged to the Inklings may seem hypocritical to some people. However, a proper fellowship, such as the Inklings (see Glossary), is a group united by a shared love of learning, a common bond of friendship,[115] and a desire to serve others. Although such a fellowship might exclude people, it does not exist for that purpose. However, when he wrote of groups or parties in the church, Lewis knew that an inner ring could also invade the body of Christ.[116] What Lewis disliked was the fellowship that arrogated authority to itself, existing not to serve others or for the sake of friendship but to serve itself. Those fellowships arise in academia, but they are not unique to that world.

Early in life, Lewis's experiences at Wynyard School (1908–1910) set the stage for his dislike of the inner ring. According to Lewis, so much of Wynyard was a few students standing against the rest, in almost the same way that he and his brother had stood against their father. Lewis never appreciated the cliquishness of schools, whether as a child, as an undergraduate, or as a professor. He wrote about the various groups he faced at Malvern College as a 15-year-old, including the Bloods or athletes: "The whole school was a great temple for the worship of these mortal gods; and no boy ever went there more prepared to worship them than I."[117]

During his undergraduate days at University College, Oxford, Lewis wrote in his diary about an older gentleman in the library of the English school who seemed to consider that library to be his private property. Apparently this annoyed Lewis.[118]

As a tutor and later as a professor, Lewis met the inner ring at Oxford and Cambridge. Early in his fellowship at Magdalen College, Lewis expressed disillusionment with his colleagues because of the intrigue, lying, and back-scratching that he saw.[119] During the 1940 Michaelmas term (see Glossary), Lewis became vice president of Magdalen College and had his first taste of administrative work. When the president became ill and Lewis had to take on the president's duties for a time, his work increased significantly and led to his decision never again to accept such an appointment.[120] As a result, instead of completing the full two-year term, Lewis resigned after one year.

Readers can see Lewis's personal disdain, experienced at Magdalen, in the example of two characters in *That Hideous Strength*. Dr. Dimble and Mark Studdock, two professors of the University of Edgestow, provide a contrast. Dr. Dimble, a professor at Northumberland College, part of the University of Edgestow, was a humble man, eager to serve through his teaching, willing to help anyone he could. Mark Studdock was the young professor striving to gain entrance into the inner ring so he could join Dr. Curry and Lord Feverstone, members of the progressive element at Bracton.[121] One cannot read this book without being drawn to the example of Dr. Dimble and repulsed by that of Mark Studdock.

Lewis was not much interested in the political side of the university as a whole. Richard Ladborough, a colleague at Magdalene College, Cambridge, once wrote: "But he was essentially a college rather than a university man. He rarely seemed to be interested in the affairs of the university as a whole, or even (and this was a fault) in those of his own faculty."[122]

Lewis did not believe that an inner ring was evil in itself. Many such groups were morally neutral. He saw the problem in the human desire to enter an inner ring.[123] Like many other areas of life, whether card-playing or dancing or attending concerts or athletic events, the evil is in the perversion of something good, something social, something capable of building friendship. Lewis also saw a problem when an inner ring existed for the purpose of excluding others.[124] Having seen the inner ring in operation in many settings, Lewis set about making the Inklings, as well as his home life, something that existed for noble purposes rather than for the purpose of exclusion. This was one reason he avoided participation in the political side of university life.

AMATEUR PHILOSOPHERS

Lewis opposed the use of the curriculum to create a new social order in Great Britain.[125] He roundly criticized the authors of *The Green Book*, complaining that those who purchased it thought they were getting a book written by professional grammarians but instead had to read the work of "amateur philosophers."[126] Lewis was concerned about the "boy who thinks he is 'doing' his 'English prep' and has no notion that ethics, theology, and politics are all at stake."[127] Although Lewis wanted people to think in an interdisciplinary manner, he deplored the use of one's academic discipline to indoctrinate. Realizing that far more was at stake than a child's education, Lewis saw in *The Green Book* an indication that subjective values don't simply destroy education, they destroy civilization and cause the abolition of man.

Every discipline has its examples of amateur philosophy, but Lewis especially opposed historicism and scientism.[128] Both viewpoints were common at Oxford during the Lewis years, and Lewis wrote the Space Trilogy in response to scientism. Historicism is the alleged ability of certain historians to discover some meaning behind the events of history. In his essay "Historicism," Lewis defined a historicist as one who believed he had discovered the inner meaning of a particular slice of history on the basis of his learning rather than on the basis of the facts, probably a reference to some Oxford historians, among them Magdalen's A. J. P. Taylor (see Appendix V).[129] According to Lewis, a historicist studies the past to learn not only historical truth but also metaphysical or transcendent truth.[130] By this method, some use history as an opportunity to re-educate people according to their personal philosophy. Lewis once remarked in a letter about the great difference between historians and the writings of those people about whom historians wrote: The former often contradicted the latter.[131] For example, some would create a revisionist history that excludes Christianity from colonial American history, but in the process they would omit one of the foundational principles of the United States.

Scientism does something similar with science. Lewis described scientism as "the belief that the supreme moral end is the perpetuation of our own species, and that this is to be pursued even if, in the process of being fitted for survival, our species has to be stripped of all those things for which we value it—of pity, of happiness, and of freedom."[132] Lewis elsewhere called it developmentalism, an "extension of the evolutionary idea far beyond the biological realm . . . as the key principle of reality."[133]

Lewis was not anti-science. He opposed "scientific materialism raised to a philosophy and imposed on society and morals."[134] This was illustrated in the character of Mark Studdock, whose education, Lewis wrote in *That Hideous Strength*, had made "things that he read and wrote more real to him than things he saw."[135] Studdock was a man whose "education had been neither scientific nor classical—merely 'Modern.' The severities of both abstraction and of high human tradition had passed him by . . . . He was a man of straw, a glib examinee in subjects that require no exact knowledge."[136]

According to Lewis, any individual who uses an academic discipline to teach a particular philosophy, rather than the discipline itself, is guilty of an *ism*, whether it is communicationism, political scientism, or the approach to English literature used by Leavis. Although pure objectivity is impossible, some effort at objectivity must at least be expended.

Cannot one criticize Lewis for doing exactly what he disliked in others? Was not Lewis an amateur philosopher because he published popular children's literature, works of theology, and philosophical works when, in fact, he was a professor of English literature? First, one must remember that Lewis had studied philosophy, earning the second of his three First Class Honours in philosophy. To publish a philosophical work such as *The Abolition of Man* was not to publish in an area outside Lewis's expertise. Although not a professional philosopher, Lewis served for an entire year (1924–1925) as a tutor in philosophy at University College in place of E. F. Carritt, and during his early years at Magdalen College, Lewis did some tutorials in philosophy. Likewise, in writing the Chronicles of Narnia, Lewis was not venturing outside of his expertise, for he was a professor of literature. Second, though he published in these areas, he did not use the classroom or the tutorial as a platform for promoting the perspective that his writings represented. His students have testified that Lewis did not use his tutorials to witness about his Christian faith. Lewis differed from some of his Oxford colleagues in his willingness to distinguish between the classroom or the tutorial (where he would teach the discipline itself rather than use the discipline to teach personal viewpoints and preferences) and the outside world of publishing, which he would use as an opportunity to express his views both within his primary teaching field and outside of it. Too many Oxford dons saw the world of publishing only as an extension of the classroom. Third, by publishing the Chronicles of Narnia, for example, Lewis was being himself. He was a man with a profound understanding of literature, myth, and theology, and to use children's literature as a vehicle for conveying Christian truth was most natural for him. Lewis did not distinguish between Lewis the Christian and Lewis the Professor.

THREE

C. S. LEWIS ON THE CURRICULUM OF EDUCATION

I wonder what they *do* teach them at these schools.
—C. S. Lewis, *The Lion, the Witch, and the Wardrobe*.[1]

THE CURRICULUM

In our summary of the type of curriculum C. S. Lewis preferred, we must first distinguish between the curricula about which Lewis wrote. At times, he wrote about the general curriculum, but at other times he wrote about the "English Syllabus."[2] At Oxford or Cambridge, students would take one course of study. They were not attending what is known in the United States as a liberal arts college. Therefore most of what Lewis said about *general education*, or a liberal arts core, must be gleaned from his comments about *education in general* and from his letters to friends, relatives, and acquaintances rather than what he said about a specific curriculum, such as the study of English language and literature.

Lewis also wrote about the choice between *breadth* and *depth*, a topic touched on briefly in the previous chapter. He wanted depth at the university level, with the undergraduate able to pursue in-depth an area of choice, but Lewis wanted students to be able to select highlights, or breadth, at the secondary school level. But in one of his letters to children, Lewis showed that he wanted more depth and less breadth even at the secondary level: "All schools, both here and in America, ought to teach far fewer subjects and teach them far better."[3] Elsewhere Lewis called such a reduction in subjects "the greatest service we can do to education today."[4]

In the university, Lewis wanted depth rather than highlights, but highlights at the secondary level would give students choices from which to select an area of study at the university level. The depth Lewis wanted at the university level included some breadth within the particular course of study selected by a student at an English university. Lewis wrote about breadth (the highlights selected by the faculty) and depth (the chamber of knowledge chosen by the student in which to concentrate), advocating both as important. However, he wanted the highlights especially to be studied in the school (i.e., before university) and the depth to be pursued in the university.[5]

We have also established Lewis's commitment to the liberal arts. What, then, does that mean for the curriculum? According to Lewis, it means the study of "the great poets, orators, and philosophers."[6] It does not mean athletic contests or physical education courses. It does not mean the curriculum of the medievals and Elizabethans, though some of the same goals ought to be attained. For Lewis, a commitment to the liberal arts means concrete knowledge combined with abstraction, practical education combined with literary appreciation, the ability to think theologically, rhetorically, and legally.[7]

GENERAL EDUCATION CURRICULUM

In general education, or core curricular subjects, Lewis championed the liberal arts. We must remember, however, that he did not favor a liberal arts major or an entire course of study in the liberal arts or in another broad selection of courses. Furthermore, he argued against the composite syllabus, or distributed core, as follows:

> In reading such a school, therefore, you would not be turned loose on some tract of reality as it is, to make what you could of it; you would be getting selections of reality selected by your elders—something cooked, expurgated, filtered, and generally toned down for your edification.[8]

Lewis saw the composite syllabus as a flawed course of study because life is not a balanced arrangement and because the student does not see a subject area in depth, from its source to its conclusion. Lewis believed that such a core could not provide an integrated approach to reality. However, the inexperienced selection of a course of study by the undergraduate is hardly an improvement on the course selections of a trained faculty. If that core, or composite syllabus, were a cohesive core, part of a carefully integrated curriculum, it is probable that Lewis would see value in such a liberal arts education, though few institutions accomplish such cohesiveness in their curriculum.

Lewis wanted philology, linguistic history, linguistic theory,[9] grammar, logic, rhetoric,[10] the classics, French,[11] history,[12] philosophy,[13] religion, literature, art, mathematics, biology,[14] music,[15] and astronomy[16] to be taught in the liberal arts. Foreign language, a subject at which Lewis excelled, was also recommended. Sports, historicism, scientific materialism,[17] and vocational subjects were among the subjects that Lewis would exclude from the university. Indeed, he would undoubtedly see the wide range of courses in many modern curricula as another aspect of the egalitarian attempt to shut no subject out, an attempt that hinders educators from teaching that which produces the good person, the good citizen.

Abstraction (logic, philosophy[18] [Plato and Aristotle]) and high human tradition[19] (literature [Dante, Milton, Spenser, Yeats, and others]), the classics (Greek and Latin), history, and religion help the individual to learn to think. These subjects irrigate the deserts of the mind. What follows is a brief look at three of the subjects mentioned in this paragraph, explaining why they are included in Lewis's curriculum.

THE CLASSICS

Lewis showed his appreciation of the classics when he placed criticism of Greek, Latin, and history in the mouth of the scientist Weston in *Out of the Silent Planet*.[20] According to Lewis, the classics do what good history also does: They prevent the mind from being isolated in its own age.[21] The classics provide an infusion of the better elements of paganism, enabling students of Greek and Latin both to believe that valuable truth could still be found in old books and to reverence tradition.[22] In the classics, therefore, paganism irrigates our minds, even as it irrigated Lewis's mind. Here Lewis stressed the value of contact with original sources as opposed to analyses of those sources, just as he wanted students to read more literature than literary criticism. He "very much emphasized text over any secondary commentary."[23] By stressing the value of original sources[24] and a respect for old books, Lewis thereby argued against chronological snobbery.

Lewis also contended that Greek and Latin were useful for other reasons. In a letter to Arthur Greeves, who had suggested that Lewis omit the Greek and Latin quotations in *Pilgrim's Regress*, Lewis wrote: "One of the contentions of the book is that the decay of our old classical learning is a contributory cause of atheism."[25] Indeed, in *Pilgrim's Regress*, the Guide told John and Vertue that the Northern people no longer had to learn the languages of the old pagans (Greek and Latin). When they had to learn those languages, they "had therefore the chance to come at last to Mother Kirk."[26] Reading the literature of the old pagans meant being exposed to the myths of those cultures, which contain many foreshadowings of the Gospel story.

When Lewis said of the classics that "they gave us Matter . . . new things to write and feel about,"[27] he was defending their role in the irrigation of deserts:

> . . . to lose what I owe to Plato and Aristotle would be like the amputation of a limb. Hardly any lawful price would seem to me too high for what I have gained by being made to learn Latin and Greek. If any question of the value of classical studies were before us, you would find me on the extreme right.[28]

LOGIC

In a variety of places, Lewis showed his appreciation of the study of logic. (1) In one essay, Lewis argued in favor of logic when he complained that people in popular audiences were interested in practicality, not the question of truth or falsehood. (2) In the next paragraph, Lewis deplored the popular skepticism of reason, the mother of logic.[29] (3) In *The Lion, the Witch and the Wardrobe*, Lewis argued for logic when Professor Kirke said that Lucy either was lying, mad, or telling the truth.[30] (4) Through the presence of MacPhee in the community of St. Anne's in *That Hideous Strength*, Lewis indicated that he saw a place for a rational skepticism.

W. T. Kirkpatrick, Lewis's tutor during the Great Bookham days, was the model for Professor Kirke, and Kirkpatrick himself may well be the reason Lewis put those words into Kirke's mouth. Notice the importance of supporting evidence for the position the Pevensie children held when Kirke placed before them what logicians call a disjunctive statement.

Notice also its similarity to the section in *Mere Christianity* on the identity of Jesus, where Lewis asked the reader to choose one of three options for Jesus: lunatic, liar, or Lord.[31]

The disjunctive syllogism states that if you have a disjunction, or separation, between two or more related ideas and if one idea is false, then the other idea is probably true. If we know that A or B or C is true (either Lucy is lying, she is mad, or she is telling the truth) and we learn that both A and B are probably false, then we should conclude that C is probably true Another name for this is "elimination of alternatives," as in Sherlock Holmes's famous statement that if you have eliminated every other alternative, then the one that remains, no matter how improbable, must be true. The major danger of this approach is the possibility of an explanation you have not thought of. There may actually be explanation D, which is the correct explanation. In the case of Lewis's argument on the identity of Jesus, for example, another alternative is that Jesus was a legend. Although Lewis did not offer the possibility that Jesus was a legend, it does illustrate a potential alternative not previously considered.[32]

HISTORY

As stated in the previous chapter, Lewis opposed historicism. For *Prince Caspian*, Lewis invented Miss Prizzle, the teacher in a modern school who taught a reconstructed history that excluded the true history of Narnia. That does not mean, however, that Lewis was opposed to the study of history. He greatly valued the subject because the study of history had the ability to expose the reader to different customs and practices, different theologies and philosophies, thereby enabling the reader to escape from the prejudices of the age. But one must study an objective history; the historian may not do as he wishes.[33] Lewis modeled this approach in his work for *English Literature in the Sixteenth Century*, which was not only an appraisal of literature but also a historical study of literature.

G. K. Chesterton's *The Everlasting Man* first offered Lewis a convincing Christian reading of history. According to Lewis, Chesterton, like the Hebrew prophets, was able to escape from the local and particular and provincial to discover the universal and eschatological, thereby providing unity in history. When Lewis wrote *The Pilgrim's Regress*, History was the allegorical figure that enabled John, the hero, to return to Mother Kirk.

History was able to bring John's entire experience together.[34] Lewis stated in his essay "Learning in War-Time":

> [W]e need intimate knowledge of the past. Not that the past has any magic about it, but because we cannot study the future, and yet need something to set against the present, to remind us that the basic assumptions have been quite different in different periods and that much which seems certain to the uneducated is merely temporary fashion. A man who has lived in many places is not likely to be deceived by the local errors of his native village: the scholar has lived in many times and is therefore in some degree immune from the great cataract of nonsense that pours from the press and the microphone of his own age.[35]

Screwtape said much the same thing in his advice to Wormwood, arguing that the intellectual climate of Europe had resulted in people being cut off from other generations by convincing them that history cannot possibly be a source of knowledge.[36]

A lack of appreciation of history was one mistake made by the realists and one strength of the idealists, two schools of philosophy that were prominent in Oxford from 1910 to 1930. By 1925, Lewis had ceased to believe in the myth of progress, but he expressed his views of history in his essays "Historicism" and "The Funeral of a Great Myth." Dependent upon J. A. Smith, who once stated that all knowledge is historical knowledge, Lewis made History a hermit in *The Pilgrim's Regress*, a person who knows "all parts of this country . . . and the genius of places" in comparison to those who have little comprehension of geography.[37] In a summary statement, Lewis wrote: "To study the past does indeed liberate us from the present, from the idols of our own marketplace. But I think it liberates us from the past too. I think no class of men are less enslaved to the past than historians."[38]

In other places, Lewis had much to say about various subjects in the liberal arts. For example, writing his essay "Learning in War-Time," Lewis indirectly stated the value of the study of literature, art, mathematics, and biology.[39] Although literature, art, mathematics, and biology seem insignificant in comparison to the problems attendant in wartime, these subjects provide students with the ability to appreciate literary, artistic, and natural beauty; to solve problems; and to understand the workings of the human body or the various realms of nature. In other words, these subjects are among the liberal arts, which develop the educated and humane person.

The English Syllabus

The English Syllabus of the English School at Oxford changed in 1931 through the reforms of J. R. R. Tolkien, reforms that were accepted in part because of Lewis's influence. Anglo-Saxon and Middle English were more important in the new syllabus, while Victorian literature, that is, that material written between 1830 and 1900, became much less important. English literature from Beowulf to the Romantics was the basic syllabus. This program of study was still in place when Derek Brewer read English from 1945 to 1947.[40] This was the syllabus that Lewis taught for most of his career.

The change in 1931 was the opposite of the curricular change that apparently had occurred in 1922 when Lewis was an undergraduate.[41] Tolkien and Lewis both held that the shift in culture after 1830, caused in large part by the industrial revolution, lessened the value of literature written after that period.[42] Lewis disliked much of modern literature because it reflected modern life,[43] something little appreciated by a dinosaur (his self-designation in "De Descriptione Temporum"). Lewis did, however, enjoy many post-1830 authors, such as G. K. Chesterton, E. R. Eddison, Rudyard Kipling, William Morris, Dorothy Sayers, J. R. R. Tolkien, and Charles Williams, so his dislike of modern literature was not universal.

In the early 1950s, Tolkien was persuaded by Helen Gardner and others that Victorian literature, as well as twentieth-century literature, should be restored to the syllabus. However, at the faculty meeting at which this recommendation was made, the proposal was voted down. Many years later the recommendation was adopted.[44] George Sayer stated that the trend toward including later literature in the syllabus was likely one of the reasons Lewis left Oxford for Cambridge in 1954.[45]

Lewis felt that the syllabus for English language and literature must include the historical and linguistic origins of the English language and a selection of authors, including the study of early literature, that would give a sense of the continuity of English literature.[46] The selection would exclude most modern literature (already familiar to many students and written from the modern mind-set)[47] and most minor authors. Lewis once complained about a modern novel that he read at one sitting, stating that he did not dislike the modern novels simply because they were modern but because most of them were "pretty sickly with their everlasting problems."[48]

Above all, the English Syllabus would exclude Greek, Latin, and French classics. It would include Anglo-Saxon[49] and some Old High German,[50] Old French,[51] and Latin works that made significant contributions to the development of Old English. In a diary entry dated November 2, 1922, Lewis wrote against the linguistic side of the English School curriculum, a position he would later modify under the influence of Tolkien: "Went to the Schools library. Here I puzzled for the best of two hours over phonetics, back voice stops, glides, glottal catches and open Lord-knows-whats. Very good stuff in its way, but why physiology should form part of the English school I really don't know."[52] But earlier that year, Lewis had spoken highly of philology, linguistic history, and linguistic theory.[53] According to Lewis, no other languages should be included, not even Greek, Spanish, Italian, or modern French and German.[54] This would mean depth in the important areas rather than breadth. It also would mean that Lewis resisted the inclusion of modern literature, which the younger members of the Oxford faculty desired to include.

Writing about Charles Williams, Lewis gave an indication of some of the authors he most wanted to see studied. He praised Williams's command of history, theology, legend, and comparative religion. Lewis also was impressed by Williams's knowledge of English literature, especially Malory, Shakespeare, Milton, Johnson, Scott, Wordsworth, Tennyson, Patmore, and Chesterton.[55]

A 1941 letter to prospective student Derek Brewer tells us more about Lewis's specific preferences for the English Syllabus.[56] He discouraged a study of Greek authors but encouraged a study of Latin classics,[57] especially the *Aeneid*, Ovid's *Metamorphoses*, Boethius's *De Consolatione Philosophiae*, and Cicero's *De Republica*. Lewis also wanted students to have a biblical background because it was assumed by most of the older English authors. He advocated especially familiarity with the historical books of the Old Testament, the Book of Psalms, and the Gospel of Luke. Next in importance came Chaucer, Shakespeare, and Milton. After them came Malory, Spenser, Donne, Browne, Dryden, Pope, Swift, Johnson, and Wordsworth. After that it was a matter of taste. Lewis stated: "The great thing is to be always reading but not to get bored—treat it not like work, more as a vice! Your book bill ought to be your biggest extravagance."[58]

Lewis was consistent in his approach both to the core curriculum and to the English Syllabus. He wanted the major authors studied, the liberal arts emphasized, a focus on primary rather than secondary works, and a strong focus on history, philosophy, religion, literature, and the rest of the liberal arts. Most modern curricula lack religion and philosophy, in particular, when compared to Lewis's views. In our haste to create a naked public square and also to separate church and state by removing religion from the curriculum, we have removed the ability to provide a strong ethical foundation for the rest of the curriculum.

FOUR

READING AND REREADING BOOKS

... and perhaps *rereading* of an old friend—a Scott with much skipping—is the best of all.—C. S. Lewis, *They Stand Together*[1]

The foundation of C. S. Lewis's educational philosophy was his love of books, for it opened vast new worlds. George Bailey wrote: "I think it is clear that the grand passion of his life was reading."[2] Some study has been done of the kind of books that Lewis read,[3] but no one has done a comprehensive study. Because it took Lewis a lifetime to read and reread various books, it would probably take a lifetime for someone to study Lewis's reading habits. But the books he read more than once (some are indicated in Appendix I) tell much about Lewis. More important, however, are the reasons why Lewis read books more than once.

Actually, the topic of this chapter will jar some modern readers. "Read something a second time?" we ask. "There are so many books and periodicals and newspapers that I hardly have time to read anything once!" We live in an age in which information is exploding, and the publishing industry is likewise mushrooming. One cannot keep up with publications in one's field, much less two or three fields. Lewis's idea of rereading literature actually offers a partial escape from that difficulty, inviting us to read and reread classics based upon an idea of how one should read literature for the first time. In *An Experiment in Criticism*, Lewis proposed that the type of reader, rather than the type of literature, be the criterion for making distinctions. He wanted to judge books by the kind of readings that people give them rather than judge the reader by the type of books he or she reads. In *An Experiment in Criticism*, Lewis most clearly set forth his thinking about the importance of reading and rereading works of literature. This chapter will connect Lewis's thinking about rereading to the training of students to be literary readers. We irrigate deserts when we train students to read as literary readers, and literary readers read and reread books.

Lewis both practiced what he preached and engendered in others this practice of rereading books. He reread Ariosto, Dante, MacDonald, Malory, Scott, Spenser, Virgil, Wordsworth, and many others. Furthermore, the quality of his own writings has led many to read a book or set of books by Lewis annually. Many a lover of Lewis has read a particular Lewis title ten, twenty, or thirty times, thereby emulating Lewis's practice.

THE LITERARY READER

In the opening chapter of *An Experiment in Criticism*, Lewis presented four major differences between literary and unliterary readers. First, most readers read a work once, while a literary person may read the same work as many as thirty times in a lifetime.[4] Second, most readers do not yearn to read, while literary people are looking for moments when they can read. Third, literary people have momentous experiences with literature that are comparable to experiences with love, religion, or bereavement. Fourth, literary people frequently think about what they have read and talk about their readings with one another.[5]

Literary people also read without preconceptions.[6] They read literature with an open mind and allow literature to affect them. Both Arthur Greeves and A. K. Hamilton Jenkin helped Lewis to read in this way. Jenkin especially helped Lewis to attempt a total surrender to whatever was being experienced at the time, whether nature or literature or anything else.[7] When Lewis wrote about the observation of nature and works of art, he was expressing also his approach to literature: "Total surrender is the first step toward the fruition of either. Shut your mouth; open your eyes and ears. Take in what is there and give no thought to what might have been there or what is somewhere else."[8] When Lewis criticized his father for being unable to empty his own mind to make room for other thoughts, he was expressing the same philosophy applied to the art of listening.[9] The student of Scripture will recognize this as an exegetical approach rather than an eisegetical approach. The word *exegesis* means "to lead out" the meaning that is in the text, and the word *eisegesis* means to read into a text the meaning you wish to find. Therefore the approach Lewis recommends is the same approach that a student of Scripture ought to adopt.

The task of reading should cause us to lay aside our preconceived ideas so the message of the text comes through to us and has the opportunity to change us. According to Lewis, when literature is read as it truly is, we open ourselves to new experiences and become more than ourselves.[10] Lewis wrote: "We are so busy doing things with the work that we give it too little chance to work on us. Thus increasingly we meet only ourselves. But one of the chief operations of art is to remove our gaze from that mirrored face, to deliver us from that solitude."[11] Here Lewis was protesting the approach to the teaching of English literature that tries to create a piece of literature in the image of the teacher, thereby reinforcing the teacher's own position. Lewis opposed the tendency to see books "through the spectacles of other books."[12] He summarized later: "The necessary condition of all good reading is 'to get ourselves out of the way,'"[13] something not being done by the critics of Lewis's day or of our own time.

According to Lewis, another advantage of judging literature by the way in which people read it is that it frees us from what he elsewhere calls chronological snobbery. It also makes us better readers by forcing us to be attentive in our reading and to read without preconceptions so we receive the message of the literature.[14]

The literary person will read different kinds of literature, will read both for the ear and the eye, will be conscious of style (that is, not satisfied with the cliché), will appreciate detail and dialogue, and will understand the importance of slow-moving narrative for character and setting development. The literary person is looking for much more than the event, just as the musical listener is looking for much more than the tune.[15] If we heed this advice also in our writing, we will become better writers. For example, we will avoid the cliché, and we will use detail and dialogue.

In the literary realm, wrote Lewis, the unliterary person *uses* literature rather than *receives* literature,[16] just as the popular view of art and music uses rather than receives, or appreciates, art and music. But the literary person allows literature to set its own agenda in the reader because the literary person reads exegetically.

READING OLD BOOKS

According to Lewis, we should not only reread books, we also should read old books. Read an old book after every new book you read, argued Lewis, or at least one old book out of every three.[17] Lewis argued that many feel that only professionals should read the old books. The problem with this is that the great writers[18] are often better writers and more intelligible than the modern author who discusses the great works. Reading literature firsthand is better than reading about it secondhand,[19] just as meeting the president of the United States is better than reading about him or driving a car is better than reading a book about driving. George Watson has noted that a footnote of Lewis in "Shelley, Dryden and Mr. Eliot" mentioned the difficulty of finding copies of Godwin's *Political Justice*. Watson wrote: "You feel sure that he will read the book as soon as he can, abstain from judgment until he has read it, and disdain the views of those who imagine that the easy dismissal of the book by fashionable critics justifies them in leaving it unread."[20]

In addition, according to Lewis, new books have this against them: They are written within a particular age whose presuppositions—both the correct ones and the mistaken ones—are shared by most writers of that age. Therefore new books are usually unable to lift themselves out of that age and write timelessly. Lewis stated: "The true aim of literary studies is to lift the student out of his provincialism by making him 'the spectator', if not of all, yet of much, 'time and existence' . . . . The student . . . is taken out of the narrowness of his own age and class into a more public world."[21] By reading old books, Lewis once wrote that a person is able to see the presuppositions of one's own age, presuppositions that are shared by most writers of that age who are usually unable to escape the mistakes of that age. In reading old books, we are reading both literature and history simultaneously, thus the reading of old books carries one of the same functions as the study of history. Only the test of time can determine whether or not a particular modern author has written a timeless classic. As an example of this combination of history and literature, Lewis cited the word *Christianity*. Many think that the word *Christianity* carries so many meanings that it means nothing at all. By stepping out of the present century and reading the books of past Christians, we discover the mere Christianity of the ages, which is "no insipid inter-denominational transparency" but a powerful and positive spirituality.[22]

Writing about the classics, Lewis stated: "The effect of removing this education has been to isolate the mind in its own age."[23] The Greek and Latin classics provide an infusion of the better elements of paganism. According to Lewis, "[i]t was natural to men so trained to believe that valuable truth could still be found in an ancient book. It was natural to them to reverence tradition."[24] Writing similarly about history, Lewis stated: "Most of all, perhaps, we need intimate knowledge of the past . . . to remind us that the basic assumptions have been quite different in different periods."[25] But here we are only rehearsing what we have already stated about Lewis's educational philosophy. In Letter 27, Screwtape wrote from the opposite point of view:

> Only the learned read old books, and we have now so dealt with the learned that they are of all men the least likely to acquire wisdom by doing so. We have done this by inculcating the Historical Point of View. The Historical Point of View, put briefly, means that when a learned man is presented with any statement in an ancient author, the one question he never asks is whether it is true.[26]

How *should* we read old books? In the opening paragraphs of *Studies in Medieval and Renaissance Literature*, Lewis argued that we ought to read old books not for what we think we see in them but for what the author intended in that day. That is, we should become literary readers who receive the text. Unless we do this, we will not find ourselves lifted out of our century, but we will merely be reading the views and prejudices of our present life back into the literature we are reading. What the book means to us today cannot be fully understood until we know what it meant to the person who wrote it. "What a poem may 'mean' to moderns and to them only, however delightful," wrote Lewis, "is from this point of view merely a stain on the lens. We must clean the lens and remove the stain so that the real past can be seen better."[27]

In summary, then, Lewis read and reread books because of his love of literature and so he could be influenced by the text. He read without preconceptions so he could learn to be attentive, to appreciate detail and dialogue and style, and to rise above the isolation of his own age and thereby learn or relearn valid and timeless truths. Lewis also reread books because those volumes he read a second time were ones that had influenced his thinking. He once wrote about the important discovery that, in rereading a book, the book had contributed much to his thinking.[28]

PART II

C. S. LEWIS AS A STUDENT

FIVE

The Early Education of C. S. Lewis

There, behind me, far away, never more beautiful since, was the fabled cluster of spires and towers.—C. S. Lewis, *Surprised by Joy*[1]

We begin this section with C. S. Lewis's own education, for this allows us insight into the origin of his views on education. Because educators often teach what and how they were taught, we must understand the education Lewis received.

At Home

Lewis's education began at home. Both his father and mother encouraged and modeled the educated life. His father was a well-educated solicitor with his own law practice in Belfast. Lewis's mother had earned a degree in mathematics and logic from Queen's College (later Queen's University) in Belfast.

From Albert James Lewis (1863–1929), his father, C. S. Lewis was reputed to have inherited an excellent memory, a strong work ethic, and a sharp mind.[2] The younger Lewis is also said to have been influenced by his father's romantic and imaginative side, in part because Albert helped to develop his son's literary interests with the many books in the home library. Albert attended three schools—the Model School, Belfast; Lurgan College, Lurgan; and Queen's College, Belfast. During Albert's years at

Lurgan College in Lurgan, Ireland, W. T. Kirkpatrick was headmaster. In 1879 Kirkpatrick helped Albert become established in a legal career as an apprentice solicitor[3] in the firm of McLean, Boyle, and McLean in Belfast. In 1881, Albert joined the Belmont Literary Society, a move reflective of his literary interests and his public speaking ability. After his apprenticeship, Albert Lewis established his own law practice in 1885 in Belfast with W. H. Arbuthnot.[4]

Lewis's mother, Florence (Flora) Hamilton Lewis (1862–1908), earned a First in logic and a Second Class Honours degree in mathematics from Queen's College, Belfast, which she attended from 1881 to 1886.[5] Lewis apparently inherited his mother's ability in logic, though not her mathematical skill (his failure to pass the mathematics portion of *Responsions* as an undergraduate is well known). Florence had sufficient linguistic ability to start Lewis in both French and Latin.

One particular feature of the household of most educated families also characterized the Albert Lewis household—books. Both parents loved to read and would often read for hours in the evening. That the two Lewis boys would later become voracious readers should surprise no one. Although neither parent read *to* the boys, Nurse Lizzie Endicott did.[6] Lewis wrote in *Surprised by Joy* about the books Albert had acquired for those evenings spent reading, books that shaped the younger Lewis's early life.[7] A lifetime of reading began in the home and formed the primary source for the irrigation of Lewis's mind. Lewis was known to have read *Paradise Lost* at age 9.[8] The young Lewis also was writing by this time, as identified both by diary entries and the tales of Boxen.[9]

WYNYARD SCHOOL AND CAMPBELL COLLEGE[10]

In 1908 Albert Lewis sent his son to Wynyard School in Watford, Hertfordshire, England. Wynyard was the first of four private schools that the young Lewis attended prior to his years with W. T. Kirkpatrick. His brother, Warren, had already spent three years at Wynyard, and both boys were two of eight or nine students who boarded at the school. A similar number attended the school but lived at home. Watford is located about 11 kilometers southwest of St. Albans on the northwest side of London.

Headed by the Rev. Robert Capron, known to the boys as "Oldie," Wynyard School may have been one of the worst ever in the history of education. In *Surprised by Joy*, Lewis renames the school "Belsen," after one of the Nazi concentration camps. He relates that Oldie beat students who did not know their lessons and assigned repetitious arithmetic problems for much of each day, thereby starving Lewis's imaginative life and teaching him almost nothing. Of his time at Wynyard, Lewis wrote: "In the meantime, the putting on of the school clothes was . . . the assumption of a prison uniform."[11] Although bullying had existed in earlier days, the dwindling population of the student body eliminated that problem, except from Oldie.[12]

Describing these two years at Wynyard, Lewis remembered longing for the end of term so he could return home to enjoy his free time. In fact, that longing, so much a part of Lewis's writings, taught him something. He later wrote of his time at Wynyard School: "To live by hope and longing is an art that was taught at my school. It does not surprise me that there should be two worlds."[13]

After leaving Wynyard in July 1910 at the age of 11, Lewis attended Campbell College in Belfast for half a term from September to mid-November 1910. The school is about a mile from Little Lea. There he encountered Matthew Arnold's poetry for the first time through the help of an excellent master, James Adams McNeill, a close friend of the Lewis family.[14] Both Lewis and Arthur Greeves, who would become a close friend, attended Campbell College, though they did not meet at that time.[15] Because of health concerns, Albert removed his son from Campbell College in November 1910.

CHERBOURG HOUSE AND MALVERN COLLEGE[16]

After Campbell College, Lewis headed to Cherbourg House,[17] a Malvern preparatory school. It was located only 100 yards west of Malvern College, where Warren Lewis attended. During his time at Cherbourg, the younger Lewis discovered the music of Wagner, which with other experiences at this time in life developed within him a love of the Northern people and culture. Lewis's mental desert was being irrigated.

Lewis won a classical entrance scholarship to Malvern College in the summer of 1913, so from Cherbourg he moved next door to Malvern,[18] which he attended from September 1913 to July 1914. Malvern College is located on the slopes of the Malvern Hills, Worcestershire, England, about

40 kilometers southwest of Birmingham and 150 kilometers northwest of London. Malvern College ran a traditional curriculum with a strong grounding in the classics, something that would bear fruit in Lewis's life despite his long-held antipathy toward the school.

Entering Malvern with a scholarship at the age of 14, his precocious feeling for both art and literature made him an unusual boy, as awkward at athletic games as he was adept at language and literature. Unfortunately, Lewis entered Malvern during a period of British emphasis upon sports.[19] The Malvern College of today continues this athletic tradition, offering soccer, swimming, badminton, scuba diving, lacrosse, hockey, tennis, rackets, and rugby. Few veterans of elementary schools will have difficulty imagining the ridicule and scorn with which Lewis must have been treated by peers and older students for his lack of prowess on the athletic field.

Despite the well-known dislike for the schools he attended early in life, Lewis gained much from those experiences, as his brother, Warren, attested. Lewis's low opinion of Malvern College became a sore spot in his relationship with his older brother, who remembered Malvern fondly. Lewis's time at Malvern College nevertheless provided a strong education. Lewis wrote about the times of intellectual growth at Malvern[20] and admitted the profound impact of a Malvern schoolmaster, Harry Wakelyn Smith (nicknamed Smugy), who taught him to understand and to love poetry. More than that, Smith taught Lewis to practice critical thinking. Lewis said: "He could enchant but he could also analyze."[21]

During this year at Malvern, Lewis learned about Celtic and Norse literature and he made friends with Arthur Greeves, with whom he continued a lifelong correspondence. Lewis also admitted that his low opinion of Malvern College was caused in part by his awkwardness at sports. However, he also disliked the social struggle to be numbered among the top students, a dislike that later surfaced in his disapproval of the inner ring.

During the next period of his life, while living and studying with Kirkpatrick and developing his literary tastes, Lewis's friendship with Greeves continued to develop. Lewis gave credit to Greeves for infecting him (a good infection!) with a taste for the classic English novelists, such as Charles Dickens, Sir Walter Scott, the Brontës, and Jane Austen.[22]

WILLIAM T. (W. T.) KIRKPATRICK[23]

On September 19, 1914, less than three months after the assassination of Archduke Francis Ferdinand, which led to World War I, Lewis traveled to Great Bookham to study with W. T. Kirkpatrick. Great Bookham was located in Surrey, a village about 25 kilometers southwest of Wimbledon on the southwest side of London. Lewis was only two-and-a-half months shy of his sixteenth birthday. Lewis's education from Kirkpatrick and his wife formed him into the logical sparring partner who would later use his skill at verbal sword-fighting with the Inklings (see Glossary), with the Socratic Club, and in tutorials.

Lewis's brother, Warren, also had studied with Kirkpatrick, who had successfully prepared Warren for entrance into Sandhurst as a recipient of a prize cadetship.[24] Albert Lewis was inclined to make the same arrangements for his youngest son, but this educational situation would be even more successful because Lewis learned to thrive in the homeschooling atmosphere of the Kirkpatrick household.

Kirkpatrick possessed a sharp and rational mind, was an avowed atheist, had liberal leanings, along with various idiosyncrasies. He had graduated from Queen's College, Belfast, Ireland, in 1868 with honors in English, history, and metaphysics. Kirkpatrick had been headmaster of Lurgan College (1874–1899) until his retirement, which is how Albert Lewis knew him.

Kirkpatrick's rational and logical mind led Lewis to write: "Born a little later, he would have been a Logical Positivist."[25] Kirkpatrick defined terms precisely and challenged the underpinnings of virtually everything that the younger Lewis said. "If ever a man came near to being a purely logical entity," wrote Lewis, "that man was Kirk."[26] In conversation with Kirkpatrick, Lewis recalled that "[t]he most casual remark was taken as a summons to disputation."[27] Later, Lewis would describe Kirkpatrick as a man who "thought not about you but about what you said."[28] Here we find *The Personal Heresy* in embryo, a work that Kirkpatrick clearly influenced.

In *Surprised by Joy*, Lewis summarized the Kirkpatrick regimen with its strong grounding in the classics. He read Homer, Demosthenes, Cicero,[29] Virgil, Greek and Latin compositions, Euripides, Sophocles, and Aeschylus. Lewis also studied French (with Mrs. Kirkpatrick), German, and Italian.[30] In January 1915, Kirkpatrick wrote to Albert Lewis about his son's exceptional abilities, indicating a premonition of his later career: "He was born with the literary temperament . . . . By an unerring instinct he detects first rate quality in literary workmanship, and the second rate does not interest him in any way."[31] Later in life, however, Lewis understood that some boredom went with the territory. When J. O. Reed complained of the boredom of reading certain texts, Lewis responded sympathetically but realistically. "I'm afraid," Lewis said, "you must accept being bored to death from time to time as one of the professional hazards of making English Literature your career."[32]

Later, Kirkpatrick wrote of Lewis's breadth of reading: "He has read more classics than any boy I ever had—or indeed I might add than any I ever heard of, unless it be an Addison or Landor or Macaulay."[33] Kirkpatrick had tremendous influence on Lewis's educational career. One example comes from a comment in Lewis's diary in 1923 when he wrote about his poem "Dymer" and the introduction of a semi-Kirkian character into the poem.[34] After Kirkpatrick's death in March 1921, Lewis wrote: "I at least owe to him in the intellectual sphere as much as one human being can owe another."[35] On the strength of his own intellect and Kirkpatrick's teaching, Lewis won a scholarship to University College, Oxford.

SIX

C. S. LEWIS AT OXFORD

Responsions is the entrance exam to the University: for you see,
tho' I have got a scholarship at one college, I don't belong
to the whole show.—C. S. Lewis, *They Stand Together*[1]

Knowledge of a portion of the English system of education will enable
us to understand both the undergraduate education that Lewis himself experienced and the educational system within which he taught.
However, this chapter does not present a mainstream English education.
We focus on Oxford and Cambridge, which accept only a small portion of
those students who would pursue a degree in higher education in England. As we focus on these two institutions, we will understand better the
education Lewis received in his late teens and early 20s.

Because Oxford and Cambridge are similar in many ways, they will be
discussed together, with the emphasis placed upon Oxford, where Lewis
studied as an undergraduate. An understanding of Cambridge will be
necessary as background for the years Lewis spent in that university as an
educator. Both institutions use similar tutorial systems, and the two universities cooperate on curriculum, examination, and in other areas. For
example, when Lewis was elected to the Chair (see Glossary) of Medieval
and Renaissance Literature in Cambridge, Oxford colleague J. R. R.
Tolkien was one of the electors.

Although the pages of this chapter will concentrate on the academic
side of Lewis's education at Oxford and elsewhere, much more than this

mattered at Oxford. Oxford "saw college life as educational in itself—cultivating tolerance, articulateness, sociability and qualities of leadership and organization."[2]

AN OXFORD EDUCATION

Only with great difficulty could prospective students gain entrance into one of the colleges of Oxford University. Furthermore, students admitted to a college within the university still had to gain admission to the university itself, and admission to the university was more difficult. Therefore when Lewis was elected to a scholarship at University College because of his successful entrance exams in December 1916, he had yet to be admitted to Oxford University. That admission would come as a result of passing Responsions (literally, responding to masters of, or experts in, various subjects).

Students could take Responsions four times a year in Oxford—September, December, March, and June. Lewis took his Responsions on March 20–21, 1917.[3] The subjects were organized into two groups: Stated Subjects and Additional Subjects. All candidates for the bachelor's degree were required to pass the examination in Stated Subjects, except those admitted to the status of Senior or Junior student, that is, transfer students. Candidates were "deemed to have 'passed Responsions' who have passed in 'Stated Subjects.' "[4] The Stated Subjects were arithmetic, elementary algebra or geometry, Greek and Latin grammar, translation from English into Latin prose, one Greek book, and one Latin book. Additional Subjects were taken only by candidates who wished to obtain an exemption from the classical part of the First Public Examination (see below) and begin early study of the subjects of the Final Honour Schools.

On his first try Lewis failed mathematics, which he described as elementary mathematics, so he was still required to pass it.[5] He once said that he could handle those aspects of mathematics that involved reasoning, such as geometry, but he could not do mathematical calculations.[6] Therefore arithmetic, one of the Stated Subjects, must have been his downfall.

There were three eight-week terms at Oxford each year when Lewis was an undergraduate—fall, winter, and spring—and undergraduates usually arrived early in October for the fall term. The fall term (October to December) was called Michaelmas term (see Glossary) and was followed by a vacation at Christmas. The second term (January to March) was Lent term and was followed by Easter vacation. The third term (April to June/July) was Trinity term (see Glossary) and was followed by summer vacation or "the Long Vac." Michaelmas term was named for the Feast of St. Michael and All Angels, normally celebrated on September 29. The Lent term, as it is called at Cambridge, was named for the Lenten season, which began after Christmas and continued to Easter. It is known as the Hilary term at Oxford, named after St. Hilary, bishop of Poitiers, whose festival is celebrated on January 13. Trinity term was named for what the Christian church used to call the season of Trinity but now calls the season of Pentecost. Trinity term, its Oxford name, is called Easter term at Cambridge. Within these terms, the tutorials and lectures occurred. Undergraduates normally took three years to complete the Bachelor of Arts degree. During the months of August and September, Lewis often took his holidays in Ireland, visiting his father and Arthur Greeves.

Candidates admitted to Oxford could choose between Pass and Honour Examinations. Pass Examinations had one standard (that is, you either passed or failed), while the Honour Examinations had four classes, each representing a different level of performance. No time limit was required for Pass Examinations, whereas Honour Examinations had a time limit. Each college and hall could set up its own rules, and some colleges required all candidates to read for Honours in one or more schools. Lewis attended University College, which was one of the colleges that required undergraduates to read for Honours in one of the Final Schools.[7]

Once admitted to Oxford, candidates for the Bachelor of Arts had to fulfill three requirements: (1) the First Public Examination, (2) the Second Public Examination, and (3) nine terms (three academic years) in residence. The First Public Examination was an intermediate examination that qualified a student to enter the Final School. The following description of the public examinations may sound tedious, but it will illustrate both the breadth and the difficulty of the curriculum. (As Lewis once suggested about reading something of little interest, if this portion does not interest you, then skip to the next section, "The University Tutorial System.")

THE FIRST PUBLIC EXAMINATION

Sometimes called the Preliminary Exam (or Prelims), the First Public Examination included an examination in Holy Scripture, required of all candidates, plus one of six other examinations, such as Mathematical Honour Moderations, the Preliminary Examination in Jurisprudence, or, the one Lewis would have taken, "an examination *in Literis Graecis et Latinis* for those who seek Honours (Classical Honour Moderations)."[8] The examination in Holy Scripture included one of the Synoptic Gospels and the Gospel of St. John, plus either the Book of Acts or the two Books of Samuel.

The First Public Examination in Greek and Latin texts included the following:

- Selections from four necessary books (Homer, Virgil, Demosthenes's *Orations*, and Cicero's *Orations*).
- Three special books (chosen from four Greek tragedies, portions of other Greek authors, certain Latin poets, and portions of other Latin authors).
- One of the following: the history of Greek drama, with Aristotle's *Poetics*; the history of Attic oratory, with Aristotle's *Rhetoric*; the history of Roman poetry to the end of the Augustan Age; the history of Latin prose style, with Cicero's *Orator*; logic; either comparative philology as applied to Greek and Latin or historical and analytical syntax of the Greek and Latin languages; Greek sculpture, 600–320 B.C.; or Homeric archaeology.

Three hours were allowed to each subject. Thus Lewis spent three hours on Latin prose composition, three hours on unseen translation from Greek, three hours on unseen translation from Latin, three hours on Greek and Latin grammar, three hours on literary criticism, and three hours on antiquities, including questions on the necessary books plus optional papers on Greek prose composition (three hours) and Greek and Latin verse composition (three hours). The examination was held once a year, beginning on the Thursday of the seventh week of Hilary term.

THE SECOND PUBLIC EXAMINATION

Those taking the Second Public Examination (or Finals) in an Honour School also followed specific requirements and procedures. The examinations of the School of Literae Humaniores, within which Lewis took his first two courses of study, would begin on the Thursday in the sixth week of Trinity term. The examination took six days, three hours on each of two papers each day, or thirty-six hours of writing. The candidate had to give notice of taking the examination and pay examination fees. The examinations were both written and oral. The interview, or *viva voce* (live interview, literally, in Latin, "with a live voice"), took place three weeks after the examiners had read the written examinations. The list of those who took the examinations would be grouped into four classes, and all the examiners would sign the list. The list would be put up in the Examination Schools, on the door of the Convocation House, published in the *University Gazette*, and published in the principal newspapers of Oxford.

In Lewis's day, there were First, Second, Third, and Fourth Class degrees. Today, however, a student can earn a First Class degree, an upper Second Class degree, a lower Second Class degree, or a Third Class degree. Few students earn a First Class degree. In fact, only about 5 percent did so at the time Lewis was a student at Oxford, though in the last fifteen years, 20 percent or more earn a First.[9] The Second Class degrees also are not easy to achieve. The level of accomplishment, naturally, depends on several factors: the intelligence and background of the student, the amount of effort, and the effectiveness of the tutor. One Oxford graduate has written: "Academic research has shown that normally pupils who soak in their tutors get firsts, those who parrot them get seconds, and those who think independently get thirds; only very good Universities and professors—such as Lewis—provide exceptions to this rule."[10]

The *Oxford University Handbook* describes the School of Literae Humaniores, or the Final Classical School, as "the premier School in dignity and importance," one that

- carries the most coveted distinction . . .
- includes the greatest proportion of the ablest students . . .
- covers the widest area of study . . .
- makes probably the severest demands.[11]

Although the case may be overstated, this is the school in which Lewis studied.

The Second Public Examination included the following:
- Greek and Latin;
- the histories of Greece and Rome;
- logic; and
- the outlines of moral and political philosophy.

In the language portion, students had to translate from Greek and Latin into English and from English into Greek and Latin prose. In history, students could choose one of two periods in Greek history[12] and one of three periods in Roman history in which to specialize.[13] Philosophy comprised three broad areas. In logic, students were recommended to study the logic of Aristotle and Francis Bacon and that of modern authors. Students had to know the outlines of the theory of knowledge from René Descartes to Immanuel Kant, especially the philosophy of John Locke, George Berkeley, David Hume, and Kant. They also had to study Plato and Aristotle on moral philosophy, the British moralists of the eighteenth century, Kant, and the Utilitarians. In political philosophy, they studied Plato's *Republic*, Aristotle's *Ethics*, Aristotle's *Politics*, some modern political thought, some political economy, and the works of Thomas Hobbes, John Stuart Mill, T. H. Green, Henry Sidgwick, and Bernard Bosanquet.[14]

Times have changed, of course, so the university setting that Lewis experienced during his undergraduate years is much different today. For example, Greek and Latin are much less common, and the study of modern literature has been incorporated into the curriculum.[15]

THE UNIVERSITY TUTORIAL SYSTEM

The Oxbridge system (see Glossary) makes use of the lecture, but the primary element of the system is the tutorial. (Generally speaking, tutorials are not a major feature of non-Oxbridge universities.)

The tutorial system, however, is much more important. It has ancient roots, though in its present form it dates to the latter part of the nineteenth century. After the Royal Commission of 1850, changes occurred to create efficiency and effectiveness in the tutorial system.[16] Tutors were specifically chosen based on their ability to teach. At first, both lectures and tutorials were carried out within the student's college, but later in the century both lectures and tutorials could be taken outside the student's college. Tutorials could be taken in another college if one's own college lacked a tutor in the subject. Teachers in each discipline were organized into faculties, and the faculties drew up plans for their curriculum. Because informal discussion does not occur in lectures, students come to the room of the tutor for private instruction, either individually or in small groups.

At Oxford, tutors conduct these tutorials, which are supplemented by lectures. At Cambridge, two positions carry the functions performed by Oxford tutors: supervisors and moral tutors. At Cambridge a supervisor is the Fellow who conducts the tutorials under the direction of the Director of Studies for the particular academic discipline at that college. The moral tutor at Cambridge is the person who carries responsibility for all aspects of the undergraduate's life, not just the academic portion.[17] The same function today would be performed at Oxford by the college's senior tutor.

In the tutorial, the student comes to the rooms of the tutor and reads a paper he or she has prepared on the topic assigned the week before. The tutor listens to the paper, discusses it with the student, critiques it, and makes an assignment for the next week. That assignment is to write another essay on a topic, and a reading list is usually provided with that assignment. Students might come in pairs or even in small groups, but the individual tutorial is more common. When more than one student participates, one reads an essay and the others join in the discussion.

As an Oxford undergraduate, Lewis took tutorials from several tutors. Summaries of tutorials he took with F. P. Wilson, Edith Wardale, and George Hope Stevenson appear in various places in Lewis's diary.[18] As a Fellow, Lewis gave tutorials. The book *We Remember C. S. Lewis*[19] contains numerous remembrances of tutorials that students took with Lewis, some of which are incorporated into chapter 9 of this book.

During the term, tutors meet with the head (see Glossary) of the college to discuss the work of each pupil. Other Fellows who know the pupil also can express their views. At the end of each term, or sometimes at the beginning, students take college examinations known as Collections (see Glossary). The tutor looks at these exams, then meets with the students to discuss them. On the last day of the term, undergraduates appear before the head of the college and five dons, who serve as the tutorial committee, and the tutors give reports on the students' work. No reports are given to parents because undergraduates are fully responsible for their education. (Now undergraduates meet with the college's senior tutor, who apprises students of the reports written on their work by the various subject tutors.)

The tutor-pupil relationship can provide students with help in adjusting to college, with advice on spending habits, and with other kinds of assistance. Sometimes the tutor assists an undergraduate in finding employment, including serving as a reference. Occasionally the relationship results in a friendship that lasts long after the student graduates. An observer of English university life once wrote: "Oxford and Cambridge establish a personal relationship between the undergraduate and his tutor, that is, despite possible personal limitations, the most effective pedagogical relation in the world."[20]

THE UNIVERSITY LECTURE SYSTEM

The other side of the Oxbridge system is the lecture. Both tutors (though not all tutors) and professors offer lectures to all students, regardless of the college in which they are enrolled. Students of New College can attend the lectures of Professor X of Merton College, and students of Brasenose College can attend the lectures of Professor Y of Christ Church (never called Christ Church College by Oxonians). No attendance records are kept at lectures nor are they compulsory. Undergraduates could conceivably complete a degree without attending a single lecture, though most tutors will recommend various series of lectures to their students. These days most Oxbridge lectures occur in the building of the particular faculty (the faculty of a given academic discipline, not the faculty of a college) and are run centrally by the university as a whole, not in individual colleges. Undergraduates may attend lectures at any of these locations, and they pay no additional fees.

British lectures carry all the same problems of lectures in the modern U.S. higher education system. On October 16, 1922, Lewis attended a lecture on the "Outlines of the History of English" at University College. The lecture was given by H. C. K. Wyld, who was the Merton Professor of English Language and Literature. After the lecture, Lewis complained that Wyld taught him nothing he did not already know.[21]

Although most tutors were required to do tutorials and lectures, professors were required only to lecture. That is why Lewis, upon being asked in 1954 about his new position at Cambridge, called it "rather less work for rather more pay."[22] At Cambridge, Lewis held the Chair of Medieval and Renaissance Literature, while at Oxford he was a Fellow and tutor. Later we will look at Lewis as lecturer and find that he was one of the few Fellows who excelled at lecturing.

THE ENGLISH SCHOOL

The third course of study for Lewis was English language and literature, which he read in the English School.[23] In 1914 the English School was new, only 20 years old, and very small. When Walter Raleigh (1861–1922, not to be confused with the sixteenth-century Sir Walter Raleigh) came to Oxford in 1904, he energized the English School, and enrollment began to grow. But enrollment soon slowed because of the school's primary focus on philology, an emphasis that was supposed to provide the rigor that a pure study of literature would allegedly lack.[24] In 1914 the English School offered two courses of study, both of which were largely philological. The first course consisted of nine or ten papers in a language course, including three literary papers, one of which covered the period since Shakespeare. The second course, which was more literary, consisted of nine or ten papers, including three language papers and two literary papers on the period since Shakespeare.

In 1916–1917 a new course of study was devised with examination in this course to begin in 1919. This new course included the study of modern literature, which was intended to attract more students. In 1922 the syllabus[25] for all three courses was revised. The first two courses increased the linguistic options, while the new course, especially designed for those who wanted to study modern literature, required three-and-a-half or four-and-a-half post-Shakespeare literary papers. All three courses[26] offered the option of nineteenth-century literature and a new list of optional subjects, including a choice of Greek literary criticism, French classical drama, or Italian influences on sixteenth-century English literature.[27] Lewis would have taken his degree in English language and literature in the new course, with its greater emphasis on literature, but still with a significant amount of study of the language. Three of his papers in this course were language papers, which is why he studied Old English (formerly called Anglo-Saxon, a subject Lewis later insisted was indispensable for the study of English language and literature) with Edith Wardale. Thus by the time Lewis was a student, Oxford offered three courses in English: one in philology, one that was half in philology and half in literature, and one primarily in literature.

J. O. Reed later took the same literary course of study as Lewis. In an unpublished letter from Lewis to Reed, Lewis summarized the three courses of study: "I am assuming you choose Course 3 which is mainly modern. If you prefer No. 1 (mainly philological & medieval) or 2 (a half way house between 1 and 3) let me know."[28] During the Trinity term of 1950, as most students did, Reed opted for the modern course, which required eleven papers covering English literature to 1832, with separate papers on Chaucer and his contemporaries, Shakespeare and contemporary dramatists, and a paper on Spenser and Milton.[29] Other philological work—Old English, Middle English, history of the language—occurred concurrently with J. A. W. Bennett.

Because of the influence of J. R. R. Tolkien, the Honours English School syllabus was changed again in 1931. Because the two philological courses were attracting only about 10 percent of the English Honours students, Tolkien presented two new philological Final Honours courses, only one of which made Shakespeare a requirement. Tolkien was assisted by H. F. B. Brett-Smith, the Reader (see Glossary) in English literature, and George Gordon, who also wished to avoid mandating the study of post-1800 literature. On May 22, 1931, the English School established a medieval philological course covering the period up to Chaucer. Another modern philological course would cover the period up to Milton. The time after Milton would be covered in the literary course, now course three, in which the literature of the period from 1830 to 1900 was optional. Under the new syllabus, however, the number of Honours finalists in English fell by 10 percent between 1933 and 1939, with 95 percent of the candidates taking the literary course.[30] The discussions and revisions of the English School continued through the decades, but during the 1930s and 1940s the English School was primarily philological. It was not until 1970 that twentieth-century literature was allowed in the English Syllabus.[31]

Thus the undergraduate in Lewis's day would seek entrance to a college, take Responsions (in Stated Subjects and Additional Subjects, which gained admission to the university), then choose Pass or Honour Examinations. Having made that choice, the undergraduate would begin studying with a tutor, writing papers, and attending lectures in preparation for the First Public Examination (the Preliminary Exam), eventually the Second Public Examination (Finals), and finally a *viva voce*, or final oral interview.

C. S. LEWIS'S EDUCATION AT OXFORD[32]

Lewis began his Oxford entrance exam in classics on December 4, 1916, and finished on December 9. His score earned him one of three scholarships for classics at University College. In a glimpse at one of the reasons for this success, E. F. Carritt had been astonished at Lewis's wide reading during the time he examined him for this scholarship.[33] Reginald W. Macan, master[34] of University College, wrote to Lewis with the news: "This College elects you to a Scholarship." On December 14, *The Times* listed Lewis as successful in winning a scholarship.[35] His scholarship secured Lewis free rooms and a monetary grant, but not entrance to Oxford University. To gain entrance to the university, he would have to pass Responsions. These he took on March 20–21, 1917. He passed every portion of Responsions except mathematics. Despite his failure in mathematics, Lewis was allowed to enter the university. He arrived on April 26 for the beginning of the summer term to train in the university Officers' Training Corps (O.T.C.). Lewis's rooms at University College were in the Front Quad, Number 5, Staircase 12, overlooking the Radcliffe Quad.[36]

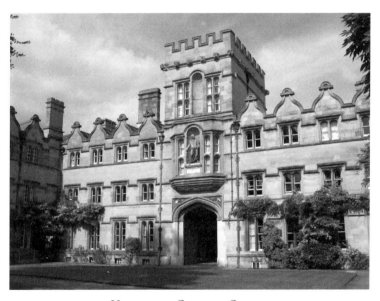

UNIVERSITY COLLEGE, OXFORD

Clearly, Lewis knew of the possibility of serving in World War I, having matriculated with the O.T.C. He was motivated by his patriotic desire to defend England (though he was Irish and was, therefore, not obligated to serve in the war). The 1917 *Oxford University Handbook* describes the O.T.C.:

> The object of the Officers' Training Corps is to give an opportunity to undergraduates to offer their services to the Country in the simplest and most practical way during peace, and to provide officers for His Majesty's Army (Regular and Territorial) from this University in time of national emergency.

> With a view to these important objects every effort is made to provide cadets with a standardized measure of elementary military training, and to inculcate some knowledge of war in its greater aspect, as taught by history.[37]

After another term with W. T. Kirkpatrick to study mathematics between Christmas and Easter 1917, Lewis took the mathematics portion of Responsions a second time in June 1917 and failed again.[38] In Trinity term 1917, he tried again with a Hertford College tutor.[39] Lewis enlisted in the military, beginning his service with the Somerset Light Infantry in June 1917. The choice to enter the service was not motivated by the knowledge that Responsions would be waived for World War I veterans, though Lewis knew of the exemption before his military service.[40] However, Lewis may never have entered Oxford University without this exemption because he never passed Responsions in mathematics. After serving in World War I, Lewis returned to Oxford on January 13, 1919, for the Hilary term. Later that month, Lewis learned he was "deemed to have passed" Responsions in mathematics and also to have passed divinity.

CLASSICAL HONOUR MODERATIONS (HONOUR MODERATIONS)

The end result of Lewis's Oxford education at University College was a liberal arts education, including the study of the classics, philosophy, history, and English language and literature. The subjects Lewis studied are well represented in the curriculum of the modern liberal arts college. The Oxford student focused on a single area of study rather than a distributed core as the foundation for completing a major, a minor, and a series of elective courses. Lewis's first area of study was Honour, or Classical, Moderations, a difficult course of study in Greek and Latin texts, which he studied under the tutelage of Arthur Poynton.[41] As a tutor, Lewis rated Poynton alongside Harry Wakelyn Smith (Smugy) and W. T. Kirkpatrick.[42] Lewis's studies prepared him for his First Public Examination, which focused on Latin and Greek. It included the following:

1. Unseen translation from Latin and Greek.

2. Rendering English prose into Latin and Greek as close to the style of the ancient classical authors as possible.

3. Competence in the writings of Homer and Virgil.

4. Competence in the classical writers, poets, orators, and historians.

5. Special subjects, one of which the candidate may choose, such as history of Greek drama, Homeric archaeology, or comparative Latin and Greek philology.

In March 1920, Lewis learned that he had earned First Class Honours in Honour Moderations. The course of study, normally taken along with Greats, takes four years; Lewis had completed the first part in sixteen months.

LITERAE HUMANIORES (GREATS)

Lewis followed his success in Classical Honour Moderations with Greats, a course of study in ancient history and classical philosophy, in the Honour School of Literae Humaniores. His tutors for this course were George Hope Stevenson and E. F. Carritt, the former in history and the latter in philosophy.[43] Lewis also studied under Arthur Spenser Loat Farquharson, a tutor in Greats. The Honour School of Literae Humaniores was defined in 1830 as including "Greek and Latin Language and History, Rhetoric and Poetics, the Moral and Political Sciences, with ancient writers illustrated from the moderns, as well as Logic."[44]

In 1852 this school had been divided into two parts, the first dealing with poets and orators and the second with historians and philosophers. Lewis's success in Classical Honour Moderations was the first part, so this second course of study in Greats was the natural next step. He probably studied Francis Bacon's logic and read Thomas Fowler's *Modern Logic*. Lewis's personal library included H. W. B. Joseph's *Introduction to Logic*.[45] According to one commentator, "[t]he philosopher most important for the Greats curriculum was Plato, the *Republic* the most important text."[46] Aristotle was added to the Greats curriculum in the 1850s, and modern philosophers, especially Immanuel Kant and G. W. F. Hegel, were added in the 1860s and the following two decades. During this course of study, Lewis adopted the realist position, a philosophical position reflected in the chapter in *Surprised by Joy* entitled "New Look," which is described more fully below.

Greats, the slang name for Literae Humaniores, was considered the most celebrated of the arts courses at Oxford. With Classical Honour Moderations, it lasted four years, including preparation for both the First Public Examination and the Second Public Examination. Most other courses lasted three years. In the second year, students took the First Public Examination (most other courses of study put students through the First Public Examination after the second term) in Classical Honour Moderations (see pp. 75–76).

After this examination, the course of study proceeded to history, including Greek and Roman history, and philosophy, especially Plato's *Republic* and Aristotle's *Ethics*. This segment also included modern philosophy beginning with Descartes. At the end of the course of study, students took the Final Honour School Examination, a series of nine or ten three-hour papers followed by a *viva voce*, or oral, examination. The *viva voce* interview especially addressed those students who lay on the margin between two classes of Honours and could determine which class they achieved. For other students the *viva voce* interview was a mere formality. The examining board reviewed the papers with much intensity, and all members of the examining board were responsible jointly for their judgments. A student who had completed one Final Honour School, as Lewis did, could take a Second Honour School. "That, however, is difficult and exacting and can only be recommended to those who are both gifted and industrious beyond the average."[47]

On June 8, 1922, Lewis began to sit for the six days of exams for Greats. The number of times Lewis cited Plato in his writings or echoed Plato's concept of forms provides ample testimony to the influence of this philosopher on his thinking. Plato's influence also can be seen in this comment by Lewis: "I think that all things, in their way, reflect heavenly truth, the imagination not least."[48] This quotation reflects Plato's concept of earthly objects having a perfect heavenly counterpart; Lewis echoes this in his concept of earth as the Shadowlands. On July 28, 1922, Lewis had his *viva voce* interview, and on August 4, 1922, it was announced that he had earned First Class Honours again. He had completed this four-year program in about three-and-a-half years.

ENGLISH LANGUAGE AND LITERATURE

During 1922 and 1923, Lewis took a second degree (Classical Honour Moderations and Greats resulted in the first degree) in English language and literature under the tutelage of Frank P. Wilson, then a Fellow of Exeter College and later the Merton Professor of English Literature, and Edith Wardale of St. Hugh's College. Wilson tutored Lewis in literature (and later gave him the idea for *The Allegory of Love*), and Wardale tutored him in Old English. Lewis also studied English literature with George Stuart Gordon.[49] At that time, the course of study for this degree focused far more on language study than it did later. Lewis began his exams with Old English on June 14, 1923, and continued through June 19 with other written exams on Middle English, Chaucer, Milton, Shakespeare, Spenser, Bacon, Sydney, Bunyan, Shadwell, and other topics. He took his oral exam on July 10, 1923. On July 16, he learned that, along with Nevill Coghill, he had earned "First Class Honours in the Honour School of English Language and Literature."[50] It had taken Lewis only one year to complete this course of study, about one-third the length of time it normally takes an undergraduate to do so.[51]

The course in English language and literature was relatively new at Oxford when Lewis studied for his third Honour School. This course of study covered both the history of the English language as well as the history of English literature with new texts and authors occasionally added. All candidates had to show competence in the English language at all periods of history, including Old English, and had to demonstrate wide knowledge of English literature. After this overarching requirement, candidates could choose to focus on philology and the history of the English language or specified authors and periods in English literature. Lewis chose the literary track, as did most students. This included Old English texts such as *Beowulf,* followed by Middle English texts up to Chaucer. Study of English literature from 1400 to 1550 then followed without a prescribed set of authors. Shakespeare and his contemporaries were a separate subject, as were Spenser and Milton, especially *Paradise Lost.* English literature from 1550 to 1830 comprised another course, as did English literature from 1830 to 1920, the conclusion of the course of study. This last course was one that Lewis fought against later in his career. Optional courses of study included Gothic, Old Saxon, Old High German, Middle High German, Old Norse, and Old French.

Later, when Lewis himself was a Fellow, Hugh Whitney Morrison followed this course of study in English language and literature with David Nichol Smith and H. C. K. Wyld at Merton College (1930–1932):

Anglo-Saxon (Old English)

Middle-English and The History of English Language

Chaucer, his Canterbury Tales, and his contemporaries

Shakespeare, in general, plus four "Set Plays" ("Love's Labour's Lost," "Henry IV—Pt. 1," "Othello," and "Anthony and Cleopatra")

Spenser and Milton, with special study of "Paradise Lost"

15th and 16th Century English

17th Century English

18th Century English

19th Century English (no 20th Century offered)[52]

Lewis had earned three Firsts at Oxford University—Classical Honour Moderations in 1920, Greats in 1922, and English Language and Literature in 1923. Few students earn a First, so to win three such honors reflects tremendous intellectual talent. In 1808 Robert Peel had been the first person to earn two firsts: in classics and mathematics. The second to do so was W. E. Gladstone in 1831,[53] so the frequency of a double first, though probably more common in later years, was not high. A triple first was even more rare.

Few people put two and two together when they consider Lewis's education. Here was one of the most effective writers of the twentieth century, a man steeped in the subjects of the liberal arts. He studied Greek and Latin texts, as well as their authors, classical philosophy, and English language and literature. These subjects are powerfully representative of the liberal arts, yet today many clamor for more vocational training and less from the liberal arts because of an alleged lack of practicality. One secret to Lewis's skill was the education in the liberal arts that he received, especially from W. T. Kirkpatrick and from University College, Oxford. That education taught Lewis to think critically, to write effectively, to pursue objective truth, to develop trained emotions, to desire transcendent truth (or what he called "Joy"), and to follow a path that allowed him to share his insights with the rest of the world.

On May 24, 1921, Lewis won the Chancellor's essay prize, apparently worth £20.[54] The assigned topic was "optimism," and as the winner, Lewis read his essay at Encaenia. This annual ceremony in commemoration of Oxford's founders and benefactors was held in the Sheldonian Theatre. At this ceremony several men received honorary degrees, including the former French Prime Minister and Minister for War Georges Clemenceau and Admiral Roger Keyes. Unfortunately, the essay no longer exists, but this accomplishment served as a premonition of Lewis's later proficiency in writing. The essay was probably never published for the following reasons, which Lewis mentioned in a 1921 letter to his father: Several dons advised Lewis not to publish it because it could eventually form the basis of a book and because he would outgrow many of the views expressed in embryo in the essay.[55]

During 1922, Lewis wrote the essay "Hegemony of Moral Value" in an effort to secure a fellowship in philosophy at Magdalen College. He failed, as Herbert Warren, president (see Glossary) of Magdalen, informed him. The essay was never published, but it was probably incorporated into his lectures and later, in part, into *The Abolition of Man*.[56]

SUMMARY

C. S. Lewis did indeed receive a marvelous and rigorous liberal arts education at Oxford University. He excelled at each stage, earning two degrees and three First Class Honours. He went on to make the most of the education he received, first, as an Oxford don but also as a writer. We now turn to Lewis's career as an Oxford don.

PART III

C. S. LEWIS AS A TEACHER

SEVEN

C. S. LEWIS AS AN OXFORD FELLOW

[H]e was a philologist, and fellow of a Cambridge college.
His name was Ransom.—C. S. Lewis, Out of the Silent Planet[1]

What was the academic climate of the Oxford University and Magdalen College of C. S. Lewis between 1925 and 1954?[2] In his chapter "Exorcising the Zeitgeist: Lewis as Evangelist to the Modernists," George Musacchio described the major influences that helped to create the Oxford and Cambridge of Lewis's day: Enlightenment reason, the scientific method, scientism, logical positivism, and life-force philosophy.[3] These factors and others will appear prominently in this chapter.

Prior to becoming a Fellow of Magdalen College, Lewis was offered a one-year, full-time job as a teacher of philosophy at University College. He would substitute for E. F. Carritt, who was to spend a year lecturing at the University of Michigan.[4] Lewis accepted, and the fellowship was announced in April 1924. This became Lewis's first experience at teaching. During this time, he apparently was flirting with realism, a philosophic position that Carritt espoused, and this may have been the reason Lewis was bypassed for a Magdalen post for which he had applied in 1922.[5] It may also have been the reason that Carritt gave Lewis his pupils while he spent the year in Michigan, thus attempting to ensure a realist succession at Oxford.

During this year, Lewis applied for various fellowships at Oxford in philosophy and English. As so often happens, the one he thought he had no chance to obtain was the one to which he was elected: to teach English at Magdalen College. Lewis was elected by Magdalen College rather than by the university's governing board because the individual colleges act autonomously in such appointments. The governing body at the men's colleges actually consists of the Fellows. Albert Lewis received a telegram on May 20, 1925, stating that his son had been appointed for a five-year term in English, with some work in philosophy. Lewis's position would begin June 25, 1925.[6] *The Times* announced Lewis's appointment on May 22, 1925:

> The President and Fellows of Magdalen College have elected to an official Fellowship in the College as Tutor in English Language and Literature, for five years as from next June 25, Mr. Clive Staples Lewis.[7]

What sets the universities of Oxford and Cambridge apart from the red-brick universities in the United Kingdom are their independent endowments, their self-government, and their history of more than seven hundred years of teaching and learning. The thirty-one colleges of Cambridge University and the thirty-four colleges of Oxford University select their own Fellows, but each college belongs to the entire university, which provides lectures, tutorials, laboratories, examinations, and degrees.[8]

A Fellow is a senior member of a particular college. He or she will be either a Bye-Fellow (a postgraduate student, often in the third year of doctoral studies, who is appointed for one year; see Glossary) or a Research Fellow (usually postdoctoral and appointed for five years; see Glossary), either of whom could teach, called supervising in Cambridge.[9] There also were permanent Fellows (usually lecturers on the university staff, though sometimes full-time members of a college staff), senior tutors (presiding over the tutors and possessing an administrative and pastoral responsibility for student members of the college), a Dean of Chapel or chaplain, and Professorial Fellows (a professor of the university who held a permanent fellowship but did not teach in the college; see Glossary).

Those Fellows who are on the university staff (the great majority) may be either a junior or senior lecturer (see Glossary), a Reader (a special title given by a faculty to honor a lecturer of distinction), or a professor (increasingly, this can be a personal title given to reward and recognize achievement, but it also denotes a full professor, the holder of a chair in a faculty, known in the United States as a chair of a department). Not everyone appointed to a university post is necessarily invited to be a Fellow of a particular college. Efforts are usually made, however, by those on the faculty to persuade a college to make such an invitation to a new professor or lecturer. Sometimes colleges compete with one another to invite such newcomers to the university to become Fellows. This is a considerable advantage because a college offers its Fellows rooms in which to study and teach. As in Lewis's case at Cambridge, this provides living accommodation for those who do not want to acquire a house in the city.

In 1925 Lewis finally became a Fellow of Oxford, which he had once described as ". . . a close corporation of jolly, untidy, lazy, good for nothing humorous old men, who have been electing their own successors ever since the world began and who intend to go on with it."[10] One can only call it poetic justice.

Lewis had rooms in New Building on the same staircase as J. A. Smith and in the same building as people such as Hugh Sinclair, which Lewis once said was a liberal education itself.[11] A typical schedule had him up for tea at 7:15 A.M., to Matins at 8 A.M., and to breakfast from 8:15 to 8:25. (Lewis was a very fast eater.) Until pupils arrived for tutorials at 9 A.M., Lewis answered correspondence. Tutorials lasted until 1 P.M., at which time he went home for lunch. In the afternoon Lewis would often walk, then return to the college after tea for tutorials from 5 to 7 P.M. After a 7:15 dinner, he attended the meetings of various undergraduate societies.

A BRIEF HISTORY OF OXFORD UNIVERSITY

Oxford University is located near a junction of the Rivers Thames and Cherwell, at the place where the oxen could ford (Oxen-ford). Popular legend reports that the Saxon princess Frideswide, or her father, founded a monastery at this site in A.D. 727. In 1121, during the Norman period, Christ Church was built at the place where the Priory of St. Frideswide was located, so she is regarded as the patron saint of Oxford. Although students came to the university to study in the twelfth century, there were no colleges until the thirteenth century. The first college, University College, was endowed in 1249. This was the college Lewis attended as an undergraduate. Balliol College was founded in 1262 and Merton College in 1264.

MAGDALEN COLLEGE, OXFORD

Christ Church, one of the better known colleges, was established by King Henry VIII in 1546. Its Tom Tower, designed by Sir Christopher Wren, stands as a visible landmark at the southern end of the university. During the Tudor period, Archbishop of Canterbury Thomas Cranmer and Bishops High Latimer and Nicholas Ridley were tried and subsequently burned at the stake in Oxford for their Protestant convictions.[12] In 1602 the library of Duke Humfrey[13] was restored by Thomas Bodley, thus the Bodleian Library has carried his name ever since. (This library is one of two libraries in the world that carry the complete works of C. S. Lewis, the other being the Marion E. Wade Center at Wheaton College, Wheaton, Illinois.) The Sheldonian Theatre, also designed by Sir Christopher Wren, was begun in 1664, and the Ashmolean Museum began in 1683. Oxford is also known as the birthplace of Methodism (1729).[14]

Today Oxford University boasts approximately 14,000 students and thirty-four undergraduate colleges. Among Oxford's famous alumni are the Bible translator John Wycliffe (1330–1384), Sir Walter Raleigh (1552–1618), Richard Hooker (1554–1600), John Donne (1572–1631),

William Harvey (1578–1657, discoverer of the circulatory system), the seventeenth-century philosopher John Locke (1632–1704), architect and astronomer Christopher Wren (1632–1723), Quaker William Penn (1644–1718), Edmond Halley (1656–1742, discoverer of Halley's Comet), General James Edward Oglethorpe (1696–1785, founder of the State of Georgia), John Wesley (1703–91, founder of Methodism), Charles Wesley (1707–88, John's hymn-writing brother), Samuel Johnson (1709–1784), evangelist George Whitefield (1714–1770), John Keble (1792–1866), Percy Bysshe Shelley (1792–1822), John Henry Newman (1801–1890), W. E. Gladstone (1809–1898, prime minister of Great Britain and Ireland), John Ruskin (1819–1900), Matthew Arnold (1822–1888), C. L. Dodgson (1832–1898, author of *Alice in Wonderland*), Lord Randolph Churchill (1849–1895), and essayist and drama critic Max Beerbohm (1872–1956).

A BRIEF HISTORY OF MAGDALEN COLLEGE, OXFORD

William of Waynflete (1395–1486), bishop of Winchester and Lord Chancellor of England, founded Magdalen Hall in 1448 and Magdalen College on June 12, 1458. It was the tenth college to be established at Oxford University. William had become Lord Chancellor in 1456 under King Henry VI and demonstrated the power of his position with the founding of Magdalen College. William convinced Henry that the Hospital of St. John the Baptist could be put to better use, so Henry gave those buildings to the president and Fellows of Magdalen Hall. The college bar (once the Old Kitchen) and part of the buildings alongside the tower facing High Street are part of the original hospital construction. Around 1480 additional work was carried out to build the hall, chapel, and library of Magdalen College. The Cloisters, built as living quarters for students and Fellows, and the tower were completed a few years later. On September 22, 1481, King Edward IV was the first royal visitor to the college. Other royal visitors have included Richard III, Henry VII, Elizabeth I, and James I. The first president of Magdalen College was William Tybard.

Located on the east end of High Street next to the River Cherwell, Magdalen College is governed according to its Statutes, the rules delivered by its founder in 1483. William of Waynflete originally envisioned that Magdalen College would be dedicated to the study of moral and natural philosophy and theology. Today its strength is in the arts and sciences and its five libraries, including the Law Library. Magdalen College is popular among Rhodes Scholars, at least thirteen of whom studied with C. S. Lewis.[15]

During the English Civil War, Oxford University was loyal to King Charles I, who made his headquarters in Oxford until April 27, 1646. In 1687 King James II tried to make Magdalen a Catholic seminary. When the Fellows resisted, King James relented, and on October 25, 1688, the Fellows were reinstated. The day is known as Restoration Day and is still celebrated. In 1733 the medieval Song School was torn down and the New Building erected on the Magdalen campus. It was in this edifice that Lewis had his rooms from 1929 until 1954. The chapel, redesigned by L. N. Cottingham from 1829 to 1834, remains arranged in much the same way as when Cottingham designed it. However, renovations in the stalls, pavement, ceiling, and other areas have occurred, some of them stimulated in 1994 by the filming of the movie *Shadowlands*. St. Swithun's Buildings were completed from 1880 to 1884 and the present entrance gate was finished in 1885. The Longwall Quadrangle was constructed from 1928 to 1930, and the New Library completed in 1932, Holywell Ford in 1992, and the Grove Buildings from 1994 to 1995.

Many have argued that Magdalen is the most beautiful of the Oxford colleges. It boasts an 11-acre grove (where deer have lived for more than three hundred years), a majestic bell tower (King James I is supposed to have called it "the most absolute tower in England"), the River Cherwell, Addison's Walk (about 100 acres named after Sir Joseph Addison [1672–1719], a former student and a Fellow of Magdalen for twenty years), and beautiful architecture. The Great Tower, built from 1492 to 1509, is 144 feet tall and one of the best-known sights in Oxford. The carved panels behind the high table in the Great Hall, dated to 1541, contain scenes from the life of the college's patron saint, Mary of Magdala. Some also say that Magdalen is one of the three richest colleges of Oxford University, along with St. John's and Christ Church.[16] Certainly, it has been one of the largest landowners in Oxford, and John Betjeman called it the richest college of Oxford for its size.[17]

Among many special features, Magdalen College boasts an outdoor pulpit, built in the fifteenth century, which is located at the entrance of the Chaplains' Quadrangle. Every year until 1766, on June 24, St. John the Baptist's Day, or the Sunday closest to it, a service was conducted in St.

John's Quad. The service began again in 1896 and continues to this day. At 6 A.M. on the first of May each year, the college choir sings *Hymnus Eucharisticus*, the college anthem, from the top of the tower, after which the bells ring (some of these bells were cast in the fifteenth century). The annual hymn sing has developed into a service and attracts large crowds by both land and river. The appearance of the ceremony in the movie *Shadowlands* made it even more famous.

Among Magdalen College's famous faculty have been seven Nobel Laureates: Sir Charles Sherrington (1932, medicine), Dr. Erwin Schrödinger (1933, physics), Professor Howard Florey (1945, medicine), Sir Robert Robinson (1947, chemistry), Sir Peter Medawar (1960, medicine), Sir John Eccles (1963, medicine), and Seamus Heaney (1995, literature). Well-known alumni have included Cardinal Thomas Wolsey (1475–1530); eighteenth-century poet and essayist Sir Joseph Addison (1672–1719); Edward Gibbon (1737–1794), author of *The Decline and Fall of the Roman Empire*; Oscar Wilde (1854–1900), poet and dramatist; and Stephen Breyer (1938–) and David Souter (1939–), associate justices of the U.S. Supreme Court. Magdalen currently has approximately 400 undergraduates and 200 graduate students.

MAGDALEN COLLEGE DURING THE LEWIS YEARS[18]

Although most people wanted to open Oxford University to students from all social backgrounds, most students of Magdalen College were socially well placed. Robert Havard described the Oxford don as "having positive philosophy, comparative religion, and superlative conceit . . . ."[19] Magdalen students were secularist, but matched by a frank and open Christianity represented by people such as Lewis, Tolkien, Adam Fox, and Robin George Collingwood. Students participated in sports, including cricket, football (soccer), rugby, lacrosse, tennis, croquet, boxing, field hockey, track, and rowing, though the works of the unathletic Lewis scarcely acknowledge this fact. Students considered reality to be the universe as revealed by the senses, all the while ascribing the words *truth*, *valid*, and *valuable* to abstract thinking, moral judgments, and aesthetic experience.[20] Magdalen students were major proponents of chronological snobbery, which James Como describes as an offshoot of Darwinism.[21]

"The dominant feature of twentieth-century Oxford is the immense proliferation of science," wrote A. L. Rowse.[22] At Oxford in 1940, penicillin was discovered by Lord Howard Florey; J. B. S. Haldane (previously at Cambridge) and E. B. Ford worked as geneticists; and Julian Huxley popularized science. Frederick Soddy,[23] Nevil Sidgwick, and Sir Cyril Hinshelwood worked as chemists; Edward C. Titchmarsh as a mathematician; Arthur G. Tansley as a botanist and plant ecologist; and Sir Henry Thomas Tizard, a Magdalen graduate who later became president of the college, worked on radar. With the arrival of the empirical method in the seventeenth century, science viewed knowledge as something to be known only through sensory experience. Along with this came scientism, the misuse of science, what George Musacchio called "a philosophical attitude toward science, sometimes even the worship of science."[24] In addition, between the materialist view of the universe and the religious view, many held to the emergent, or creative, evolution of Henri Bergson. Lewis satirized this view in Weston, the Un-Man in *Perelandra*, who believed that an "unconsciously purposive dynamism" explained the origin and purpose of life.[25] Emergent evolution allowed a person to avoid the emptiness of materialism without having to believe in God.

During the early part of the twentieth century, much discussion was held concerning the continuing role of a medical school at Magdalen College. But with the establishment of a chair of biochemistry, the work of the Medical Research Council under Sir Walter Morley Fletcher, the establishment of the Dunn School of Pathology in 1927, a Rockefeller endowment for a new department of biochemistry (opened in 1927), the generosity of Lord Nuffield (who contributed £2 million for the clinical school, now known as the Nuffield Institute), and many other developments, the medical school began to grow. In the 1940s, it was approved as a full medical school. The last major construction at the medical school was the Radcliffe Infirmary, which was completed in 1970.[26]

Some would argue that the Christian faith was the largest single influence at Oxford during the twentieth century and that Lewis was at the center of this influence. Describing the religious atmosphere during and after the Second World War, John Wain wrote: "It was impossible, at that time, to take in 'Oxford' without taking in, if not exactly the Christian faith, at least a very considerable respect for Christianity. . . . Everybody to whom an imaginative and bookish youth naturally looked up, every figure who radiated intellectual glamour of any kind, was in the Christian camp."[27] Lewis himself was a significant part of this Christian influence, a fact that undoubtedly provided encouragement to him as he wrote *The Screwtape Letters*, gave the BBC broadcasts that led to *Mere Christianity*, and led the Socratic Club.

Non-Anglicans had come to Oxford with the opening of the Congregational Mansfield College (1886); the arrival of Manchester College (1893); the arrival of Regent's Park College, a Baptist seminary (called a Theological Training College in England) (1927); the return of Roman Catholicism (1896); the founding of a Jewish Society (1904); and in many other ways. However, the Anglican Church continued to dominate the university. Wycliffe Hall trained evangelical clergy, Ripon Hall was associated with modernism, the Cowley Fathers were based in Oxford, and St. Stephen's House and Pusey House produced high church clergy. Pusey House was heir to the Oxford Movement, the nineteenth-century move toward Catholicism within the Church of England that was led by John Henry Newman, Edward Pusey, and John Keble, all of whom were connected to Oxford University. The most evangelical Anglican churches were St. Aldate's and St. Ebbe's, and St. Aldate's helped to bring evangelists Dwight Moody (1882 and 1892) and Billy Graham (1954, 1955, and 1980) to Oxford.

When H. Wheeler Robinson came to Oxford as principal (see Glossary) of Regent's Park College, he was the most respected British Old Testament scholar of the day. The Theology Faculty immediately appointed Robinson an examiner, and he became a Reader in biblical criticism in 1934. Between the two world wars, Father Martin C. K'Arcy, S.J., became master (see Glossary) of Campion Hall (1927) and actively sought converts, the most famous being Evelyn Waugh. He also made the intellectual case for a resurgent Roman Catholicism at Oxford.

Student Christian organizations, such as the Student Christian Movement (SCM) and the Oxford Inter-Collegiate Christian Union (OICCU), helped to maintain a student presence in the religious life of the university. The student missionary movement of the 1890s produced the former, and the latter had origins in the Inter-Varsity Fellowship of Evangelical Unions. The SCM left its evangelical moorings during the first quarter of the twentieth century, and the OICCU maintained its evangelical stance throughout the Lewis years. The university church, St. Mary the Virgin, where

Lewis preached on at least two occasions, served as a worship center and the focus of religious organization at Oxford. Daily chapel services at the various colleges also enhanced religious life.[28]

Lewis entered Oxford as an undergraduate and later as a don at a time when the exploration of English language and literature was becoming a legitimate field of study at both Oxford and Cambridge. As Terry Eagleton exaggerated: "In the early 1920s it was desperately unclear why English was worth studying at all. In the early 1930s it had become a question of why it was worth wasting your time on anything else."[29]

Among its many prominent dons and students, Oxford welcomed novelist Evelyn Waugh to Hertford College as a student in 1922, the eventual British poet laureate John Betjeman (a student at Magdalen College who took tutorials under Lewis in the 1920s), Lancelot Phelps (1853–1936, a member of Oriel College for sixty-four years), W. H. Auden (who wrote poetry at Christ Church), and Maurice Bowra (warden [see Glossary] of Wadham in the 1930s).

The many talented writers of the twentieth century who hailed from Oxford—from T. S. Eliot, John Buchan, Graham Greene, William Golding, and Aldous Huxley to Dorothy Sayers, John Wain, J. R. R. Tolkien, and C. S. Lewis—are the result of, among other things, the university's emphasis upon the fine arts and English literature and the presence of bookshops, libraries, and publishers in the city (there were twenty booksellers, thirty-one printers, and nine publishers in Oxford in 1952). Throughout the years, the literary journals of Oxford University have included in their number such diverse publications as T. S. Eliot's *The Criterion*, Cyril Connolly's *Horizon*, Alan Ross's *London Magazine*, *The Calendar of Modern Letters* (1925–1927), and the socialist literary paper *Left Review*, which was published in the 1930s.[30] (Much more concerning the literary culture of the time can be found in the biographical sketches of the English faculties of Oxford and Cambridge that appear in Appendix V.)

"While much of scholarly Oxford was hard at work unraveling the traditional relation between philosophy and theology . . . the Magdalen metaphysicals[31] [see below on R. G. Collingwood, Lewis, J. A. Smith, and C. C. J. Webb] seemed impelled toward belief by their philosophic interests."[32] During the last quarter of the nineteenth century, a new school of philosophy emerged at Oxford, a school under which Lewis himself was to study at University College. Thomas Hill Green began an anglicized version of

Hegelianism, known as idealism, and Francis Herbert Bradley became its most distinguished proponent. Lewis had studied Green and Bosanquet during his undergraduate days, and he once called this English Hegelianism an approach that provided "all the conveniences of Theism, without believing in God."[33] True knowledge, the idealists maintained, can be achieved by reason, which recognizes nature as a product of the mind, or at least something formed and articulated by the mind. Lewis always held reason in high esteem, capable of freeing us from error, and he owed this commitment in part to Kirkpatrick, in part to idealism, in part to Chesterton and other authors, and in part to the Scriptures. According to Lewis, a reason enlightened by grace could discover truth. Indeed, Lewis once wrote that reason was the natural organ of truth and imagination the organ of meaning.[34]

Idealism also holds to an absolute, transcendent reality, not unlike Plato's idea of forms, after which much of human life is patterned. Therefore many idealists, Christians, and other philosophers saw idealism as connected to, or at least compatible with, Christianity. Idealism was superseded by the realism of Thomas Case, John Cook Wilson, Horace William Brindley Joseph, and Harold Arthur Prichard, but when Lewis matriculated to Oxford in 1917, he considered idealism still powerful, though it was considerably diminished.[35] Realism maintains an emphasis upon the universe as revealed by the senses, claiming also that there is no necessary relation between the world of facts that we know and a knower, other beings, or God. Realism also states that knowledge is objective, leaving both the knower and the known unchanged, whereas idealism would argue that knowledge changes both the knower and the known and would, therefore, see reason as a friend of faith.[36] Both schools of philosophy were Hegelian, yet also critics of Hegel.[37]

The classicism of T. S. Eliot and *The Criterion*, the new idealism of the 1920s, and modernism were three movements whose thought overlapped that of Lewis. Eliot began the literary journal *The Criterion* in 1922. After 1927, it showed the influence of neo-scholasticism (see Glossary), but it also defended the intellectual and rational content of Christian theology and, like the Magdalen metaphysicals, demonstrated a philosophy similar to that which Lewis had studied in his Greats curriculum.[38] Although Lewis originally disliked Eliot because of the modern verse that Eliot wrote and also because of his neo-scholasticism, Lewis's conversion to Christianity tempered that dislike, especially later when Eliot helped Lewis in the publication of a *Festschrift* for Charles Williams in 1943. In 1926 Lewis and some friends attempted to write parodies of Eliot's poetry for publication in *The Criterion*. In the hope that Eliot would publish them, they submitted the works from a fictional brother and sister, Rollo and Bridget Considine, who lived in Vienna. The plot, however, never saw the light of day because the poems were never submitted. Later, Lewis and Eliot worked together on a revision of the Anglican Prayer Book, and their friendship further developed in the 1950s. Although their approaches were different, both men defended reason, tradition, and the Christian faith for three decades. Eliot, who had studied philosophy under H. H. Joachim, an idealist from whom he learned his English prose style, had discovered from philosophy that the arts "without intellectual content are vanity."[39]

Neo-scholasticism consisted of a renewal of the study of St. Thomas Aquinas and other medieval writers, spurred by Pope Leo XIII's 1879 recommendation. It centered at the University of Louvain and, by 1920, in the writings of Jacques Maritain and Etienne Gilson. Although closely tied to Roman Catholicism, the rise of neo-scholasticism coincided with the rise of the study of medieval writers, something encouraged by C. C. J. Webb and the other Magdalen metaphysicals. Thus the two movements fed upon each other. However, "[b]oth Lewis and Webb probably considered Neo-Scholasticism an arrogant rationalism bound too closely to Rome."[40]

The new idealism of the 1920s described those philosophers who disagreed with the idealism of T. H. Green and F. H. Bradley but who also rejected realism. These new idealists showed interest in Immanuel Kant, the Italian idealists Benedetto Croce and Giovanni Gentile, and both history and the philosophy of history, stressing the unity of the European mind with the past. Therefore, unlike the earlier idealism, this new movement recognized the importance of history.

Modernism in England challenged many traditionally held Christian beliefs, including belief in miracles and the historicity and reliability of many of the sources of Christianity, especially the Bible.[41] Modernists claimed that truth arose from experience. They attempted to commend the Christian faith on rational grounds but conceded too much to the attempt to redefine Christianity in terms congenial to a cultural and "modern" Christianity. The two periodicals of the modernist movement were the *Churchman* and the *Hibbert Journal*. In 1910 modernist views were responsible for Burnett Hillman Streeter's formation of a group of Oxford dons that held to the reasonableness of religion. These dons met weekly to discuss theological topics and became known as The Group.

In an effort to present a more rational Christianity, though repudiated by nearly everyone, James Matthew Thompson, Dean of Divinity (chaplain) at Magdalen, wrote in 1911 that the miracles of the New Testament were to be explained as religious psychology.[42] This was another example of modernism's attempt to join faith and reason, as Lewis himself did later, but Thompson also surrendered a significant portion of the Christian faith in the process.

During Lewis's early years as a tutor at Oxford, Samuel Alexander and G. K. Chesterton influenced his thinking tremendously.[43] Alexander wrote *Space, Time and Deity* (1920), a book that distinguished between enjoyment and contemplation. According to Alexander, one enjoys the act of thinking but contemplates the object of that thinking; therefore one cannot both enjoy and contemplate an object at the same time. This concept helped Lewis to realize that "Joy," a longing for something otherworldly, could not be had while he was contemplating it. Joy was only a pointing to God, but the moment he tried to contemplate God, that Joy would disappear. This distinction would appear later in Lewis's essay "Meditation in a Toolshed." Lewis read six books by Chesterton from 1922 to 1927.[44] Reading Chesterton's *The Everlasting Man* enabled Lewis to see a coherent Christian view of history, thereby removing for Lewis one of the intellectual obstacles to a serious consideration of the Christian faith.

During this same decade (the 1920s), laying the foundation for A. J. Ayer was I. A. Richards's *The Meaning of Meaning* (coauthored with C. K. Ogden and published in 1923) and *Principles of Literary Criticism* (1929). Richards, a naturalist, argued that metaphorical language could not describe a scientific matter and that there were two uses of language: one to refer to facts in the world of verifiable experience and the other to refer to the subjective states of the poets. The first use of language corresponded to the first kind of meaningful statement in Ayer's thought. The second use of language, from the world of poetry and including religious statements, was neither true nor false because it was not scientific. This created a category of subjective statements unrelated to reality.[45] Ayer and Richards were among the reasons that many of Oxford's faculty during the years leading up to World War II taught that there was no such thing as truth, and they both illustrate the influence of science on the fields of literary criticism and philosophy. This led to an atmosphere at the university that some have described as intellectual despair.[46] Against Richards stood Lewis's friend Owen Barfield, whose book *Poetic Diction: A Study in Meaning* (1928), argued that all language was metaphorical in nature and that even the terms used by Ogden and Richards were not exempt from this fact. Furthermore, Tolkien held that myth was a bearer of truth, a position that would be powerfully supported years later in *The Lord of the Rings.*

Around the same time as Richards, Edwardian realism also laid the groundwork for the positivism of A. J. Ayer. Edwardian realism appeared in the writings of both Gilbert Ryle and Ayer. R. G. Collingwood, the only practicing philosopher at Magdalen College in the 1930s, carried the responsibility for responding to positivism. Perhaps because of attacks against his work, Collingwood changed from a dispassionate to a passionate critic of realism and, later, of positivism.[47] Others joined in the argument against positivism, including H. J. Paton, a disciple of J. A. Smith.[48]

During the years 1925 to 1929, Lewis set aside realist philosophy and adopted an idealist philosophy, which held to a transcendent truth. Eventually, with the help of Tolkien and Hugo Dyson, Lewis saw that myth contained a germ of truth, which had reached its fullness in Jesus Christ. Lewis's midnight conversation with Tolkien and Dyson about myth and metaphor took place on September 19, 1931. Tolkien and Dyson convinced Lewis that, though he was attracted by the myth of the dying and rising god, he was prejudiced against it in Christianity and therefore inconsistent in his view of this myth. They also convinced Lewis that the myth actually had taken place once in history, namely, in Jesus Christ. Lewis's conversion took place on September 22, the single most important irrigation in Lewis's educational life.

The Pilgrim's Regress, Lewis's first book after his conversion, recounted the road he traveled back to Christianity. In this book, his protagonist avoided the northern road of rational aridity and the southern waste of sentimentality, allowing the pilgrim, John (Lewis himself), to regress to the Christianity of his childhood. The book created a difficulty for Lewis at Oxford because it made public his conversion to Christianity.[49] Publications such as *The Pilgrim's Regress,* as well as his involvement in the controversial election of Adam Fox as professor of poetry in 1938,[50] led to Lewis being bypassed for a full professorship in Oxford.

Things changed philosophically in 1936 when A. J. Ayer's *Language, Truth, and Logic* provided the classic statement in English for logical positivism. Ayer, who had come to a lectureship at Christ Church in 1933, believed there were only two kinds of cognitively meaningful statements: those that are empirically verifiable and those that are analytically true. Because religious and metaphysical statements fit into neither category, the atheist Ayer concluded that they were meaningless. Therefore the principle of verifiability became a central doctrine of positivism. This comes as no surprise, given that logical positivists had great admiration for science, which is founded upon the empirical method. Later, when ordinary language philosophy became popular, Ayer moved away from his early doctrinaire position, but he retained much of the spirit of his early work, advocating empiricism but treating metaphysics with respect.

Lewis made fun of empirical verification in *That Hideous Strength* when the N.I.C.E. measured progress with a pragmatometer and when Mark Studdock entered the objectivity room of N.I.C.E. and submitted to its argument that thought is subjective. N.I.C.E. failed to convince Studdock, and during this experiment, he learned to trust his reason.[51]

Alec King and Martin Ketley's *The Control of Language* appeared only three years after Ayer's work on language. In part the work of King and Ketley was indebted to Ayer. Lewis referred to *The Control of Language* as *The Green Book*[52] in *The Abolition of Man*. In *The Control of Language*, King and Ketley agreed with the positivists that the primary meaning of some sentences was their emotive or evocative meaning. To say "x is good" is to say "I like x," the positivists argued. To say "the waterfall is sublime" is to mean "I have sublime feelings about the waterfall," argued King and Ketley.

A flavor of the elitist attitude at Oxford can be demonstrated by reference to the most famous debate in the history of the Oxford Union Society. The following question was debated on February 9, 1933: "That this House will in no circumstances fight for its King and Country." The topic illustrates both the attitude of Oxford and the state of England and Europe as a second World War approached. After five speakers, including C. E. M. Joad of Balliol College, the motion passed by a vote of 275 to 153. History later proved, however, that Oxford did fight. For example, Jan Morris reported that the entire Trinity boat crew, which won the Eights Week races in 1939, fought in the war and that all but two died.[53] Numerous other students and faculty fought as well.

Three poets dominated the 1930s in Oxford: Louis MacNeice of Merton College; Stephen Spender of University College; and W. H. Auden of Christ Church, the best known of the three who was known in part for his Marxist stance. Before them, poet laureate Robert Bridges had returned to live in Oxford from 1907 to 1930. Bridges is considered by some to be "the dominating literary figure in the landscape."[54] A. E. Housman (1859–1936) was a brilliant Latin scholar who eventually moved to Cambridge, and Gilbert Murray (1866–1957) became the foremost Greek scholar of his day, introducing Euripides to the reading public and becoming better known for his service in the initiation of the League of Nations. The poets John Masefield and William Butler Yeats, novelists Evelyn Waugh and Graham Greene, and playwright and novelist Dorothy Sayers also called Oxford home.[55]

In the summers of 1931 and 1932, Albert Einstein, the brilliant physicist, came to Oxford and lived at Christ Church. During the 1930s, Maurice Bowra, Fellow of New College and later warden (see Glossary) of Wadham, was the best-known Oxford don of his day. He was known especially for his catty tongue and his sense of humor, once saying, "I'm a man more dined against than dining."[56]

Common in many European circles during the time that Lewis was an undergraduate and a Fellow was a love affair with socialism. As mentioned earlier, Lewis's tutor in philosophy at University College, E. F. Carritt, was a devoted socialist.

The Anglican Austin Farrer, who had read Greats at Balliol College as an undergraduate, came to Oxford as chaplain of St. Edmund Hall (1931–1935) and later as chaplain of Trinity (1935–1960). He then became warden (see Glossary) of Keble College and remained in this post until his death in 1968. He became a close friend of Lewis, was a member of the Inklings (see Glossary), and was often in attendance at the Socratic Club. Farrer was a romantic whose central insight was "his insistence that knowledge is a poetic unity involving reason and imagination, and in the case of knowledge of God, revelation."[57] Like Lewis, Farrer counted poetic vision and amatory passion as friends of religion. E. L. Mascall considered Farrer's greatest contribution to be in the area of natural theology, and he considered Farrer's *Finite and Infinite* a most compelling defense of theism and a challenge to logical positivism.[58] According to F. M. Turner, "[m]ore than any figure of his generation in the University, Farrer embodied the highest ideal of the college chaplain-theologian."[59]

Lewis won the Sir Israel Gollancz[60] Prize in 1937 for *The Allegory of Love* (1936). This study of the allegorical love poetry of the Middle Ages was Lewis's first great scholarly and literary work. It grew out of his interest in medieval literature and served, in part, as a response to D. H. Lawrence's *Lady Chatterley's Lover*,[61] which had been published in 1932. Peter Bayley described *The Allegory of Love* as a "magisterial and brilliant book."[62] Elsewhere John Lawlor wrote: "If anyone can be said to have ended a tradition of dullness in scholarly writing, it is surely Lewis in this great, forever readable book."[63]

Being asked in 1938 by F. P. Wilson to write *English Literature in the Sixteenth Century* for the Oxford History of English Literature series was one indication of the esteem with which Lewis was held by the scholarly and publishing world. That work furthered Lewis's reputation as a literary critic and literary historian, which had been firmly established by the publication of *The Allegory of Love.*

J. R. R. Tolkien was professor of English language at Leeds University (1919–1926). He moved to Oxford University where he was Rawlinson and Bosworth Professor of Anglo-Saxon (1925–1945), then Merton Professor of English (1945–1959), succeeding H. C. K. Wyld in that position. He published *The Hobbit* in 1937, and Lewis published *Out of the Silent Planet* in 1938. Both works of fantasy would have an impact for truth and for an objective standard of right and wrong. Tolkien would later write a sequel to *The Hobbit* in *The Lord of the Rings* (published in 1954 and 1955), which was judged in four different polls as the best book of the twentieth century.

Much of the literary, religious, and philosophical thought to which Lewis was reacting in the publication of *The Personal Heresy* (1939), and also in *The Abolition of Man*, was prevalent at the time in Oxford. It had become fashionable to believe that a piece of literature was more about the personality of the author than about the subject matter the author was addressing. A discussion Lewis had in 1924 with a fellow undergraduate had shown that William Robson-Scott thought of a poem as being more about the author and the effect of the poem on the reader than on the subject of the poem, thereby demonstrating this viewpoint much earlier than

1939.[64] In a collection of point-counterpoint essays with E. M. W. Tillyard published in 1939,[65] Lewis challenged this view, and both men moved toward a better understanding of each other as a result of the series of essays. Lewis believed that Richards's theory—that poetry had nothing to do with objective truth—created a false division between fact and poetic language, and this was one of the targets of *The Abolition of Man,* a work that grew out of the Riddell Memorial Lectures given by Lewis on February 24, 1943, at the University of Durham. Lewis accused Richards and F. R. Leavis of "a tradition of educated infidelity" because of their denial of any objective standard.[66] One of the graduate tutors at Magdalen College, Robert Browning, hailed the new criticism of Leavis and others at Cambridge,[67] thereby reflecting the majority viewpoint.

Many at Oxford believed at this time that science would eliminate the need for religion. The topics of the Socratic Club, which held its first meeting at Somerville College on January 26, 1942, provide ample evidence of the issues commonly under discussion at Oxford University during the time that Lewis was president of the club (1942–1954). The first meeting addressed the topic "Won't mankind outgrow the advance of science and modern ideologies?" Oxford physician and philosopher Robert E. Havard, Lewis's personal physician, said no. A selection of topics throughout the next decade indicates the debate over science and religion during this time:

1942   "Can Science Render Religion Unnecessary?" H. A. Hodges

1943   "Science and Faith," Frank Sherwood-Taylor
       "Is the New Testament Reliable Evidence?" Richard Kehoe

1944   "Materialism and Agnosticism," J. K. White, G. B. Preston
       "The Grounds of Modern Agnosticism," H. H. Price
       "Has Psychology Debunked Sin?" L. W. Grensted, Barbara Falk

1945   "Marxist and Christian Views of the Nature of Man,"
       Archibald Robertson, Emile Cammaerts

1946   "Can Science Provide a Basis for Ethics?"
       C. H. Waddington, Austin Farrer
       "The Limits of Positivism," Friedrich Waismann

1947   "Did the Resurrection Happen?" R. E. Davies, T. M. Parker

1948 "Rudolf Steiner and the Scientific Outlook,"
     Alfred Heidenreich, Frank Sherwood-Taylor
     "Atheism," J. B. S. Haldane, Ian M. Crombie

1949 "Can Science Create Values?" J. Bronowski, Basil Mitchell
     "Philosophy and Psychoanalysis," John Wisdom, Leycester King

1950 "Freudian Psychology and Christian Faith," B. A. Farrell, R. S. Lee
     "The Relation of Psychical Research to the Scientific Method,"
     N. M. Tyrell, L. W. Grensted

1951 "The Philosophical Basis of Marxism," Marcus Wheeler, S. F. Mason

1952 "Rational Existentialism," E. L. Mascall, Iris Murdoch
     "The Notion of Development in Psychology and Its Bearing
     upon Religion," R. S. Lee

1953 "The Gospels: Myth or History?" R. Creham, A. R. C. Leaney

1954 "The Anatomy of Atheism," E. W. Lambert, John Lucas[68]

During 1943, as astronomers discovered that the universe was much larger in size than previously thought, some in the scientific community began to claim that Christianity was no longer needed.[69] The smaller man became, the less the value of mankind and the earth in such a huge universe. In response to this thinking, Lewis wrote a two-part essay for *The Guardian*: "Dogma and the Universe" and "Dogma and Science."[70] Therein Lewis argued that the size of the universe had no effect upon Christian theology and that, in fact, we ought to expect a massive universe if it was created by an omnipotent God. Lewis wrote: "I should be suffocated in a universe that I could see to the end of."[71]

Freudian psychology was prominent during the days of Lewis. Psychology as a discipline had arrived in Oxford during the mid-1920s, and Freudian psychology came soon thereafter. In *Surprised by Joy*, Lewis called a concern about fantasy and wishful thinking the new psychology and had to determine if his longings were self-created or were actually longings for something else, even a longing for God.[72] Nine chapters of *The Pilgrim's Regress* (1933) addressed Freudian psychology, and within those chapters, the pilgrim, John, escaped from the giant called Spirit of the Age by common sense and with the help of Reason, a female knight. On May 28, 1944, Lewis preached the sermon "Transposition" at Mansfield College in response to the Freudian charge that Christianity was simply a psychological projection. Lewis argued instead that God had placed within each person a desire to know God.[73]

During the 1920s, Frederick A. Lindemann (1886–1957), professor of experimental philosophy at Christ Church (1922–1957) and later Lord Cherwell, became known as the father of modern physics at Oxford. "The Prof," as he came to be known, was Churchill's indispensable scientific advisor during World War II. Without Lindemann, Britain may not have survived the German attempts at invasion.[74]

After World War II, government spending opened undergraduate education to nearly everyone, thus the focus shifted from education to training, from culture to certificates, a shift inimical to Lewis's way of thinking. The growing number of undergraduates necessitated many more dons at the universities.[75] This appears in the following graph, which demonstrates the increased tutorial workload of Lewis in the post-World War II era. This graph includes only those undergraduates of Magdalen College assigned to Lewis to read English language and literature. It does not include, for example, Peter Bayley, who took tutorials with Lewis in English while an undergraduate at University College, and Donald Whittle and Charles Wrong,[76] Magdalen undergraduates who read political science in the modern history degree with him for a time. It shows a drop in the number of students during World War II and a large increase in the five years after the war.[77]

The publication of *The Great Divorce* in 1946 was a challenge to the liberal views of the Church of England. The portraits of Anglican clergy in *The Pilgrim's Regress* and *The Screwtape Letters* had not flattered them.[78] The picture of an Anglican bishop in hell who did not believe in a literal heaven or hell demonstrated Lewis's opposition to a growing denial of many historical Christian beliefs, a good deal of them in his own denomination. Such positions did nothing to endear Lewis to the Oxford dons who already thought he was out of character for writing theological works without theological training. In the next year Lewis was passed over for the Merton Chair of English Literature.

In March 1948, Lewis was elected a Fellow of the Royal Society of Literature. He was elected a Fellow of the British Academy[79] in 1955. In 1951 Lewis declined appointment as Commander, Order of the British Empire.[80] In response to a letter from Sir Winston Churchill's secretary, Lewis wrote that the acceptance of this honor would only strengthen the

The Tutorials of C. S. Lewis

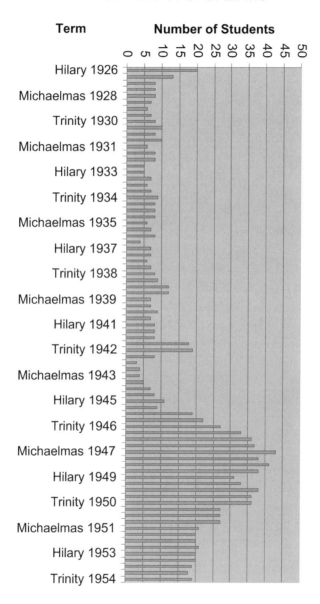

case of those who thought his writings full of anti-leftist propaganda. Although he felt honored personally, he was obligated to decline.[81]

During the 1950s, the new trend in philosophy was to study language and make a break from theology.[82] Philosophy became logical analysis rather than metaphysics, that is, the analysis of language rather than the study of the nature of reality. The question was not "Does God exist?" but "What do we mean when we use the word *God*?" It was a short distance from this trend to the "God is dead" philosophy of the 1960s.

The impact of Owen Barfield and Charles Williams upon Oxford University came especially in their impact upon C. S. Lewis. Barfield's destruction of Lewis's chronological snobbery and Williams's understanding of Plato's doctrine of real forms, evident in Lewis's references to Shadowlands, greatly influenced Lewis during this period of his life. More than that, Lewis shared with Williams an approach to romantic theology that led to the Chronicles of Narnia and their interpenetration of the external world and a parallel world. The move of the offices of Oxford University Press to the city of Oxford during World War II increased contact between Lewis and Williams, thereby developing their friendship, which ended abruptly with Williams's death in 1945.

Lewis's success as a defender of mere Christianity and R. G. Collingwood's defense of thought as leading to truth and truth to action violated the rules of an Oxford academia that did not think ideas could be true, that truth could be defined, that fact *and* judgment about fact could be objective and related to each other. That modern philosophy, for the most part, does not see metaphysics as a legitimate school of thought or religion as a relevant topic for philosophy explains the silence with which the philosophical academy has greeted Lewis and Collingwood in the history of twentieth-century philosophy.

In summary, Magdalen College took its place in the midst of an Oxford University that adopted a scientific and materialistic worldview, philosophized the difficulty of discovering truth, and flirted with Freudianism, socialism, and many other trends of the day. However, there was a Christian presence in the person of Lewis and others that brought a stabilizing influence to the university, a strength in its scholarship, and a contrasting worldview.

PUBLISH OR PERISH

Many academics, especially academics in the United States, work in universities where they must write for publication or lose their job or their tenure track. They must publish or perish. The ironic thing about Lewis is that though he was one of the most published academics of his day, he did not approve of the publish-or-perish situation.[83] He thought of writing as a natural outgrowth of the life of the scholar but something that should not be forced. He prized the teaching and learning that took place far more than the publishing.

ADVANCED DEGREES AND ACCOMPLISHMENTS

Although Lewis received five honorary doctorates, he never earned a doctorate, though in those days few bothered to earn one. In July 1923, shortly after Lewis had learned the results of his First in English, F. P. Wilson suggested an advanced degree in literature or philosophy.[84] In March 1924, Lewis discussed with Mrs. Moore the possibility of pursuing a doctorate in philosophy on the thought of the Cambridge Platonist Henry More. Mrs. Moore considered it a waste of time, and he wondered if it might hurt his chances of obtaining a fellowship because he would have to focus his efforts on that degree rather than on history, philosophy, English, and Greek. Lewis also felt a doctorate would add little to the Firsts he already had earned.[85]

Lewis disliked the advanced degree and much of the research in English literature that produced dissertations on obscure and insignificant subjects. George Sayer wrote that Lewis "was fond of saying that there were three kinds of literacy at Oxford: the literate, the illiterate, and the B. Litterate, and that personally he preferred the first two."[86] On this topic, however, Lewis was typically Oxonian. Most Oxford dons believed that a First from an Oxford college was the ultimate achievement and that a doctorate actually detracted from the value of the First.[87]

Lewis did, however, hold the Master of Arts degree as of 1925. The 1954 Oxford *Handbook* states: "The Degree of Master of Arts is open without further examination to candidates who have taken the Oxford degree of Bachelor of Arts and have had their names on the books of a society (i.e. have paid university and college dues) for a period of twenty-one terms."[88] This would mean that, having been on the books of University College since 1917, Lewis would have been eligible for the Master of Arts in 1924, twenty-one terms (seven years at three terms per year) later. *The Times* reported on May 22, 1925, that "Clive Staples Lewis, M.A.," had been elected to a fellowship as tutor in English language and literature.[89] Therefore Lewis had earned that Master of Arts before May 22, 1925.

On April 8, 1946,[90] Lewis received an honorary Doctor of Divinity from St. Mary's College, part of the University of St. Andrew's in St. Andrews, Fife, Scotland.[91] In 1952 Lewis received the honorary Doctor of Letters from L'Université Laval in Laval, Quebec, Canada. On May 13, 1959, he received the Doctor of Letters from Manchester University in Manchester, England. In 1962 he received an honorary doctorate from the University of Dijon in Dijon, France, and in 1963 he was given an honorary doctorate from the University of Lyon in Lyon, France.[92]

EIGHT

C. S. Lewis at Cambridge

You were never safe from the philosopher at Oxford;
here, never from the Critic.—C. S. Lewis, "Interim Report"[1]

What was the academic climate of the Cambridge University and Magdalene College of C. S. Lewis between 1955 and 1963?

In 1947 F. P. Wilson filled the Merton Chair of English Literature upon the retirement of David Nichol Smith, and in 1951 Cecil Day Lewis (no relation) was elected to the professorship of poetry by nineteen votes over C. S. Lewis. Either of these positions Lewis could easily have filled had forces not been arrayed against him. The failure to be elected professor and the changing nature of Oxford University, especially after World War II, contributed to Lewis's willingness to accept a position at Cambridge when it was offered to him.

When in 1954 the University of Cambridge appointed Lewis to the Chair of Medieval and Renaissance Literature, Magdalene College was eager to have him as a Professorial Fellow (see Glossary). To strengthen its claim, Magdalene College emphasized its nominal association with Magdalen College, Oxford. After considerable personal struggle concerning this decision, Lewis was happy to accept the invitation from Magdalene. He continued to live in Oxford, commuting by train to Cambridge during the week and to Oxford on the weekends. Lewis delivered his inaugural lecture at Cambridge on November 29, 1954, his 56th birthday. The lecture was titled "De Descriptione Temporum,"[2] and he spoke to a packed house. In this lecture, Lewis denied that the barrier between the medieval age and the Renaissance was large, preferring instead the year 1830 as "the Great Divide." This year marked the end of the work of Jane Austen and Sir Walter Scott (who died in 1832), the advent of the Industrial Age, and the arrival of the full impact of the Age of Enlightenment.

Magdalen College, Oxford, elected Lewis to an honorary fellowship in 1956,[3] and University College, Oxford, did the same on March 26, 1959, but Lewis continued his work in Cambridge. In 1957 when F. P. Wilson retired from the Merton Chair of English Literature at Oxford, an unsuccessful attempt was made to lure Lewis back.[4] Because of ill health, Lewis missed both the Michaelmas term 1962 and the Hilary term 1963 (see Glossary), returning for his final term, the spring 1963 Trinity term (see Glossary). After resigning his fellowship later in 1963, the year of his death, Magdalene College made Lewis an Honorary Fellow.[5]

A Brief History of Cambridge University

Built along the River Cam, Cambridge University boasts medieval and modern colleges of great variety and beauty. The Romans built a fort north of the river on the road to the garrison in Colchester. Saxons later began to build south of the river and developed the town known in the Anglo-Saxon Chronicle as early as A.D. 875 as Grantebrycge (i.e., Granta Bridge because the River Cam used to be known as the River Granta). After the Norman conquest, William the Conqueror built a castle as a military base on Castle Hill.

The town began to grow as a commercial presence. Churches were built, and fairs were held to which many traders came. A group of undergraduates, allegedly fleeing the riots of Oxford, arrived in 1209. These undergraduates and a group of teachers were set up under a chancellor seventeen years later. The Bishop of Ely founded the first college, Peterhouse, in 1284, and the pope recognized the school as a place of study in 1318. The second college, Clare College, was founded in 1326 by Lady Elizabeth de Clare, the granddaughter of Edward I. The Countess of Pembroke founded Pembroke College, Cambridge's third college, in 1347.

Among Cambridge's architectural notables are the King's College Chapel, with its vaulted ceiling; the chapel of Jesus College, which was constructed in 1496 and features a nave ceiling that combines medieval and nineteenth-century Gothic with Pre-Raphaelite decoration and glass; the Bridge of Sighs that links St. John's College's New Court with the older part of the college; Trinity College's Great Court and its library, which were designed by Sir Christopher Wren; the Great Gate of Trinity College, which was founded by Henry VIII; and the Pepys Library and the Round Church, which date from about 1130. Cambridge now consists of thirty-one colleges with more than 15,000 undergraduates.

Today, Cambridge, a city of more than 100,000, enjoys international fame for its high-tech industry, which is rooted in the scientific strengths of the university. The city mingles town and gown, and the people of Cambridge live alongside the university population. The city's bookshops are among the best in England, and it has a wide range of theater and cinema. The city hosts a major arts festival each July. The oldest surviving building in Cambridge is the Saxon tower of St. Bene't's Church, which was built around 1025. The city also maintains important museums, including the Fitzwilliam Museum, Kettle's Yard (for the visual arts and music), the Museum of Classical Archaeology, the University Museum of Archaeology and Anthropology, the University Museum of Zoology, the Sedgwick Museum, the Whipple Museum of the History of Science, the Scott Polar Research Institute, and the Cambridge and County Folk Museum.

Cambridge's more famous alumni include Oliver Cromwell (1599–1658), John Harvard (1607–1638, founder of Harvard University in the United States), poet John Milton (1608–1674), writer Samuel Pepys (1633–1703), Isaac Newton (1642–1727), British Prime Minister William Pitt (1759–1806), and Charles Darwin (1809–1882).[6]

A Brief History of Magdalene College, Cambridge

In 1428, with permission from Henry VI, the area of Cambridge that would become Magdalene College was purchased by Abbot John Litlington of Crowland Abbey. There he founded a hostel for Benedictine monk-scholars, an institution that would be open to all Benedictine monks who wished to study at the university. The Benedictine monasteries of England contained the best libraries of the age, and this institution would be no exception. Buildings were erected in the 1470s, and the name was changed from Monks' Hostel to Buckingham College. Various people have attributed the college's change of name to the patronage of Henry Stafford, second duke of Buckingham (1455–1483),[7] or, perhaps more likely, to Henry's grandmother, the Duchess of Buckingham, Anne Neville.

When Henry VIII dissolved the monasteries, including Crowland Abbey, on December 4, 1539, the hostel was converted to a college. Magdalene College, located at the north end of the center of Cambridge, adjacent to the River Cam, was allegedly founded in 1542 by Lord Audley of Walden, but it was probably begun by Henry VIII, who issued the Letters Patent on April 3, 1542, that actually founded Magdalene College.[8] The institution's official name was the College of St. Mary Magdalene. Lord Audley, Lord Chancellor under Henry VIII and the judge at the trials of Anne Boleyn and Sir Thomas More, seems to have had some role in the founding of the college. The choice of Mary Magdalene as the patroness of the new college may have been an act of arrogance by Lord Audley because in the pronunciation of the day, the college would have been pronounced "M-AUDLEY-N."[9] Whatever his precise role, Lord Audley is responsible for the crest of the college and for its motto: "*Garde ta foy*" ("Keep your faith").[10] Robert Evans was named the first master (see Glossary) of Magdalene. In 1546 the college had eleven people resident, including faculty, undergraduates, and servants. The curriculum followed the medieval Trivium (grammar, logic, rhetoric), the Quadrivium (astronomy, arithmetic, geometry, music), and the three philosophies (natural, moral, metaphysical).[11] By 1589 Sir Christopher Wray and John Spendluffe had infused the college with much needed support, enabling the institution to complete the construction of buildings necessary to its success.

For much of its history Magdalene College has suffered from the loss of benefactors, some of whom were executed and others of whom did not follow through on their original intent. Significant loss of income came when a piece of land was granted in 1574 to Benedict Spinola in perpetuity for £15 a year. This helped lead to Magdalene's reputation as the poorest of the colleges of Oxford and Cambridge.

A. C. Benson, Fellow from 1904 and master from 1915 to 1925, built the reputation of the college and the undergraduate enrollment. Some would argue that "Magdalene today is very largely Benson's creation."[12] During Benson's time, the first Pepys Dinner took place in 1905, the Kingsley Club began in 1906, the first issue of the *College Magazine* appeared in 1909, and the first May Ball was held in 1912.[13]

Sir Henry Willink was named master of Magdalene in 1948, one year after the formal admission of the first female undergraduates in Cambridge University but forty years before Magdalene College admitted women. Retiring in 1966, he was the master under whom Lewis lectured as a Fellow of Magdalene College. During Willink's tenure, there was almost continuous improvement in the buildings. Two new buildings appeared in Benson Court in the 1950s, a new college library was opened in 1960, and the old library was remodeled to enable the creation of the Parlour in 1966. The Porter's Lodge was enlarged in 1965–1966, and a new Master's Lodge was built in 1966–1967.[14]

Magdalene's most famous alumnus is Samuel Pepys (1633–1703), the writer known for his diaries written between 1660 and 1669 that told the story of the coronation of Charles II (1660), the Plague of 1665, and the Great Fire of London (1666). Pepys was formally admitted to Magdalene on October 1, 1650, as an undergraduate and earned his degree in 1654. Later, Pepys bequeathed to the college his library of 3,000 books and manuscripts.

Other distinguished alumni include Edmund Grindal, a later master of Pembroke College (Cambridge) and archbishop of Canterbury (1575–1583); novelist Charles Kingsley (1819–1875); George Mallory, who is remembered for his ill-fated attempt to climb Mt. Everest (June 1924) "because it was there"; Professor I. A. Richards (1893–1979), the founding father of the English faculty whose work of literary criticism *The Meaning of Meaning* changed the teaching of English literature around the world; Lord Blackett (1897–1974), who won the Nobel Prize for physics in 1948; Archbishop of Canterbury Michael Ramsey (1904–1988); and actor Sir Michael Redgrave (1908–1985). Between the mid-1780s and the mid-1790s, Magdalene graduated five men who would help lay the foundation of the Protestant missionary movement in India and the southern seas: Richard Johnson, John Crowther, Samuel Marsden (1764–1838, known as the apostle of New Zealand), David Brown, and Thomas Thomason.

Other famous names from Magdalene's past include Thomas Cranmer (1489–1556), who held a theology lectureship briefly in 1515 or 1516; Henry Dunster, president of Harvard College and probably the designer of the Harvard coat of arms (1643), which features the word *Veritas* (Latin for "truth") distributed upon three open books; Edward Waring, the best Cambridge mathematician of the eighteenth century (an undergraduate and later a Fellow); Charles Stewart Parnell (1846–1891), who became the leader of the Irish Parliamentary Party (1880–1890); and Henry Chadwick, known for his work in patristics and the early history of Christianity. Today Magdalene numbers approximately 305 undergraduates, 130 postgraduates, and 35 fellows.

MAGDALENE COLLEGE DURING THE LEWIS YEARS[15]

Curiously, when Lewis moved from Oxford to Cambridge in 1955, he moved from a lower salary to a higher salary, though he moved from one of the wealthiest colleges of Oxford to the poorest college of Cambridge. Lewis also moved from a fellowship that required tutorials to one that did not. His last tutorial had been given in Oxford on December 3, 1954, and his first night in Cambridge was January 7, 1955. Lewis had rooms in the North Range on the second floor of staircase 3, the "chapel staircase."

Magdalene College had had a reputation for conservatism at the start of the 1930s, but it became enthralled with materialism and Moscow. Thus many of its Fellows embraced socialism and the Left during that decade. The 1930s saw a strong devotion to team games, rowing, and the rituals that go with those activities. The 1940s and 1950s brought complacency in material security for some, but for others, Christianity still held an important place. In 1954 Lewis wrote to Don Giovanni Calabria: "The Christian Faith . . . counts for more among Cambridge men than among us; Communists are rarer and those plaguey philosophers whom we call Logical Positivists are not so powerful."[16]

Many Cambridge academics were happy to have the breath of fresh academic air that Lewis brought to the university. The feeling was mutual. Simon Barrington-Ward described Lewis as becoming increasingly happier for two reasons. First, Lewis enjoyed what he described as the rather old-world piety of Magdalene, Cambridge. Lewis once said, "And I think I shall like Magdalene better than Magdalen. It's a tiny college (a perfect cameo architecturally) and they're all so old fashioned, and pious, and gentle and conservative—unlike this leftist, atheist, cynical, hard-boiled, huge Magdalen."[17] Robert E. Havard said that Lewis used to refer to Magdalene as the Penitent Magdalene and the Magdalen of Oxford as the Impenitent.[18] The pelican that adorns the gable of the roof just south of the Porter's Lodge suggests this because the pelican was a medieval symbol of penitence, allegedly wounding its breast so its young could drink the blood of the mother.

In Cambridge there was much less hostility to Lewis's efforts at Christian apologetic than there had been at Oxford. In fact, he found a warm and congenial welcome from Fellows who enormously appreciated the imaginative and intellectual gifts he brought and the astonishing range of his learning and his power of recall in conversation. Lewis's reputation as a Christian writer was already established before he came and was probably more widely appreciated in a Cambridge where the Christian heritage of the university was still more widely valued. A stronger low-church tradition at Cambridge could more easily appreciate the popularization of Christianity that Lewis accomplished. Dame Helen Gardner, Lewis's chief rival for the post he accepted at Cambridge, expressed the feeling of many at Oxford when she wrote: "[A] good many people thought that shoemakers should stick to their lasts, and disliked the thought of a Professor of English Literature winning fame as an amateur theologian."[19] Also, Lewis was growing personally and spiritually through his constantly deepening relationship with Joy Davidman. He enjoyed the greater freedom from college teaching that his new appointment brought, which meant he had more time for undisturbed reading and writing.

Because of an Edwardian widening of the curriculum, history, English, and music prospered in the twentieth century at Magdalene College. Magdalene was one of the first institutions to have a Fellow in English, I. A. Richards, who arrived in 1926 and made Britain a world center of critical theory.[20] In the 1940s Richards moved to Harvard, so John Stevens and Arthur Sale developed English as a major subject for undergraduates in the 1950s and 1960s.

As at Oxford, so also at Cambridge, during the 1950s the new trend in philosophy was to study language and separate philosophy from theology.[21] During the early 1960s, Bishop J. A. T. Robinson's *Honest to God* (1963)[22] challenged traditional ways of thinking by suggesting that Christians must recast the Christian faith in modern, secular terms, preferring Paul Tillich's description of God as the "ground" of all being and writing that "[n]othing can of itself be labeled as wrong."[23] God is not up there or out there, coming to earth as a visitor from outer space. Ethical conduct, according to Robinson, then bishop of Woolwich, is bound only by love, and moral decisions depend upon the situation. The Bible is little more than a collection of religious opinions. This is not to suggest that modernism or liberalism was only now making its way into Cambridge, but Robinson's book was a watershed in the Church of England.

Four Cambridge deans—James Stanley Bezzant of St. John's College, Alec Vidler of King's College,[24] H. A. Williams of Trinity College, and Donald MacKinnon (who spoke several times at the Socratic Club)—published *Objections to Christian Belief* (1963), a work in which Vidler wrote of the "striking inconsistencies" in the New Testament writers and others wrote unfavorably of traditional Christian beliefs. Lewis rejected such rewriting of New Testament theology, much of it a demythologizing of the Scriptures in the tradition of Rudolph Bultmann. For example, Vidler had claimed that the miracle of turning water into wine at Cana was actually a parable.

For Lewis and for many others, the central figure at Cambridge was F. R. Leavis (1895–1978), a Fellow of Downing College from 1936 until 1962 and the most influential literary critic of his time after T. S. Eliot. Whereas the English Syllabus at Oxford focused more on the linguistic roots of modern literature, the English Syllabus at Cambridge focused much more on literary criticism. Leavis's first major book, *New Bearings in English Poetry* (1932), argued that T. S. Eliot, G. M. Hopkins, Ezra Pound, and W. B. Yeats were the more important and creative of the modern writers. Leavis disliked most of the parts of Milton's *Paradise Lost* that Lewis loved, largely because of Milton's Christian theology. When Tolkien's *Lord of the Rings* came out, Lewis wrote to Christopher Derrick in reflection of its Christian origin: "And it shows too, which cheers, that there are thousands left in Israel who have not bowed the knee to Leavis . . . ."[25] Leavis, therefore, was part of the intellectual climate in both Oxford and Cambridge, though he never taught at Oxford. His years of influence spanned some of Lewis's Oxford years and most of his Cambridge years. Lewis saw Leavis as accepting the error of much of literary criticism, namely, that writing was largely a function of the writer's personality.[26]

Leavis was cofounder and editor of *Scrutiny*, a quarterly journal of literature and cultural criticism published between 1932 and 1953. In *Scrutiny*, he described literature as a moral resource to address the problems of everyday life; provided a canon of worthwhile English literature; criticized mass culture, especially politics, commercialism, technology, and science; described the university as a place where human responsibility and courage should be developed; and warned against turning the university into a business enterprise.[27]

The emphasis of Leavis, then, in summary, "was on the imperative need to create a critical readership able to maintain standards, to preserve and protect the values of the tradition."[28] For Leavis the standards were egalitarian, anti-capitalistic, moral though not Christian, viewing English as the new classics, and able to criticize the culture and its media environment in order to bring about change.[29] English was not only the new classics but the new religion. Leavis claimed to be able to reveal both the meaning of literature and the meaning of life.[30]

Indeed, one of the differences between Oxford and Cambridge was the predominance of the philosopher at Oxford and the literary critic at Cambridge. Lewis commented on the lack of philosophers at Cambridge, writing:

> To me, one of the oddest things about Cambridge is the absence of the philosopher . . . there is something at Cambridge which fills the same place philosophy filled at Oxford; a discipline which overflows the faculty of its birth and percolates through all the others and about which the freshman must pick up something if he means to be anybody. This is Literary Criticism (with the largest possible capitals for both words). You were never safe from the philosopher at Oxford; here, never from the Critic.[31]

Almost all the books that Lewis wrote at Cambridge were a reflection of the changed environment in Cambridge compared to that of Oxford. Lewis attacked Leavis and the various contributors to *Scrutiny* in his book *The Personal Heresy* and in the essay "Christianity and Literature" because of what Lewis saw as a subjective criticism of literature that was based on feelings and preferences rather than an objective criticism based on facts.[32] Especially in *The Discarded Image* and *An Experiment in Criticism*, Lewis opposed the Leavis approach, contending instead that too much theory and too little actual reading of literature prevented the reader from truly appreciating literature. Lewis opposed Leavis's prescriptive approach, which argued that only a certain selection of poets, named above, and a certain canon of prose writers (Jane Austen, Joseph Conrad, George Eliot, Henry James, and D. H. Lawrence) formed a good literary canon. Lewis believed that reading was an unprescriptive activity, something to be enjoyed rather than to be used for social or political purposes. Lewis challenged Leavis with *An Experiment in Criticism* (1961), in which he suggested judging readers by what they read rather than judging books and writers according to the criteria of the critic, in the manner of Leavis, who wanted to "scrutinize" literature for its moral, social, and political value.[33] In describing the combative positions of Leavis, whom Noel Annan portrayed as proud of being both persecutor and persecuted,[34] Donald Davie remarked that the charm of *Scrutiny* lay in the fact that each issue provided the reader with "a dozen authors or books or whole periods and genres of literature which I not only need not, but *should not* read."[35] That fifty years later most of Lewis's books are still in print while Leavis's are scarcely known suggests the lasting influence of the approach that Lewis took. The demise of *Scrutiny* for its self-imposed canon is further testimony to the limiting nature of the Leavis school of thought.

In summary, then, during the Lewis years, Magdalene College and Cambridge University were more conservative, Christian, and low church; more focused on science than at Oxford; but with the literary critic as obvious in Cambridge as the philosopher was at Oxford.

One should not underestimate the prestige of these two universities, both of which are undergirded by centuries of tradition and a long list of distinguished dons and graduates. The history of England is bound up in the history of Oxford and Cambridge, while many academic disciplines in many countries owe much to the contributions these two institutions have made to learning. Within Oxford and Cambridge, one of England's brightest minds, C. S. Lewis, learned and taught for more than four decades. How Lewis taught is the subject of the next chapter.

NINE

C. S. Lewis as Tutor
and Lecturer

> . . . whose lectures are still among the most rapturous memories
> of my undergraduate days.—C. S. Lewis, *Preface to Paradise Lost*[1]

The previous chapters said much about the setting in which C. S. Lewis worked. But they excluded one important aspect of his work as an educator—the undergraduates, the reason for which he taught and the beneficiaries of his irrigating work.

As an educator at Oxford and Cambridge, Lewis functioned primarily in two roles: as tutor and as lecturer. Here we must recall the tutorial system of Oxford and Cambridge, described in earlier chapters. For the Fellow, tutorials were the rule and lectures the exception. For the professor, lectures were the rule and there were no exceptions, though there were graduate students to supervise.

Those in higher education can learn from an educator such as C. S. Lewis. He spent twenty-nine years as a Fellow at Oxford University (1925–1954) and nine years as a professor at Cambridge University (1955–1963), from which he retired. Lewis excelled as a lecturer and a tutor, as well as in his writings. George Bailey once wrote that it was "almost impossible to exaggerate Lewis's prestige in postwar Oxford." He was ". . . the most eminent scholar in his field . . . perhaps the most powerful and best trained intellect in the world."[2] In this chapter, through the eyes of those who studied with him, we take a firsthand look at the impact of Lewis's lectures and his tutorials.

LEWIS AS TUTOR

Students of Lewis began the term with Collections (see Glossary), much like the Collections described in chapter 6. Every student would write two three-hour papers, one on Old or Middle English during the morning and the other on later literature during the afternoon. Each paper was based on the previous term's work and work done during vacation. Lewis would conscientiously grade these papers, thirty to forty of them, during the first week of the term so he would know what sort of progress the students had made and how much they remembered from the previous term.[3]

In 1925 Lewis averaged four tutorials a day, though not every weekday—three in the morning and one in the late afternoon. Each tutorial usually had one or two students.[4] Later, he tutored many more students, reaching a peak of 43 during the 1947 Michaelmas term (see Glossary). The five years immediately after World War II saw the largest number of students at Magdalen College, Oxford, as many soldiers returned from the war to continue their education.

Insight into the course of study in tutorials comes from Edward L. Edmonds:

> Lewis' approach to English Literature was strictly chronological. We started with Anglo-Saxon and finished at 1832. We began with the early Anglo-Saxon prose à la Sweet, e.g. *The Voyages of Ohthere and Wulstan* and through the Saxon Chronicle, to the fiery, more polemical prose of the sermon of Bishop Wulfstan, Archbishop of York, 1002–1023. We also "did" a considerable number of the poems, including "The Fall of the Angels," "The Seafarer," "Judith," "The Phoenix," and "The Battle of Maldon." Thence to Spenser, Shakespeare, Milton, the 18th century and early 19th century.
>
> In language-study, etymology of words may be out of fashion today, but Lewis insisted on it. He picked up Tyndale's use of "scapegoat" (in his translation of the New Testament from the Greek in 1525). Milton's coinages, "pandemonium" or "ethereal," for example, received close attention. We noted Milton's strikingly transitive use of the verb "scowl" in "scowls o'er the darkened landscape snow and showers." His reference to "charm of earliest birds" took us back to Anglo-Saxon "cyrm"; to the

"charms" too, which we had already studied, as well as to other later usages, by Sir Walter Scott, for example.[5]

But taking tutorials with Lewis was not simply a course of study designed to prepare the student for the Second Public Examination. Studying with Lewis was starting on a lifetime pursuit in literature; it was an entry into a life of scholarship.[6]

Lewis the tutor received mixed reviews from his former undergraduates. Most of them, however, especially the better undergraduates, appreciated his tutorials. Humphrey Carpenter claimed that many undergraduates were frightened by his manner of conducting tutorials.[7] George Bailey wrote: ". . . Lewis's great fault, perhaps his only one as a teacher, was his basic lack of interest in his students as individuals."[8] J. I. Packer felt similarly, writing about both tutorials and lectures:

> When I say I did not know him, I mean I had no personal link with him. (Nor did most of his pupils; they found him an awesome academic who hid his sensitive heart behind a debater's façade of urbane, loud-voiced pugnacity. "I'm a butcher, a rough and brutal man," he told one of them.) I heard him speak once, on the medievalism of the Anglican theologian Richard Hooker. He was supposed to be the best lecturer in Oxford, and on that showing it could have been true, though in the Oxford of my day the compliment meant less than you might think.[9]

However, many of his students would challenge that characterization. Charles Arnold-Baker stated:

> Intellectually arrogant he certainly was not—he was actually tolerant—but he would not accept the weak and insipid undergraduate who thought that the world owed him a degree. It was said that he would eat an undergraduate for breakfast. Not so! He respected anyone who had done their homework. If sometimes he bit deeply into an intellect, he did so because it was his job.[10]

Edward Edmonds agreed with this characterization of Lewis the scholar, who held high standards and would accept nothing but the student's best effort:

> Lewis made no concessions; and perhaps for the first time I learned to submit to stringent criticism. But, he was never cynical or sarcastic; and his own frequent change of intellectual stance taught me one very valuable lesson for my own students later on, namely that no one should be regarded as an absolute authority. Thus, much as he respected Tillyard,

Tillyard for him was not the only authority on Milton, any more than A. C. Bradley's views of Shakespeare were the exclusive ones.[11]

Another of Lewis's former students, Paul Piehler, also challenged the view of Carpenter, Bailey, and Packer. Stating that Lewis's affectionate soubriquet in one group of students was "Papa Lewis," Piehler went on to say that "the idea of Lewis being intimidating among those guys [a group of his students] would have raised incredulous laughter."[12] Lest one think that Piehler came to Oxford already enthralled with Lewis, he wrote that

> [a]ll my Catholic relatives were crazy about Lewis, thought it marvelous that I would be in HIS college. I was correspondingly dubious, envisioning a tall cadaverous clerical type who would doubtless be maddeningly prone to reduce all literary questions to moral or religious platitudes, so no doubt he'd prove a serious distraction from the studies I intended. I was at that time an almost totally convinced anti-clerical atheist, having read something of all the great iconoclasts of that era, Freud, Frazer, Robertson, etc.[13]

W. J. B. Owen, an English professor at McMaster University in Hamilton, Ontario, Canada, and Pat Wallsgrove, an English teacher, also considered Lewis a gifted educator. Owen stated: ". . . he was a splendid tutor . . . . I learned much of scholarly method and clear thinking from this process, and also, perhaps, a gracious approach to pupils which I tried to adopt as a teacher myself."[14] Wallsgrove said:

> We presented ourselves weekly at Mr. Lewis's rooms in the charming eighteenth-century block of Magdalen College known as the New Building. Mr. Lewis, in his carpet slippers and surrounded by piles of books and papers, always treated us with courtesy and listened to our essays with charity, and encouraged us to talk . . . I encountered Mr. Lewis in my first year in Oxford by attending (with as many other undergraduates of all schools as could cram into the medieval hall at Magdalen) his lectures on "Prolegomena to Sixteenth-Century Studies."[15]

Lewis seems to have been received differently by different students. Those who were shy probably did not appreciate Lewis's direct style nor did those who were not dedicated to their studies, such as John Betjeman.[16] John Lawlor has written: "Lewis valued time as few men I have met, before or since, have done."[17] Those who were wasting Lewis's time, then, would know it. Alastair Fowler wrote: "Those who called Lewis bully and brute probably included some who shrank from discussing matters of substance."[18] But the students who came to learn, who came to be challenged and to grow, with some notable exceptions, soon discovered flowers blooming in the deserts of their minds.

Peter Bayley and Derek Brewer described this Lewisian approach to tutorials in more detail. Bayley wrote: "Even more alarming was his ceaselessly active, almost aggressive conduct of the tutorial . . . . There was something unintentionally rebuffing about Lewis's intellectual supremacy."[19] Brewer wrote: "He spoke to everyone on the same terms of equality, and this led occasionally to inadvertent rudeness . . . ."[20] Lewis was a brilliant man, confident in his learning, anxious to impart it to students, and not willing to put up with less than a student's best effort. As Luke Rigby once noted, by showing his appreciation and his enthusiasm for learning, Lewis instilled confidence in his students and also demanded effort, both of which resulted in learning.[21] The expectation of effort would have rebuffed some students, but most of them appreciated this approach. Perhaps most important, however, Lewis directed his opposition to the views that were held and never to the people who held them.[22] Those who were unable to distinguish between the viewpoint and the person failed to see the charity with which Lewis treated people. Instead, they saw only the challenge with which he treated poor logic, unirrigated minds, or unsubstantiated views.

John Lawlor wrote: "One quickly felt that for him [Lewis] dialectic supplied the place of conversation." After some time, Lawlor came to appreciate "the weekly bout in which no quarter was asked or given."[23] Edward Edmonds wrote: "Always he was probing, always testing to see how far a particular student could go. He once handed me the philosopher Owen Barfield's book *Poetic Diction* and asked me to read and comment on it . . . . He loved to throw out challenges and see if a student would pick them up."[24] Rachel Trickett, English tutor at St. Hugh's College, Oxford, brought both disparate viewpoints together when she wrote: "Pupils who survived the combat of his tutorials learned to love and rely on his humanity and loyalty and his stealthy generosity."[25]

Indeed, in "the combat of his tutorials," Lewis irrigated deserts. A tutor who did not challenge did not irrigate. When Lewis once wrote on a student's paper "Load every rift with ore," he was encouraging the use of examples and quotations, inviting the student to read widely and incorporate concepts from that reading into his writing.[26] Lewis could just as easily have written "Fill that irrigation ditch with water." A. E. F. Davis summarized Lewis the person and Lewis the tutor when he wrote: "He was, above all, a gentlemanly and jovial man of learning, exact in factual accuracy but ready for any form of argument."[27]

TAKING A TUTORIAL WITH LEWIS

Because the tutorial was a formal event, undergraduates would arrive at the New Building, third staircase (of six), third set of rooms, wearing gowns for their tutorial with Lewis. Upon being invited in by Lewis, they would cross a threshold into a large room that faced north and had a view of the famous Magdalen College deer park. They would cross into a smaller sitting room that faced south toward the cloisters of Magdalen. Students would see Tintoretto's *The Origin of the Milky Way*, a reproduction of a painting from the National Gallery in London with its depiction of Jupiter, Hercules, and Juno, whose milk formed both the Milky Way above and the lilies below. Two armchairs, a large sofa, a dining table, and chairs sparsely adorned the room.[28]

Lewis would sit in his armchair, chain-smoking Wills Gold Flake cigarettes or smoking a pipe. He wore a Harris Tweed jacket and carpet slippers.[29] The student would take the easy chair on the left-hand side of the fireplace. According to one former student, Lewis's

> study was shabby and comfortable, very masculine, with lots of books and papers around . . . he wore comfortable shabby clothes, a brown tweed jacket and grey flannel trousers, and smoked a pipe thoughtfully while we read aloud. He was always perfectly polite, but rather distant in manner . . .[30]

As described in chapter 6, the undergraduate would then read the essay assigned the previous week, perhaps three thousand words or more, while Lewis listened carefully.[31] He would jot down notes on a pad as the essay was being read.[32] Lewis always did some of the same reading as the students because of his conscientious concern to provide appropriate critique. His prodigious memory did not obviate the need to reread books; instead, Lewis chose to use the tutorial assignment as an opportunity to reacquaint himself with old friends (see chapter 4). After reading the essay, there would be a pause, then Lewis would critique the essay, following the pattern that W. T. Kirkpatrick had instilled in him, challenging the use of inexact words or phrases or the undergraduate's interpretation of the previous week's readings.

Some who took tutorials with Lewis have commented on the routine of the tutorial. Edward Edmonds described what happened after the reading of the essay: "He would then ask one or two questions, usually requiring further elaboration of particular points I had made. We then got into discussion, with Lewis sometimes suggesting at intervals that I might care to read what so and so had said on this, etc."[33] A. E. F. Davis stated that Lewis "would only comment upon one's tutorial essay after one had read it fully through—he would remember precisely anything he wished to discuss or talk on."[34] Joan O'Hare wrote: "We would each prepare a weekly assignment. One of us would write an essay on the assignment and read it aloud in tutorial. The other would then discuss the points made and criticize. Writing and criticism would alternate."[35]

Examples of a Lewis critique appear below, as J. O. Reed describes a tutorial with Lewis addressing an essay he wrote about the two plots in Shakespeare's *King Lear*:

> I am a little nervous before the tutorial (when I am to read the essay which is upon the two plots in *King Lear*) but all goes well . . . . When I have finished Lewis says my essay was good, well-written, & bringing in an interesting new theory of my own. The epithet "well-written" is most surprising—tho' perhaps, touched up, it does not read too badly. Also I think he is surprisingly tolerant of my theory, which at the time had seemed very flimsy to me. When the tutorial finishes, he says my essay was good again & I go off contented.[36]

Another tutorial with Lewis is described in a subsequent diary entry by Reed:

> Down at 10 to the tutorial. This continues 'til 11.15, & contains much interesting discussion on the Relationship of Art & Life—Lewis sees a fullness in our everyday perceptions gained through art—poetry gives us, as it were, emotional or aesthetic "proverbs" to apply to life—We see in a tree all that our reading has told us of trees—Both of their imaginative values through literature and art & their construction and processes through our scientific study.[37]

A third tutorial between Lewis and Reed gives us still more insight because Lewis offered constructive criticism of Reed's writing, as well as appreciation of a new idea:

For my tutorial with Lewis I am alone. He returns me my Collection for which I have the satisfactory mark of beta-alpha. Indeed I think my main trouble is carelessness in composition when writing in haste. As Lewis writes on the paper "You must learn to steer while driving quickly." Also among his comments is this

> If, following your satiric muse,
> You chanced to meet a satyr
> I'm sure you'd ne'er again confuse
> The former with the latter.[38]

He seems quite satisfied with my essay on the Minor Poems,[39] & from his comments I get a great deal of information & am amazed at his tremendously wide acquaintance with English—& any other literature. He confesses my suggestion that the August Eclogue[40] is written in imitation of French syllabic metre is new to him, but is willing to think there may be something in it.[41]

Sometimes, though rarely, friendly conversation would be included in one of Lewis's tutorials, but never to the detriment of the tutorial itself. The tutorial would end after about an hour with an assignment of the next week's work, including a reading list for the assignment.

Lewis as Lecturer and Scholar

As Stan Mattson[42] has stated, few scholars have all their scholarly works still in print forty years after their death. However, this is true of Lewis, with the exception of *English Literature in the Sixteenth Century*, volume 3 in the multivolume Oxford History of the English Language. From *The Abolition of Man* to *The Discarded Image* to his first scholarly work, *The Allegory of Love*, Lewis's scholarship remains in print.

But Lewis was not only a scholar. He had the ability to draw widely on his reading, to grasp the issues with breadth and depth, and to convey those concepts in a way that readers can understand. John Lawlor once wrote of Lewis's gift of scholarly writing: "With Lewis your feet are everywhere on the ground; the skyline is always in view."[43] Few writers have this ability. Kenneth Tynan wrote:

> The great thing about him [Lewis] as a teacher of literature was that he could take you into the medieval mind and the mind of a classical writer. He could make you understand that classicism and medievalism were

really vivid and alive—that it was not the business of literature to be "relevant" to us, but *our* business to be "relevant" to it.[44]

Lecturing and scholarship go hand in hand for many people—so also for Lewis. Several of Lewis's published works were based on lectures. *A Preface to Paradise Lost* (1942) was based on the Ballard Matthews Lectures he gave in 1941 at University College, North Wales.[45] The Riddell Memorial Lectures that Lewis gave in 1943 at Durham University, Newcastle-upon-Tyne, were later published as *The Abolition of Man*. In 1944 Lewis delivered the Clark Lectures at Trinity College, Cambridge University,[46] lectures that formed a significant portion of his major work *English Literature in the Sixteenth Century* (1954). After his death, Alastair Fowler edited Lewis's lecture notes to produce *Spenser's Images of Life*. Lewis's lectures at Cambridge on "Some Difficult Words" were later published as *Studies in Words*. His "Prolegomena to Medieval Literature" lectures were published as *The Discarded Image*, and his lectures on "Prolegomena to Renaissance Literature" later formed the introduction to *English Literature in the Sixteenth Century*.[47]

Although he lectured only twice a week, Lewis's lectures drew crowds. George Bailey wrote: "While I was at Oxford, he was by far the most popular lecturer at the university."[48] In 1947 *Time* magazine reported that same opinion about Lewis.[49] Gervase Mathew claimed that Lewis's "influence on his contemporaries was at least as much as orator as writer."[50] Derek Brewer mentioned that around four hundred attended many of Lewis's lectures in the Examination Schools.[51] Helen Tyrrell Wheeler stated: ". . . people crowded out the lectures of both Williams and Lewis."[52] Patricia Hunt wrote about "his lectures in Magdalen Hall on 'Prolegomena to English Mediaeval Literature' and 'Prolegomena to English Renaissance Literature,' which were always crowded out . . . . I will add that they were absolutely enthralling, both in their content, which was satisfyingly informative, and in the manner of their delivery, which was authoritative, humorous, and forthright."[53] Mary Wright added her voice to the almost unanimous testimony of others: "As a commoner [see Glossary] out of St. Hilda's College, Oxford (1947–1950) I attended C. S. Lewis on Milton, always in packed halls . . ."[54] No one seems ever to have suggested that the lectures of Lewis generally drew anything but large crowds.[55]

When Lewis gave his inaugural lecture at Cambridge, "the largest lecture room in Mill Lane was packed and people coming late had to sit on the floor."[56] George Sayer called the lecture "a brilliant performance acknowledged by an ovation rarely given to an academic."[57] Some of those in attendance had come all the way from Oxford to support Lewis. However, he did not thereafter draw students in the same numbers as he had at Oxford.[58]

CONTENT

Lewis attracted undergraduates because of the content of his lectures. Peter Milward, English literature teacher at Sophia University in Tokyo, said regarding Lewis's lectures on prolegomena to medieval and Renaissance literature: "These lectures were by far the most popular of all those provided by the School of English, since the content was so fascinating, the presentation was so lucid, and the delivery so clear and considerate for note-taking students."[59] Other authors cite these lectures as those that established Lewis as one of the leading lecturers in Oxford. When he gave those lectures, the information they contained was not yet published. The lectures, therefore, provided insight nowhere else available, demonstrating Lewis's ability to show in prose and poetry the development of ideas across the centuries.[60]

Former student Roger Poole wrote both of the content and of the style of Lewis's lectures, showing that his lectures irrigated and, at times, irritated, much like his tutorials:

> For what exactly was the magic element in Lewis's lecturing technique? It was the ability to ask questions no one had thought of, and to start towards an answer of them by reference to sources no one had read. It was, in other words, the exact antithesis of clear lecturing. There were many obscurities, and the audience felt itself being shoved and bustled past many things it had not time to stop and examine. Clarity, indeed, in the sense of spelling things out, explaining, waiting until the back row had caught up, was never offered. Indeed, the boot was very much on the other foot. The assumption was that only those who were committed, interested, and prepared to put a great deal of work into thinking these lectures through were really part of the audience anyway. The lectures were, without a word being said about the matter, remorselessly elitist. But it was not any shade of social or economic elitism that was in question. It was simply that the audience for Lewis was made up of two classes of people: there were those who were fascinated by the subject itself, and those who weren't. And to the latter, he had nothing to say.[61]

Lewis, therefore, maintained high standards in his lectures, refusing to aim for the lowest common denominator, expecting students to keep up with him, take notes, and do the necessary reading or be left behind. Lewis knew the importance of beginning with the known before moving into the unknown,[62] and he used this technique well.

The best way to learn about the content of the lectures of Lewis is to read some of the works that later made their way into book form, especially *The Abolition of Man*, *The Discarded Image*, and *The Allegory of Love*.

PRESENTATION

In his biography of Lewis, George Sayer called Lewis "the best lecturer in the department."[63] Although Lewis wrote to his father in 1924 about the necessity of learning the slow deliberate style of the lecturer, Sayer says that Lewis never learned that method and that this is one of the reasons he became "the only Oxford lecturer of the thirties and forties to attract and hold large audiences."[64] Some would challenge Sayer, however, because Lewis said on at least one occasion: "I shall adapt myself to the slowest note-taker among you."[65]

When Lewis moved to Cambridge, he did not lose anything, for Roger Poole, lecturer in the Department of English at the University of Nottingham, said of one of Lewis's lectures at Cambridge, "It was a virtuoso performance."[66] One feature that apparently helped Lewis as a lecturer was the decision to learn to talk rather than to read, to practice his lectures, and to lecture to an imaginary audience.[67] At the same time, because Lewis used lecturing as a way to develop material for a book, his complete and careful notes provided him with an accurate text from which to lecture.

We must keep Lewis's lecturing style in context, for as Charles Arnold-Baker has written: "Moreover attendance at lectures, outside the scientific schools, was not compulsory (I hardly ever went to them) . . . And this was or might be exacerbated by the fact . . . that the standard of lecturing was abysmally low. Some, indeed, were inaudible. I have seen audiences fall to 3."[68] J. I. Packer was correct in stating that "in the Oxford of my day the compliment meant less than you might think."[69] Lewis's style was not ordinary, but his excellence in lecturing stood out more brightly against a background of mediocrity.

Among various other techniques, Roger Lancelyn Green described the lecturing style of Lewis as one from a written text with added examples and explanations.[70] Another technique, the universal practice at Oxford for both lectures and tutorials, was to respect the tradition of the university and to wear the academic gown while lecturing and to expect undergraduates to come similarly garbed. A third technique is the use of humor in teaching, sometimes at his own expense. Fourth, at times, when late in arriving, Lewis would begin to lecture before he entered the room. If not late, as former undergraduate Penelope Fitzgerald notes, ". . . he saved time by beginning just inside the door."[71] His lectures would end abruptly with Lewis stepping down from the dais after his last sentence, returning the watch he had borrowed from Roger Lancelyn Green, and heading down the hall at top walking speed. This means that he did not take questions from students or engage them in discussion, also a universal practice at Oxford.[72] Although questions and answers occurred at the Socratic Club, they did not occur in Lewis's lectures nor in the lectures of other dons. This efficient use of his lecture time may be demonstrated in the way in which Lewis once stated that a good lecture should be given. He said that the lecturer should start 5 minutes late and end 10 minutes early. Indeed, Lewis was not one to use a circumlocution when a direct statement would do.[73]

One of his former students, Paul Piehler, aptly describes Lewis the lecturer:

> I remember so well attending Lewis's lectures on medieval civilization which became the basis of his *Discarded Image* book. He would stride in with heraldic authority, his bouncy gait in perfect accord with his somewhat roly-poly figure, thrusting his way through the crowd milling around in the largest lecture hall the university could boast. He would stand there massively on the high podium and boom out resonantly over the disorderly mass below the same first sentence every lecture of the term. "Would Members of the University be seated first please!"
>
> An awed hush would fall over the crowd, a silence broken only by the shuffle of seats as a hundred or so mere "visitors"—often elderly, gave up seats to us bright young gowned undergraduates and shuffled uneasily to the back of the hall. (Well this was a university lecture and the students did have to take notes!) A glance at *The Discarded Image* book that came out of the lectures would remind you that the material was hardly of a character that most lecturers would choose in order to cram a hall to bursting point.

Macrobius or Andreas Capellanus might be quoted in Latin, Langland or Gower in equally fluent Middle English.

But one could not, would not miss a word, and I carried those notes around with me for years, until the book came out. I would say I got (or at least kept) my first job at Columbia largely on the strength of what I took from those lectures, inspiration and fact alike.

Oddly enough he seemed quite honestly innocent of the immense effect of these performances. He had had to miss one lecture, and, walking back with him to Magdalen from the Lecture Halls one day, I happened to ask him about when we were going to get a chance to hear this one lecture that he had been forced to omit. He seemed most genuinely surprised that I was evidently so eager to catch up on the missing talk, as if, after all, the grandeur of his performance and my dazzled appreciation were just part of the required academic routine, rather than a life-changing experience. Beneath the boom, it seemed, lay a genuine personal humility.[74]

Mary Wright once said of Lewis's "boom" and delivery: "But his particular unique grand rolling delivery was a delight in itself."[75] Lewis had a rich, deep voice that carried an air of authority. Charles Arnold-Baker wrote: "He was highly influential outside the College because he was an excellent expositor with an enormous voice which always emptied the front three rows."[76]

Those who have heard any of the recordings of Lewis's voice will understand this to be one of the reasons for the success of his broadcasts over the BBC in 1941, 1942, and 1944. They will understand why that voice, with its authoritative tone, could be accused, unfairly, of running roughshod over speakers at the Socratic Club or undergraduates in their tutorials.

TEN

LESSONS FROM C. S. LEWIS

"But, before I go, I must give you a few lessons, my fine hock brown."
—C. S. Lewis, *Boxen*[1]

What can we learn from C. S. Lewis for modern education? We can learn that education is far more a positive experience than a negative one, a matter of irrigating deserts rather than cutting down jungles. Students can and must learn to think outside the box, to think creatively, to explore, to analyze and synthesize, and teachers must so teach.

Beyond that, the most important concept we can learn from Lewis is that truth is objective rather than subjective. The waterfall is not sublime because I have sublime feelings; it is sublime in and of itself. The waterfall is objectively awesome, thunderous, impressive, and that creates a sense of awe within me. Likewise, a given text contains objective truth about the subject of the text rather than a record of what the author was feeling. That objective truth is a reflection of the objective truth of God.

The educator can learn that education focuses on learning (the pursuit of knowledge) rather than training (the learning of skills). We can learn the potential for the well-delivered lecture, the place of breadth and the need for depth, the importance, even the necessity, of objective truth and transcendent truth. We can learn that education is not necessarily learning and that education must serve the purpose of learning rather than the reverse. We can learn that inner rings are inevitable but that we ought not allow the desire to enter an inner ring to dominate our thinking. We can learn that we must not be so concerned about egalitarianism that we fail to allow for the gifted student to excel. We can learn the wisdom of spurning amateur philosophy. But are we not all amateur philosophers? Do we not all have unique hobbyhorses that we ride almost daily into, around, and out of the classroom? Probably so, but a commitment to transcendent truth can help us to escape this trap.

We can also learn the strong commitment that Lewis had to his students. His many years of tutorials, his dedication to student learning, his time spent grading Collections (see Glossary), and his irrigation of deserts through questioning and encouraging are some of the examples of that commitment. Students are the reason for our work, not in a self-centered consumer mentality but in the sense that professors teach so they can serve, convey truth, and irrigate mental deserts.

We can learn from Lewis that lecturing and scholarship go hand in hand as we see that lectures formed the basis for several of Lewis's published works. Those who wish they could find the time to write may need only to look at what they are currently teaching and determine how they could incorporate those insights into a book. We can learn that wide reading, and rereading, feeds this scholarship. More than that, rereading enables us to be influenced by the text, to learn to be attentive, to appreciate detail and dialogue and style, and to rise above the isolation of the age to learn timeless truths.

Lewis combined high goals with relational skills. Too often academics conclude that they must choose between the camaraderie of the academy and the scholarly acclaim of a published author, as if the two do not mix. Yet Lewis prized friendship highly and made ample room for people, both colleagues and undergraduates, while publishing both within his academic field and outside of it. He combined the basic tenets of the Christian faith with each of these enterprises. Although he was at times distant and on occasion unintentionally contentious, especially in the years before he met Joy Davidman, he was always a charitable and generous man, humble in a certain way, and unassuming. These personal qualities, demonstrating that Lewis was both saint and sinner, may be exemplified in the last lectures that both he and F. R. Leavis gave in Cambridge.

Dr. Richard Luckett, librarian of the Pepys Library at Magdalene College, Cambridge, attended those lectures. He characterized Lewis as a benign and caring lecturer, anxious to draw you into his enthusiasm for his subject matter. Leavis, however, began his last lecture on *Bleak House* with ten minutes of brilliance, followed by a vicious personal attack on John Holloway, a notable Cambridge critic at the time, who had also written on *Bleak House*.[2]

A look at the three major categories of the modern university—teaching, scholarship, and service—shows that Lewis scored high in each area. As documented on the pages of this book, his teaching was superb and his scholarship of the highest quality. His dedication to service is seen especially in the time Lewis spent with undergraduates, his tour of duty as vice president of Magdalen College, Oxford, and his participation in college activities. It is also seen externally in his willingness to fight in World War I, his willingness to speak to members of the RAF during World War II, and his willingness to serve during the Second World War in the Home Guard, patrolling a part of Oxford for the Local Defence Volunteers from 1:30 to 4:30 A.M. every Saturday. That Lewis opened his home to children from London during the war speaks of another type of service to his country. That he answered his voluminous correspondence shows still another side of his service to the general public.

Lewis was, first and foremost, an educator. In his writings, he wrote in favor of the liberal arts and objective truth and against the negative effect of democratizing the curriculum, the lack of discipline, the presence of historicism and scientism, and the problem of the inner ring. But Lewis did not simply criticize, he also wrote about the importance of both reason and imagination in the learning process, and he modeled that in his teaching. Lewis promoted a particular approach to education that emphasized a few subjects in depth rather than many subjects covered briefly. Although he did not expect British society to champion the truths of Christianity in the classroom, Lewis nevertheless encouraged the religious side of education as a crucial part of the moral fabric of society. We can learn much from this champion of education. Perhaps the best characterization of Lewis comes from a colleague and an academic, J. A. W. Bennett, the man who succeeded Lewis in the chair of Medieval and Renaissance Literature at Cambridge University. Bennett characterized Lewis as a clear and forceful writer, a master of the aphorism and the comparison, a writer with wit, a man whose wide reading made him one of the most quotable authors of all time. For Bennett, Lewis combined the Christian faith, vivid imagination, unique powers of disputation, and a poetic sensibility with an understanding of the human condition to achieve a wide and lasting appeal.[3]

APPENDIX I

BOOKS C. S. LEWIS READ:
1922–1927

Between 1922 and 1927, Lewis was taking his third course of study in English language and literature (1922–1923); filling a one-year position as a philosophy tutor at University College, Oxford, in place of E. F. Carritt (1924–1925); being elected Fellow at Magdalen College (1925); and embarking on his academic career. During that time, Lewis kept the only extended diary he ever kept. It has been published as *All My Road before Me*. This appendix contains a list of all the books that Lewis read, as reported in this diary.

The books Lewis read during these years are listed alphabetically by author's last name. The date in parentheses is the year or years when Lewis read the book, usually all of it, but sometimes only a portion. Only those books that appear in *All My Road before Me*, his diary from April 1, 1922, through March 2, 1927, appear in this list. In some cases, I could not determine the title of the work read, so only the author is listed. In some cases I could not determine the author, so only the title is listed.

The authors and/or works appear here for three reasons: (1) They form a rather complete record of books Lewis read during a formative period in his life, though his diary is empty for about thirty months or slightly more than half the total duration; (2) they come from some of the important Lewis years, though that could probably be said of every period of his life; and (3) they provide documentation of his wide reading and rereading. The period of time during which he wrote in his diary comprises about 870 days. If Lewis read works at the same pace as indicated below, he read part or all of a work approximately every two days. It is no wonder that many considered him the best-read man of his day.

Because Lewis was taking another degree in English during the first two years covered in the diary, one would expect a great deal of reading during that time. However, a comparison of the works read shows that he read even more during his first years as an Oxford don than he did as an undergraduate.

Year	Works Read	Length of Time in Diary	Dates No Diary Was Kept	Days per Work Read
1922	121	9 months	Jan. 1–March 31	2.23
1923	93	7 months	Apr. 12–19, Apr. 29–May 21, Aug. 7–Sept. 7, Sept. 19–Oct. 10, Oct. 22–Dec. 31 (156 days)	2.26
1924	66	6 months	Feb. 1–19, Aug. 4–Dec. 31	2.95
1925	25	2 months	Jan. 1–Feb. 5, March 2–Aug. 15, Sept. 6–Dec. 31	2.4
1926	59	2 months, 22 days	Jan. 1–Apr 26, July 19–Dec. 31	1.39
1927	43	1 month, 25 days	Jan. 1–8, March 3–Dec. 31	1.28
TOTAL	407	29 months, 2 days (ca. 2 years, 5 months)		2.14

Authors, Various (Prose, Literary Criticism)

Lascelles Abercrombie, *Idea of Great Poetry* (lectures, 1926)

Joseph Addison, ed., (1923), *The Spectator* (periodical, 1926)

Hans Andersen (1925)

Roger Ascham, *Schoolmaster* (1922), *Toxophilus* (1926)

Owen Barfield, *The Tower* (unpublished, 1922), *The Silver Trumpet* (fairy tale, 1923)

Hilaire Belloc, *Mr. Emanuel Burden* (1925)

Arnold Bennett, *The Human Machine* (novel, 1923)

James Boswell (1922) (1923)

Thomas Browne, *Hydriotaphia: Urn Burial* (1924)

John Buchan, *Path of the King* (novel, 1926)

John Bunyan, *Pilgrim's Progress* (allegory, 1924)

Robert Burton, *Anatomy of Melancholy* (satire, 1922)

Samuel Butler, *Erewhon Revisited* (novel, 1923), (1927), *Erewhon* (novel, 1924)

Thomas Carlyle, *The French Revolution, A History* (history, 1923)

G. K. Chesterton, *Browning* (literary biography, 1922, 1924), *Life of St Francis* (literary biography, 1924), *Club of Queer Trades* (parody, 1926), *Eugenics and Other Evils* (social criticism, 1926), *Bernard Shaw* (literary biography, 1926)

Edward Clarendon, *The True Historical Narrative of the Rebellion and Civil Wars in England (1702–1704)* (history, 1922)

J. Storer Clouston, *The Lunatic at Large* (science fiction, 1926)

Sidney Colvin, *Life of Keats* (biography, 1923)

Joseph Conrad, *Typhoon* (novel, 1923), *Chance* (novel, 1925), *Lord Jim* (novel, 1926)

William John Courthope, (1926), chapters on Wit (1927)

William Cowper, (moral satires, 1923)

George Crabbe, (moral satires, 1923)

Sir William Alexander Craigie, *Icelandic Sagas* (1927)

Walter de la Mare, *The Return* (novel, 1922)

Charles Dickens, *David Copperfield* (novel, 1924)

Goldsworthy Lowes Dickinson, *The Magic Flute: A Fantasia* (1922)

Charles Montagu Doughty, *The Cliffs* (1923)

Gavin Douglas, *Prologues to Virgil* (translation, 1926)

Dunbar (1926)

Havelock Ellis, *World of Dreams* (1922), *Studies in Psychology of Sex* (1922)

George Eliot, *Middlemarch* (novel, 1923)

Oliver Elton, *A Sheaf of Papers* (literary criticism, 1924)

Thomas Elyot, *Boke of the Governour* (treatise on education and politics, 1924, 1926), *Titus and Gisippus* (novella, 1926)

Robert Emmet, *The Broken Heart* (short story, 1922)

Erasmus, *Institutio Regis Christiani* (?) (1926), *Institutio Principis Christiani* (1926)

St. John Ervine, *Alice and a Family* (novel, 1925)

Sir Charles Fellows, *A Journal Written during an Excursion in Asia Minor* (journal, 1923)

Henry Fielding, *Tom Jones* (novel, 1924), *Amelia* (novel, 1926)

Anatole France, *The Revolt of the Angels* (novel, social criticism, 1924)

Sir James George Frazer, *The Golden Bough* (a study in magic and religion, 1923)

C. Charles Freeland, *History of Sicily* (history, 1922)

Sigmund Freud, *Introductory Lectures* (lectures on psychoanalysis, 1922)

John Galsworthy, *The Forsyte Saga* (novels, 1922, 1926)

H. W. Garrod, *Wordsworth* (literary criticism, 1923)

Edward Gibbon, *The History of the Decline and Fall of the Roman Empire* (history, 1924)

Alfred Denis Godley, *Unpublished Works* (1926)

Johann Wolfgang von Goethe, *Dichtung und Wahrheit* (1924)

Oliver Goldsmith, *The Citizen of the World* (cultural criticism, 1926)

Robert Graves, *Poetic Unreason* (literary criticism, 1926)

John Richard Green, *Short History of the English People* (history, 1922)

Gregory I, *Cura Pastoralis* (translated by King Alfred, 1922)

J. B. S. Haldane, *Daedalus or Science and the Future* (essay, 1924)

Sir Ian Hamilton, *Gallipoli Diary* (wartime diary, 1922)

Thomas Hardy, *Jude the Obscure* (novel, 1922), *Tess of the d'Urbervilles* (novel, 1923)

Arthur Hassal, *European History Chronologically Arranged* (history, 1922)

Ian Hay, *A Man's Man* (fiction, 1922)

William Hazlitt, "On Going a Journey" (essay, 1923)

Heitland (1922)

Herodotus (1923)

Maurice Hewlett, *Fool Errant* (fictional memoirs, 1924), *The Lore of Proserpine* (fantasy, 1926)

R. H. Hingley, *Psychoanalysis* (lecture, 1922)

Thomas Hoby, *The Courtyer of Count Baldesser Castilio* (translation, 1926)

Richard Hooker, *Of the Laws of Ecclesiastical Polity* (1926)

Laurence Housman, *Trimblerigg* (1927)

Richard Hurd (1923)

Aldous Huxley, *Antic Hay* (novel, 1924)

Ralph William Inge, *Outspoken Essays* (essays, 1922)

Henry James, *Turn of the Screw* (fictional horror story, 1922), *Roderick Hudson* (novel, 1923)

William James, *Varieties of Religious Experience* (lectures, 1922),

Samuel Johnson, *Lives of the Poets* (biography, 1922, 1923), *Life of Waller* (biography, 1927)

Elias Henry Jones, *The Road to Endor* (novel, 1922)

William Paton Ker, *Essays on Mediaeval Essays* (essays, 1922)

Thomas Babington Macaulay, *The Earl of Chatham, Lord Clive* (essays, 1924)

Rose Macaulay, *Potterism* (novel, 1926), *The Lee Shore* (literary fiction, 1926), *Mystery at Geneva* (novel, 1927)

George MacDonald, *Phantastes* (fantasy novel, 1923), *Lilith* (fantasy novel, 1926)

William Hurrell Mallock, *New Republic* (satire, 1922)

Thomas Malory, *Le Morte d'Arthur* (legend, 1924)

Archibald Marshall, *The Eldest Son* (1923)

Marshall, Calamy, Young, Newcomen, and Spurstow, *Apology for Smectymnuus* (ecclesiastical pamphlet, 1927)

Masson (1922)

Sarah McNaughton, *A Lame Dog's Diary* (book, 1923)

George Meredith, *The Ordeal of Richard Feverel* (novel, 1923), letters (1923)

Alice Meynell, *The Colour of Life* (essay, 1924)

Miller, *The New Psychology and the New Teacher* (1922)

John Milton (prose works), *The Doctrine and Discipline of Divorce* (1922, 1927), *Tractate on Education* (1922)

George Moore, *Confessions of a Young Man* (fictional autobiography, 1924)

William Morris, *The Life and Death of Jason* (romantic narrative, 1922, 1924), *Troilus* (1922), "In Prison" (poem, 1922), *The Well at World's End* (novel, prose romance, 1926), translation of *Volsunga Saga* (1927)

Gilbert Murray, *Greek Epic* (1924)

Alfred Noyes, *William Morris* (literary criticism, 1924)

Ferdinand Ossendowski, *Man and Mystery in Asia* (cultural study, 1924)

Thomas Stewart Omond, *Study of Metre* (literary study, 1922)

Edward Abbott Parry, *What the Judge Thought* (essays, 1922)

Francesco Patrizi, *De Regno* (treatise, 1926)

Mark Pattison, *Milton* (biography, 1922)

Fredrick Pollock, *Spinoza: His Life and Philosophy* (biography, 1925)

Sir Walter A. Raleigh, *Six Essays on Johnson* (essays, 1923), preface to Hoby (1926), letters (1927), *Milton* (literary criticism, 1927)

George Rawlinson, *The History, Geography, and Antiquities of Chaldæa, Assyria, Babylon, Media, and Persia* (1922)

Charles à Court Repington, *After the War: A Diary* (diary, 1922, 1923)

William H. R. Rivers, *Instinct and the Unconscious* (history of psychology, 1922)

William Roberts, *Memoirs of the Life and Correspondence of Mrs. Hannah More* (1926)

Denis Saurat, *Milton: Man and Thinker* (literary criticism, 1927)

Sir Walter Scott, *Waverley* (novel, 1923), *The Bride of Lammermoor* (novel, 1925), *Quentin Durward* (novel, 1926), *Guy Mannering* (novel about Scotland, 1927)

Frederic Seebohm, *Oxford Reformers* (history, 1926)

George Bernard Shaw, *Irrational Knot* (novel, 1922)

(Kenneth?) Sisam, the Bruce passage (1923)

Walter William Skeat, introduction (possibly *English Dialects from the Eighth Century to the Present Day*) (1926)

Pearsall Smith, (grammar, 1927)

William Ritchie Sorley, *Moral Values and the Idea of God* (lectures published as book, 1924)

William Force Stead, *The Sweet Miracle* (1922), *Shadow of Mt. Carmel* (1926)

Sir Leslie Stephen and Sir Sidney Lee, editors, *The Dictionary of National Biography* (1924)

James Stephens, *Irish Fairy Tales* (fiction, 1922), *Deirdre* (novel, 1923), *The Crock of Gold* (novel, 1924)

Robert Louis Stevenson, *Travels with a Donkey* (humor, 1925), *The New Arabian Nights* (short stories, 1923)

Lytton Strachey, *Queen Victoria* (biography, 1922),

St. Loe Strachey, *Adventure of Living* (autobiography, 1923)

Snorri Sturluson, *Younger Edda* or *Prose Edda* (Icelandic Epic, 1927)

Henry Sweet, *Anglo-Saxon Reader* (reader, 1922, 1923, 1927)

Jonathan Swift, *The Battle of the Books* (mock-Homeric epic, 1923), *Gulliver's Travels* (fiction, 1923)

Tacitus, *The Life of Gnaeus Julius Agricola* (biography, 1922, 1923)

William Makepeace Thackeray, *Vanity Fair* (novel, 1924), *Henry Esmond* (historical novel, 1925)

Henry David Thoreau, essay on walking, speeches on John Brown (1924)

Leo Tolstoy, *Where God Is, There Is Love* (story, 1922), *The Godson* (story, 1922), *Anna Karenina* (novel, 1923)

Richard Chenevix Trench, *The Study of Words* (1927)

George Macaulay Trevelyan, *England under the Stuarts* (history, 1926), *England in the Age of Wycliffe* (history, 1927)

Anthony Trollope, *Autobiography* (1923), *The Warden* (novel, 1926)

Turner, *Journey to Cytherea* (1923)

Hugh Seymour or Horace Walpole, (1923)

William Morris, *Völsunga Saga: The Story of the Volsungs and Niblungs, with Certain Songs from the Elder Edda* (Icelandic story, 1927)

Richard Ward, *Realm of Ends* (lectures, 1924), *Life of Henry More* (biography, 1924)

Mrs. Humphrey Ward, *Lady Rose's Daughter* (novel, 1924)

Edith E. Wardale, *An Old English Grammar* (grammar, 1922)

Joseph Warton, *Essay on the Genius and Writings of Pope* (literary criticism, 1923)

H. G. Wells, *A Modern Utopia* (novel, 1922, 1926), *The Country of the Blind* (novel, 1926)

Leonard Whibley, *Political Parties in Athens during the Peloponnesian War* (history, 1922)

Joseph and Elizabeth M. Wright, *Old English Grammar* (grammar, 1927)

Wulfstan, *Address to the English* (sermon, 1927)

Henry Cecil Kennedy Wyld, *A Short History of English* (linguistics, 1922), *The Historical Study of the Mother Tongue* (linguistics, 1927)

DRAMA AND OPERA

Aeschylus, *Prometheus Bound* (1927)

Sir James Barrie, *The Admirable Crichton* (1922), *Mary Rose* (1925)

G. K. Chesterton, *Magic* (1922)

Euripides, *Heracleidae* (1924), *Hippolytus* (1924)

James Elroy Flecker, *Hassan* (1923)

John Fletcher, *Philaster* (1922), *The Maid's Tragedy* (1922), *The Faithful Shepherdess* (1923)

Robert Greene, *The Honorable History of Friar Bacon and Friar Bungay* (1926)

Henrik Ibsen, *Master Builder* (1925), *Peer Gynt* (1925)

Ben Jonson, *The Alchemist* (1922)

Thomas Lodge, *Rosalynde* (1923)

Christopher Marlowe, *Edward II* (1926), *Tamburlaine the Great* (1926)

John Masefield, *The Tragedy of Pompey the Great* (1922)

Thomas Middleton and William Rowley, *Changeling* (1922), *Women Beware Women* (1922)

Thomas Otway, *Venice Preserv'd* (1923)

Shakespeare, *Henry VI*, Part I (1922), *Othello* (1923), *Richard III* (1923), *Twelfth Night* (1923), *Henry IV* (1922), *Henry V* (1922), *Love's Labour Lost* (1922), *Antony and Cleopatra* (1923), *Coriolanus* (1926), *The Merry Wives of Windsor* (1926), *Two Gentlemen of Verona* (1922), *Timon of Athens* (1923)

George Bernard Shaw, *Candida* (1923)

Sophocles, *Antigone* (1922)

Cyril Tourneur, *Revenger's Tragedy* (1927)

John Webster, *White Devil* (1922)

William Wycherley, *Country Wife* (1923)

PHILOSOPHERS

Robert Adamson, *The Development of Greek Philosophy* (1922)

Samuel Alexander, *Space, Time and Deity* (1924)

Aristotle (1926), *Metaphysics* (1927)

Arthur James Balfour, *Theism and Humanism* (1924), *Theism and Thought* (1924)

Henri Bergson, *L'Evolution Créatrice* (1923), *Energie Spirituelle* (1924), *Matière et Mémoire* (1925)

George Berkeley, *Principles of Human Knowledge* (1924)

Bernard Bosanquet, *Theory of the State* (1922), *Suggestions in Ethics* (1924)

Francis Herbert Bradley, *Ethical Studies* (1922), *Appearance and Reality* (1922), on Spinoza (1925)

Edmund Burke, *Thoughts on the Cause of the Present Discontents* (1922)

Cicero, *De Finibus* (1922)

Benedetto Croce, *Essence of Aesthetic* (1922)

Rene Descartes, *Meditations* (1926)

Harald Hoffding, probably *History of Modern Philosophy* or *Outlines of Psychology* (1925)

David Hume, *An Enquiry Concerning the Principles of Morals* (1922), (1924), (1926)

Thomas Henry Huxley, "Ethics and Evolution" (1924)

Harold H. Joachim, *A Study of the Ethics of Spinoza* (1925)

Horace William Brindley Joseph, *Introduction to Logic* (1922)

Immanuel Kant (1922)

Leibnitz, *Monadologie, Sur L'Entendement Humain, Systeme Nouveau* (1924), (1925)

John Locke, *On Education* (1923), (1924)

James Martineau, *Types of Ethical Theory* (1924)

George Moore, *Philosophical Studies* (1925)

Henry More, *Philosophical Works* (1924), *Defence of the Moral Cabbala* (1924), *An Explanation of the Grand Mystery of Godliness* (1924), "Appendix to the *Defence of the Philosophic Cabbala*" (1924), *An Antidote against Atheism* (1924), *Enthusiasmus* (1924), Latin correspondence (1924)

Friedrich Nietzsche, *Beyond Good and Evil* (1924)

Plato, *The Republic* (1922) *Phaedrus* (1924), *Erastae* (1927), *Theaetetus* (1927)

Bertrand Russell, *Philosophical Essays* (1924), "Worship of a Free Man" (1924), *Icarus* (or *The Future of Science*) (1924), *Problems of Philosophy* (1925)

George Santayana, *Reason in Art* (aesthetics, 1923), *Winds of Doctrine* (essays, 1924)

J. Seth, *English Philosophers and Schools of Philosophy* (1924)

Baruch Spinoza, *Ethics Part II, Problems* (1925), *The Tractatus Theologico-Politicus* (?) (1927)

POETS

Matthew Arnold, *Empedocles on Etna* (1922)

William Blake, *Gnomic Verses* (1923)

Matteo Maria Boiardo (1923)

Robert Bridges (1925), *New Poems* (1927)

Emily Brontë, poems (1926)

Elizabeth Barrett Browning, *Sonnets from the Portuguese* (1924)

Robert Browning, *The Ring and the Book* (1923)

Robert Burns (1922)

Lord (George Gordon Noel) Byron, *Beppo*, (1923) *Vision of Judgement* (1923), *Childe Harold's Pilgrimage* (1923), *Don Juan* (1924)

George Chapman, *Bussy D'Ambois* (1922), *Iliads* (1923)

Geoffrey Chaucer, *Book of the Duchesse* (1922), *Canterbury Tales* (*Miller's Tale, Reeve's Tale, Clerke's Tale*) (1922), *The Legend of Good Women* (1922), *Troilus and Cressida* (1922, 1927), *Hous of Fame* (1922), *The Man of Lawes Tale* (1922), *The Flower and the Leaf* (1923), *Knightes Tale* (1927)

William Cowper, *The Task* (1925)

Walter John de la Mare, *Veil* (1922), *Ding Dong Bell* (1924)

Ernest de Selincourt, *The Prelude* (critical edition, 1926)

Sir John Denham, *Cooper's Hill* (1927)

John Donne, *Second Anniversary* (1922), *The Progresse of the Soule* (1923)

Gavin Douglas, *The Palice of Honour* (allegorical poem, 1926)

John Dryden, *Astraea Redux* (1923), poetry (1927)

Geoffrey of Monmouth, *Sir Gawain and the Green Knight* (1923)

John Gower, *Vox Clamantis* (1922), poetry (1927)

Robert Henryson, *The Testament of Cresseid* (1923)

Thomas Hoccleve (1926)

Homer, *Odyssey* (1922), *Iliad* (1922), *Iliad* 16 (1923)

King James I, *The Kingis Quair* (1925)

Kalevala (national epic poem of Finland, 1926)

John Keats, *Endymion, Letters* (1922), "The Eve of St. Agnes" (1923), *Odes* (1923)

William Langland, *The Vision of William Concerning Piers the Plowman* (1922)

William Ellery Leonard, *Two Lives* (1926)

John Lydgate, *Story of Thebes* (1925)

John Lyly, *Endimion* (1922)

John Masefield, *The Everlasting Mercy* (narrative poem, 1922), *Daffodil Fields* (1923), *Right Royal* (1924), *Dauber* (narrative poem, 1926)

George Meredith, *Beauchamp's Career* (1922, 1923), *The Egoist* (1923)

John Milton, *Paradise Lost* (1922, 1927), *Samson Agonistes* (1923), *Il Penseroso* (1922), *L'Allegro* (1922), *Lycidas* (1922), *Reformation in England*, (1927) *Prelaticall Episcopacy* (1927), Minor Poems (1927), *Comus* (masque, 1922,

1923), *The Reason of Church Government Urged against Prelaty* (1927)

Ovid, *Metamorphoses* (1922, 1923)

Alexander Pope, *The Dunciad* (1926)

Francis Quarles (1927)

Edwin Arlington Robinson, "For a Dead Lady" (1922)

W. M. Rossetti, collation of *Troilus* and *Il Filostrato* (1922)

William Shakespeare, *The Phoenix and the Turtle* (1923)

Percy Bysshe Shelley, *Hymn of Apollo, Prometheus Bound* (1922, 1923), *The Cenci* (1922), *Prometheus Unbound* (1925)

Edmund Spenser, *The Faerie Queene* (1922, 1923, 1924), *The Shepheardes Calendar* (1926)

James Stephens, *Insurrections* (1923)

Torquato Tasso, *Jerusalem Delivered* (1923, 1925)

Turold, *Chanson de Roland* (1922)

Virgil (1922)

Edmund Waller (1927)

William Wordsworth, *The Prelude* (1923, 1924), *Excursion* (1923), *White Doe of Rylstone* (1924)

F. A. Wright, translator, *Girdle of Aphrodite* (1924)

William Butler Yeats, *Two Kings* (1922), *Wanderings of Oisin* (1926)

ANONYMOUS

Ancrene Riwle (Middle English religious classic, 1923)

Battle of Maldon (Anglo-Saxon account, 1922, 1923)

The Anglo-Saxon Chronicle, the passage on Cynewulf and Cyneheard (1922), the reign of Stephen (1923)

King Alfred, *The Voyages of Ohthere and Wulfstan* (Old English text, 1922, 1927)

Sweet, ed., *Beowulf* (1922, 1923)

Riddles, probably Anglo-Saxon riddles from the Exeter Book in Old English (1922)

Rubezahl (German fairy tale, 1923)

Sir Gawaine and the Green Knight (1923)

The Fall of the Angels (medieval English drama, 1923, 1926, 1927)

The Owl and the Nightingale (poem, 1923)

The Wanderer (Old English poem, 1922)

AUTHOR UNKNOWN

History of Seventeenth Century France (1922)

Isabella (1923)

APPENDIX II

THE NORWOOD REPORT

The full title of the 151-page Norwood Report is *Curriculum and Examinations in Secondary Schools: Report of the Committee of the Secondary School Examinations Council Appointed by the President of the Board of Education in 1941.* Lewis criticized the so-called Norwood Report in two essays: "The Parthenon and the Optative" and "Is English Doomed?" What does the Norwood Report actually contain? Why did Lewis criticize the report? In reality, Lewis criticized only a small portion of this lengthy report, and much of the document contains a common sense approach to secondary education.

One of the things recommended in the Norwood Report became a feature of the British educational system in the years ahead. This was the initiation of three kinds of secondary schools at three different levels: Grammar (knowledge for its own sake, in most cases leading to the university), Technical (leading to industry and commerce), and Secondary Modern (a more general education for the average British pupil). The feature was subsequently adopted in Great Britain under Minister of Education R. A. (Rab) Butler in the 1944 Education Act. This 1944 Education Act, designed to prepare the country for the postwar era, provided universal free schooling and raised the age for leaving school to 15.

Following an introduction on the purpose of education, the authors of the Norwood Report described three types of curriculum: study for its own sake, data and skills associated with a particular kind of occupation, and training of body and mind to enable students to take up the work of life. These three types of education correlate with the three levels of secondary schools proposed later in the document. Next, the authors described three things: secondary education as it was before their report, criticisms of secondary education (primarily criticism of a "one size fits all" approach to education), and secondary education as they wished to see it after their report.

In Part II of the Norwood Report, the authors described the School Certificate and the Higher Certificate examinations, which had been in place since 1918. They described the problem of teaching to the test, the tremendous amount of emphasis placed upon the examinations, and other difficulties incumbent in the examination process. They proposed an alternative method of examination, one that would include an exemption from university entrance examinations.

In Part III of the report, the authors stated that they wished the individual school to have the freedom to establish the curriculum. They rejected various proposed additions to the curriculum. They emphasized three primary elements in education: physical welfare (referring to physical education classes), the ideals of character (promoted by religious instruction, modeling by teachers, and other parts of the curriculum), and English ("clear expression in English, both spoken and written, based on the logical arrangement of ideas"[1]).

The Norwood Report recommended that during Fifth (ages 13–15) and Sixth Forms (ages 16–18), the number of subjects taken should be reduced from the seven, eight, or more subjects required at this time. In Sixth Form, the authors of the Norwood Report wrote, students should study natural science, foreign languages, Colonial and American history, the British Commonwealth, and public affairs and administration.

C. S. Lewis apparently read only the portion of the report in Part III on the teaching of English.[2] Lewis criticized the proposed elimination of outside examiners. He claimed, however, that if the report's authors stopped there, he might sympathize with the proposal. Then he claimed that the authors of the Norwood Report wanted literary appreciation to be taught, and he felt that the basics of English language and grammar should be the emphasis at this age. In this, Lewis revealed the fact that he did not read carefully part III, chapter 4 of the report. Earlier, the authors had written: "[T]oo many boys and girls after leaving the Secondary School show themselves deficient in ability to master the thought of a passage or chapter and to express their ideas in writing or orally with precision and clarity."[3] Hence, the authors recommended that more time spent be spent on the basics. On that same page, they claimed: "English has come to be too closely associated with (*a*) the study of literary texts and (*b*) the essay."[4] Then they suggested that the ability of the pupil to appreciate literature was yet to be formed and "to some extent beyond the help of the teacher."[5] Later, the authors stated: "While it is desirable that enjoyment of English literature should be fostered in as many pupils as possible, it is essential that every pupil should be trained to understand his own language and to use it with ease and correctness, both in speech and in writing."[6] In this, the authors of the Norwood Report appear to agree with Lewis that the basics of the English language must take priority over the study of literature at a secondary education level and that appreciation of literature is not something easily formed in the teenage years.

THE NORWOOD REPORT: CONTENTS

Part I: Secondary Education

Chapter I. The Nature of Secondary Education

What is secondary education?—variety of capacity—types of curriculum—secondary education as it exists in fact

Chapter II. Secondary Education as It Is

The distinguishing feature of the Grammar School—its expression in terms of curriculum—the curricula of the Secondary Schools today—the diverse functions of the Secondary School—criticisms of the Secondary School, favourable and unfavourable—the criticisms considered—conclusions

Chapter III. Secondary Education as It Might Be

Preliminary sketch—age of entry upon secondary education—the problem of differentiation—a "lower school"—schools combining types of secondary education—the secondary Technical School—the secondary Modern School—the secondary Grammar School—part-time education—a break between school and University—Universities and Colleges

Part II: Examinations

Chapter I. Existing Examinations

Appendix III

THE GREEN BOOK

Alec King and Martin Ketley authored *The Control of Language*, which C. S. Lewis described in *The Abolition of Man* as *The Green Book*. Writing four years after King and Ketley, Lewis referred to the authors as Gaius and Titius to hide their identity. At the time *The Control of Language* was published, King was lecturer in English at the University of Western Australia and Ketley was assistant master at St. Peter's College, Adelaide, Australia. And, yes, its cover is green—light green.

King and Ketley intended the book "for boys and girls in the upper forms in schools"[1] (i.e., 13–18 years of age), as Lewis mentioned in *The Abolition of Man*. The second chapter of *The Control of Language*, on reference and emotive meaning, deals with the two meanings of words. According to King and Ketley, the word *reference* means the thoughts, ideas, and images that are associated with a word. *Emotive meaning* is the emotional content of the word, the feelings associated with a word.[2] In this distinction, the authors are dependent upon the writings of I. A. Richards. In the second chapter of *The Control of Language*, the authors used as an example the story of Coleridge at the waterfall. In this story, according to King and Ketley, one tourist called the waterfall "sublime" while the other tourist called it "pretty." According to King and Ketley, Coleridge endorsed the first reaction and rejected the second. The quotation from the actual account (see below) demonstrates that King and Ketley misread or misunderstood the story or perhaps were working with a secondary version of the story. Throughout *The Control of Language*, the authors assumed that values reflected the emotional state of the speaker rather than the objective state of their topic. Therefore in the story of Coleridge and the waterfall, King and Ketley stated that the phrase "That waterfall is sublime" actually meant "I have sublime feelings." For King and Ketley, the matter of the waterfall's beauty or sublimity is no different from the viewers' feelings at the time of viewing.

The actual event was related by Dorothy Wordsworth, who, with her brother William Wordsworth, had joined Coleridge for a walking tour of Scotland in 1803. Dorothy recorded in her diary that on August 21 they were walking through the Falls of Clyde, a wildlife reserve south of Glasgow, now in the care of the National Trust of Scotland.[3] The Clyde River is known for several impressive waterfalls, and on this day, the trio saw the waterfall Cora Linn. Although time has changed the landscape considerably, this waterfall consists of two impressive sloping falls about a hundred yards apart. The area contains rocks and birch, ash, and hazel trees. On this particular occasion, Coleridge, a gregarious sort, engaged two tourists, a lady and a gentleman, in conversation. The gentleman called the waterfall majestic and sublime. Just the day before, Coleridge had been discussing with Wordsworth the precise meaning of the words *majestic, sublime, grand*, and others. Here follows the full text of that portion of the conversation as recorded in Dorothy Wordsworth's *Recollections*:

> After having stayed some time, we returned by the same footpath into the main carriage-road, and soon came upon what William calls an ell-wide gravel walk, from which we had different views of the Linn. We sat upon a bench, placed for the sake of one of these views, whence we looked down upon the waterfall, and over the open country, and saw a ruined tower, called Wallace's Tower, which stands at a very little distance from the fall, and is an interesting object. A lady and gentleman, more expeditious tourists than ourselves, came to the spot; they left us at the seat, and we found them again at another station above the Falls. Coleridge, who is always good-natured enough to enter into conversation with anybody whom he meets in his way, began to talk with the gentleman, who observed that it was a *majestic* waterfall. Coleridge was delighted with the accuracy of the epithet, particularly as he had been settling in his own mind the precise meaning of the words grand, majestic, sublime, etc., and had discussed the subject with William at some length the day before. 'Yes, sir,' says Coleridge, 'it *is* a majestic waterfall.' 'Sublime and beautiful,' replied the friend. Poor Coleridge could make no answer, and, not very

desirous to continue the conversation, came to us and related the story, laughing heartily.[4]

The mistake of King and Ketley, according to Lewis, was that they elevated their own feelings above an objective sense of good and bad; they treated a predicate of value as a word descriptive of the speaker's emotions. In this Lewis was right. Throughout *The Abolition of Man*, Lewis argued for objective truth, for the objectivity of trained emotions in calling a waterfall "sublime." King and Ketley also have some of their details wrong. According to these authors, one tourist, the gentleman, called the waterfall "majestic" while the other one, the lady, called it "sublime and beautiful" or "pretty." According to Dorothy Wordsworth, the same gentleman provided all the comments, showing that he really did not understand the difference between *sublime* and *beautiful*. That's why Coleridge laughed. Lewis's example, drawn from *The Control of Language*, formed the starting point for his philosophical argument against subjectivity and subjective values.

Lewis did make one small mistake in one of his arguments against *The Green Book*, namely, that the statement "I have sublime feelings" is not the corollary of the statement that "The waterfall is sublime." King and Ketley wrote that the feelings associated with the statement about sublimity were "awe, deeply felt pleasure, and a kind of profound and calm excitement" (see below). Here follows the full text of the section of *The Control of Language*, which Lewis criticized:

> Apart from exclamatory and gesture words, there is another kind of word which may often have little or no reference, namely, the adjective. This is a story told by Coleridge: he was standing with a group of tourists beside a waterfall, and, after a silence, one of the men in the party said, "That is sublime." Coleridge felt that "sublime" was exactly the right word. And then one of the women in the party added "Yes, it is pretty," and Coleridge turned away in disgust, feeling that "pretty" was exactly the wrong word. Why did Coleridge think the one word was exactly right, and the other exactly wrong? Obviously not because the one adjective described correctly, as we say, a quality of the water or the rocks or the landscape, and the other adjective described this quality incorrectly. It is not as if the man had said "That is brown" (referring, say, to the water) and the woman (also referring to the water) had added, "Yes, it is green." No, Coleridge thought "sublime" exactly the right word, because it was associated in his mind with the emotion he was himself feeling as he looked at the waterfall

in its setting of rock and landscape; and he thought "pretty" exactly the wrong word, because it was associated with feelings quite different from those he was actually feeling at the time, and with feelings that, to his way of thinking, no sensitive person would ever have while looking at such a sight.

Now let us look at these four adjectives, "brown," "blue," "sublime," and "pretty." The first two say something about the waterfall, they describe its colour (one rightly, the other wrongly); that is to say, both these words have a reference, they refer our minds to a quality of the water. As to the second pair of adjectives the man's remark, "That is sublime," did not refer the tourists' minds to anything in the water or the rocks or the land-scape, or to any shape or colour or texture; nor did the woman's remark, "Yes, it is pretty," refer the tourists' minds to anything. In fact, these two adjectives, as they were used, had no reference. They were associated, how-ever, with certain emotions; "sublime," let us say, with feelings of awe, deeply felt pleasure, and a kind of profound and calm excitement; "pretty" with feelings of a more superficial and transitory delight. These adjec-tives have no reference, but both have emotive meaning. We can realize why Coleridge turned away in disgust. The emotive meaning of "sublime" was the feelings he had; the emotive meaning of "pretty" was the feelings he had not.

You will find, if you begin to think about adjectives, that a number of them tend to have little or no reference, just as these two adjectives "sub-lime" and "pretty" had no reference on the occasion given above. Com-pare, for instance, the two following sentences: "It was a wonderful, beau-tiful fire," and "It was a big, red, fire." Do the adjectives "wonderful" and "beautiful" tell you something about the fire? You may think, at first, that they do, because to use such adjectives in connection with a fire means that the fire must have been, say, brightly burning and not dully smoking, must have been of a decent size and not some insignificant little combus-tion. But actually these adjectives did not tell you this; they did not refer your mind to the brightness and bigness of the fire. The brightness and bigness were suggested to you because only at the sight of a bright and big fire would you feel the emotions associated with the two words "wonder-ful" and "beautiful." The emotions associated with these two words would not have been aroused by a fire that was dully smoking or an insignificant little combustion. On the other hand, "big" and "red" both tell you some-thing definite about the fire; they refer your mind to an idea of its size and its colour. The reference of these two words is, in fact, obvious and clear.

We must, at this point, clear up a confusion which may already have puzzled you. We construct our sentences, our written or spoken speech, as if this distinction between emotive meaning and reference did not exist. When the man said, "That is sublime," he appeared to be making a remark about the waterfall. The form of the sentence is exactly similar to the form of "That is brown," a sentence which does make a remark about the waterfall, about its colour. Actually, when the man said, "That is sublime," he was not making a remark about the waterfall, but a remark about his own feelings. What he was saying was, really, "I have feelings associated in my mind with the word 'sublime,'" or, shortly, "I have sublime feelings." There is the same confusion, also, in the sentence, "It was a wonderful, beautiful, fire." And you will find that this confusion is continually present in language as we use it. We appear to be saying something very important about something; and, actually, we are only saying something about our own feelings. We continually use emotive words, words with emotive meaning, as if they had a definite reference.[5]

Obviously, to suggest that Coleridge turned away in disgust is to overstate the case. Although Coleridge apparently laughed about the conversation and felt the word *majestic* to be accurate and the word *pretty* to be lacking in appropriate content, he did not turn away in disgust. Furthermore, it was not a reflection of the emotive meaning of the words but of the true meaning that Coleridge felt each word contained. To say that the adjectives *sublime* and *pretty* "have no reference" is simply false. In *The Abolition of Man*, Lewis challenges this because the word *sublime* refers to an objectively sublime waterfall. But it also says something about the speaker, perhaps that the speaker had seen few waterfalls and therefore was more easily impressed by this particular waterfall. Lewis, the opponent of "the personal heresy," did not want to say that the adjectives said *anything* about the speaker. At the least the words say far more about the object than about the speaker.

THE CONTROL OF LANGUAGE: CONTENTS

words—one of the essential difficulties of communicating by speech or writing caused by the way language works.

II. Introductory: Reference and Emotive Meaning

Words may have two kinds of meaning: reference and emotive meaning—the nature of these two kinds of meaning—the structure of language tends to call attention only to the reference—the importance of emotive meaning.

III. Scientific Prose

Prose that uses words with as clear reference and as little emotive meaning as possible—used by scientists, but also by all writers who wish to refer their reader's mind, clearly and dispassionately, to facts, ideas, etc.—the difficulties of writing the simpler kinds of scientific prose—science, technology, the material world.

IV. Emotive Prose

Prose that uses words for the sake of their emotive meaning as well as their reference—the two kinds of emotive prose, responsible and irresponsible—irresponsible emotive prose rouses feeling about what is not clearly defined, rouses "unthinking emotion"—"advertising" and "devertising" prose—propaganda prose—use of metaphor and similar and other devices of poetry and rhetoric.

V. Emotive Prose (continued)

Responsible emotive prose—rhetoric and the prose of persuasion—the danger of using metaphorical language in emotive prose—metaphorical language tends to lack clear reference—further examples of distinction between responsible and irresponsible emotive prose.

VI. Scientific Prose (continued)

The more difficult kinds of scientific prose—the discussion and exposition of ideas—emotive prose masquerading as scientific prose—an examination of a passage of prose on "idealism" as an illustration of what to avoid—the need, in writing about ideas, for a constant definition of terms—the construction of a piece of prose on the subject of education as an illustration of what this definition of terms means in practice.

VII. Prose of "Self-Expression"

What makes "self-expressive" prose interesting—when is scientific prose interesting?—"reporter's" prose as a contrast to self-expressive prose—bad reporting and journalese—the need, in the prose of self-expression, for clear, particular feelings and impressions—the communication of personal feeling—the need for sincerity.

VIII. Critical Prose

The nature of criticism—two kinds of critical prose, "scientific prose" criticism and "emotive" criticism—the nature of scientific prose criticism—the meaning of well-informed or fair criticism—the need for definition of terms.

IX. Emotive Criticism

Emotive description as criticism—poetry as a "criticism of life"—base uses to which emotive criticism can be put—when emotive criticism is useful and when it is not—a discussion of examples of critical prose of a mixed kind.

X. Narrative Prose

Three kinds of narrative, the impersonal narrative in scientific prose, the impersonal narrative in emotive prose, the personal narrative in emotive prose—a discussion of these three kinds of narrative—technical points: devices for suggesting the internal life of the characters, their feelings, etc.; speed in narrative writing; relevance of detail; etc.—impersonal narrative and reporter's prose—personal narrative and the prose of self-expression.

XI. Style

An examination of the meaning of "style"—style a reflection of three things: (a) clarity of thought or feeling or observation; (b) the attitude of the writer to his work or his reader or both; (c) the relative artifice in the workings of the writer's mind—these three things examined and illustrated in relation to passages of prose of different styles—a practical consideration of these three things from the point of view of the writer—how to achieve clarity of thought and feeling—what may be done about the attitude of the writer to his work or his reader—the meaning of artifice in the workings of the writer's mind—the need for a natural, easy, language—idiom and slang—what the writer's attitude to his own style should be in practice.

XII. Metaphor and Simile

The falsity of regarding metaphor and simile as ornaments of language—metaphor and simile as tools of thought, as tools of language—the relative uselessness of these tools in the writing of scientific prose—a discussion of metaphors and similes ranging from the simple to the complicated—dead metaphors, and the advantage to clear thinking of reviving them—acquiring a command of metaphor and simile—the necessity of avoiding worn-out metaphor and simile.

XIII. Poetry and Prose

A discussion of poetry as a particular way of using language in contrast to the prosaic way of using language—writing poetry as well as writing prose—a note on "aesthetic value."

APPENDIX IV

ORBILIUS

In *The Abolition of Man*, shortly after concluding his critique of *The Green Book*, Lewis wrote about Orbilius, that is, E. G. (Ernest Gordon) Biaggini (1899–?), who authored the book *The Reading and Writing of English*, a book primarily about teaching methods and written by an Australian teacher of English. Lewis is probably using the name because Orbilius Pupillus was a grammarian who beat the Roman poet Horace while teaching him Homer's *Odyssey*.[1] The book is for students "from the higher school-forms upwards."[2] In the preface, Biaggini wrote: "This book is an attempt to bridge the widening gulf between those who know what a literary value is and the larger number who do not" and for those who wish "to improve their literary taste."[3] Biaggini's preface gives us a summary of the contents of *The Reading and Writing of English*:

> The introductory section contains a brief statement concerning the importance of literary values to the individual. This is followed (in Part I) by five chapters containing exercises and discussions intended to help the student to appreciate what literary values are. In Part II occurs a further development: the exercises and discussions are continued as before, but some actual evidence of what are normal responses to the texts of the exercises are given; this enables the discussion to begin from what is likely to be the student's own opinion. Part III contains a single exercise which, besides being useful in itself, is intended to serve the purpose of providing a means of selecting the student of promise, and of providing a background for some of the general statements made elsewhere in the book. It

can be omitted by those teachers who find it too difficult for their classes. Part IV contains some elementary instruction on how the essay should be written, and how what has been said in certain chapters bears on the student's own work. The book closes with an epilogue which very briefly indicates the importance to society of the development of good literary taste in the individual.

Most of the tests contained in Parts I and II consist of two associated extracts, of which one is definitely better than the other; and the work of the reader is to decide which is which, and to make a statement of the grounds of his decision before he reads the analysis which follows the exercise.[4]

In this book, Biaggini did much the same thing as Alec King and Martin Ketley did in *The Control of Language*. Biaggini wrote about horses, criticizing a piece of writing in which the horses were praised as the "willing servants" of the early colonists of Australia. He stated that horses were not interested in colonial expansion, failing to mention even the possibility of anthropomorphism, that is, an author treating a horse as if it were a human. He also failed to explain why the composition in which that phrase occurred was bad writing. The literary problem of the passage, that is, the use of expressions that are literally false, Biaggini did not address. Lewis complained that Biaggini merely used a straw man to criticize a piece of writing for something for which it should not be criticized, without providing any explanation on good and bad writing. Nor do students learn anything from Biaggini about the person who really loves horses or about the person who thinks of horses merely as a means of transportation. From the first person the student could learn something good, and from the second person they could also benefit, learning how not to view animals as mere things. But students learn from neither, Lewis wrote, because Biaggini did not take advantage of that setting, either to teach about good writing or to teach about horses.

Here follows the section from page 5 of chapter 1 in part I of *The Reading and Writing of English*. Part I consists of "Exercises in Reading," designed to "help you to improve your taste in reading,"[5] "to effect the desirable revolution of making people want to read what they ought to read,"[6] and "to develop within you the power to criticise and appreciate English literature."[7] In chapter 1, the reader is invited to read two passages and judge which is better. Passage A begins: "About horses I know very little and the only actual experience I have ever had with one showed that the beast knew more about me than I knew about him." The story continues for about 400 words. The following is Passage B:

The horse is a noble animal and not the least of man's dumb friends. Without such a willing servant as the horse civilisation would not have developed to the present stage.

The early pioneers of this country can bear witness to what has been said. When they first came here the prospect before them was a heart-breaking one indeed. There were no roads; in many places the country was rough and well-timbered; developmental material was hard to procure; and above all tractors, bush-devils, motor-cars, and other mechanical inventions had not come to the help of man. In these circumstances then the horse was invaluable, and without him Australia would certainly not have become the country it is. In spite of summer's heat and winter's cold; in spite of the dangers of drought, bush-fires, and flood; and in spite of the indescribable discomforts of life in a new country, man with the aid of the horse has won through and made the Australian wilderness smile.

A farmer friend of mine keeps one of his old horses in the best paddock and gives him no work whatever to do because once the faithful old creature had saved him from ruin. One night when everybody was asleep he came to the verandah of the homestead and whinnied until he woke the farmer. My friend, wondering what was wrong and how the horse had got out of the yard in which he had been locked up, hurried from his bed and immediately saw sparks and smoke going up from a post at the corner of the horse-yard. He rushed across and found that the horse had broken out and given him the alarm. The season was dry and the standing crops might easily have caught fire, but in a twinkling the farmer got the blaze under control. Naturally he was grateful to the horse and said it should work no more.

Such instances as these could be multiplied indefinitely; but enough has been said to show the goodness of this fine species. We should all be kind to animals in general and to horses in particular.[8]

The comments from Biaggini after the two passages demonstrate that he thought the first passage the better of the two. For example, he wrote:

The horse, you will notice, is spoken of as if he had been a conscious and willing agent in the development of a new country. Is this not completely ridiculous? . . . You should, then, be able to see that B is twaddle. The horse is, of course, of untold use to the pioneer, but to speak of him in the sentimental fashion of passage *B* is almost as silly as thanking the hen for laying eggs or the sheep for growing wool.[9]

Biaggini concluded his analysis of these passages by revealing that he was the author of both. The former he wrote in a diary during a holiday, and he never expected anyone but his friends to read that diary. The latter he wrote tongue in cheek as a deliberate attempt to demonstrate what insincere writing looks like.

Lewis was undoubtedly unhappy with the book not only for its failure to teach about literary taste or good writing but also because its foreword was written by F. R. Leavis, the Cambridge Fellow described elsewhere in this book.

THE READING AND WRITING OF ENGLISH: CONTENTS

Foreword by F. R. Leavis
Preface
Introductory
Part I: Exercises in Reading
    Chapter 1   Exercise 1
    Chapter 2   Exercise 2
    Chapter 3   Exercise 3
    Chapter 4   Exercise 4
    Chapter 5   Exercise 5
Part II: Further Exercises in Reading: Evidence
    Chapter 6   Exercise 6
    Chapter 7   Exercise 7
    Chapter 8   Exercise 8
    Chapter 9   Exercise 9
Part III: A Final Exercise in Reading
    Chapter 10 Exercise 10
Part IV: On Writing
    Chapter 11
        I. General
        II. The Essay and the Composition
        III. The Essay
        IV. Unity—general
        V. Unity of the sentence

VI. Unity of the paragraph
VII. How a paragraph should be concluded
VIII. Link phrases
IX. The length of the paragraph
X. Airs and graces
XI. False attitudes
XII. Conclusion
Epilogue
Sources of supplementary exercises
Some suggestions for further reading

THE COLLEAGUES OF C. S. LEWIS

A 1928 photo of the Fellows of Magdalen College, Oxford, shows C. S. Lewis in a group of thirty-five faculty, many of whom are detailed below.[1] This appendix provides a glimpse of some members of the Magdalen College faculty who taught alongside Lewis between 1925 and 1954, as well as some faculty members who taught with Lewis from 1954 to 1963.

The first portion of this appendix focuses on the individuals with whom Lewis worked, sometimes worshiped, and often interacted socially and professionally. Those who served at the same college were those who lived with Lewis, ate with him, sometimes wrote about him, drank with him, and joked with him. Those who served on the English faculty with Lewis were those who shared his curricular interests, devising and revising curriculum, recommending one another's lectures, and talking shop. The exchange of ideas within the faculty of a college and among faculties of colleges served to irrigate the minds of these dons.

In this appendix, you may encounter the following abbreviations:

B.A.	Bachelor of Arts
B.Ch.	Bachelor of Chemistry or Bachelor of Surgery
B.Litt.	Bachelor of Literature
B.M.	Bachelor of Medicine or Bachelor of Music
B.Sc.	Bachelor of Science
CBE	Commander of the Order of the British Empire
DBE	Dame Commander of the Order of the British Empire

DCL	Doctor of Civil Law or Doctor of Comparative Law
D.D.	Doctor of Divinity
DFC	Distinguished Flying Cross
Dipl.	Diploma
D.Litt.	Doctor of Literature or Letters
D.Phil.	Doctor of Philosophy
D.Sc.	Doctor of Science
FBA	Fellow of the British Academy
FRS	Fellow of the Royal Society
FRSE	Fellow of the Royal Society of Edinburgh
FRSL	Fellow of the Royal Society of Literature
FSA	Fellow of the Society of Antiquaries or
	Fellow of the Society of Actuaries
Hon.	Honorary
LL.D.	Doctor of Laws
LSE	London School of Economics
M.A.	Master of Arts
MBE	Member of the Order of the British Empire
M.C.	Military Cross
M.Sc.	Master of Science
OBE	Officer of the Order of the British Empire
O.P.	Order of Preachers
Ph.D.	Doctor of Philosophy
Sc.D.	Doctor of Science

THE FELLOWS OF MAGDALEN COLLEGE, OXFORD[2]

Among Lewis's colleagues for at least part of his tenure at Oxford were the following individuals. Each one held a key position at Magdalen College or was mentioned in the writings and correspondence of Lewis. This list and subsequent lists are not, therefore, exhaustive.

PAUL VICTOR MENDELSSOHN BENECKE (1868–1944), M.A., was the great-grandson of the composer Felix Mendelssohn. He was elected Fellow in ancient history and classics at Magdalen in 1893 and taught classics until his retirement in 1925. This made him the senior Fellow of Magdalen at the time of Lewis's appointment. Lewis said Benecke was considered by many to be a saintly man, in part because he never missed a chapel service, was familiar with his prayer book, and was gracious to guests. Benecke was never seen to be angry, and he spent time in charitable works. He was one of the faculty whose company Lewis enjoyed and had been a tutor to Lewis.

J. A. W. (JACK ARTHUR WALTER) BENNETT (1911–1981), M.A., D.Phil., FBA, came to Oxford to study English at Merton College in 1933. Born in New Zealand, Bennett was educated at Auckland University, earning a First Class in the Auckland master's examination (1933) before coming to Merton College, Oxford. He earned a First Class in the bachelor's English course in 1935 and a doctorate in philosophy in 1938. He was elected to a junior research fellowship (see Glossary) at The Queen's College, Oxford, in 1938. After working for the Ministry of Information at the British Information Services in the United States, Bennett returned to Queen's College in 1945, and in 1947 he was elected to a Magdalen tutorial fellowship as an Anglo-Saxon and medieval scholar, Fellow, and tutor. Although Lewis taught the literature side of the English course, Bennett took up the language side.[3] Bennett was a devout Roman Catholic and an Inkling (see Glossary). He published editions of medieval texts, including *The Knight's Tale* and *Devotional Pieces in Verse and Prose*, and he wrote three books on Chaucer.[4] Bennett worked with C. T. Onions to edit the medieval journal *Medium Aevum*, succeeding Onions as sole editor in 1956. In 1964, Bennett succeeded Lewis at Magdalene College, Cambridge, as Fellow and professor of medieval and Renaissance literature. His inaugural lecture at Cambridge was dedicated to Lewis and published as *The Humane Medievalist* in 1965. During the 1950s, 1960s, and 1970s, Bennett was a general editor of the Clarendon Medieval and Tudor series of annotated texts.[5] He was elected FBA in 1971 and retired in 1978.

FRANK EDWARD BRIGHTMAN (1856–1932), M.A., FBA, liturgiologist, ecclesiastical historian in patristic studies, exacting scholar, and co-editor of the *Journal of Theological Studies* (1904–1932). Brightman came to Magdalen in 1902. He had matriculated in 1875 to University College, Oxford, Lewis's alma mater, earning a First Class in Mathematical Moderations and Second Class in Classical Moderations, Literae Humaniores, and Theology. Brightman was ordained a deacon in 1884 and a priest in 1885. He was one of five people (with Smith, Benecke, Onions, and Webb) who provided Lewis with the ideal of the learned life.[6] Brightman strongly supported the study of medieval history and literature and among liturgical scholars was especially knowledgeable in oriental rites, publishing *Litur-*

gies, Eastern and Western (1896) and *English Rites* (1915). He never married, devoting himself instead to his students and his colleagues. He received the honorary D.Phil. from the University of Louvain in 1909 and the D.D. from the University of Durham in 1914.[7]

ROBIN GEORGE COLLINGWOOD (1889–1943), FBA, matriculated at University College in 1908, earning a First Class in Classical Moderations (1910) and Literae Humaniores (1912). He became a philosophy tutor at Pembroke before his First Class in Literae Humaniores was even announced. He eventually left Pembroke to become a Fellow and Waynflete Professor of Moral and Metaphysical Philosophy at Magdalen in 1935 upon J. A. Smith's retirement. Collingwood was one of four Magdalen faculty members—along with Webb, Smith, and Lewis—who were philosophical idealists in the tradition of T. H. Green and Francis Bradley.[8] This philosophical approach shared four tenets:

> (1) an interest in classical sources typified by the revival at Oxford of Aristotelian studies and by the persistence of the influence of Plato's *Republic*; (2) participation in the revival of historical studies, especially interest in classical and medieval texts, and in the status and character of history as a discipline; (3) the belief that philosophy was essentially literary, with affinities to poetry; and (4) the conviction that religion, though it might begin with experience, was finally a matter of truth.[9]

This last tenet explains why Lewis once wrote: "What I learned from the Idealists . . . is this maxim: it is more important that Heaven should exist than that any of us should reach it."[10] By this he meant that religion, Christianity in particular, was an historical religion, heading for a consummation, which would include heaven. Furthermore, this was not simply a philosophical position but truth, not simply a myth but a *true* myth.

Collingwood was a Christian who considered Christianity fundamental to historical and philosophical thinking. He challenged the idea that religion was a type of thought that was intuitive and, therefore, inferior to philosophy. He met with the modernist group organized by B. H. Streeter, known as The Group, though he did not subscribe to many of their views. Collingwood's writings included *The Idea of History*, possibly the most important twentieth-century work on the philosophy of history.[11] Ill health led to the first of a series of strokes in 1938, and Collingwood eventually resigned his chair in 1941.

EDWIN STEWART CRAIG (1865–1939), M.A., matriculated to University College, Oxford, and was later a demonstrator (see Glossary) in the Oxford Electrical Laboratory (1905–1913). Born in Belfast, Craig was a Fellow of Magdalen (1918–1930), during which time he was vice president of the college (1926–1928), assistant registrar to the Board of Faculties (1907–1924), and registrar of the University of Oxford (1924–1930). Craig was the parliamentarian among the Magdalen faculty. He was "fond of sport, notable for his quiet humor and good manners, and popular in Magdalen."[12]

CANON ADAM FOX (1883–1977), like Lewis, did his undergraduate work at University College, Oxford, and earned his B.A. in 1906. He joined Magdalen in 1929 as Fellow and Dean of Divinity. He became a member of the Inklings, sharing his poetry and hearing the writings of the other members. In 1938 he was elected professor of poetry, in large part because of the support of Lewis, who opposed the election of a Shakespearian scholar, 70-year-old E. K. Chambers, to a chair (see Glossary) of poetry. At breakfast one morning, Fox stated regarding the possible election of Chambers: "This is simply shocking; they might as well make me Professor of Poetry." Immediately, Lewis said, "Well, we will." And they did.[13] In this election, Lewis gained some new enemies, who would later thwart his election to two other Fellowships. Fox served as professor of poetry until 1943, when he became a canon of Westminster Abbey. He published the narrative poem *Old King Coel* (1937), *Meet the Greek Testament* (1952), and *Dean Inge* (1960). He retired in 1963.

GEORGE STUART GORDON (see p. 193).

COLIN GRAHAM HARDIE (1906–1998), M.A., brother of Frank (see next), was educated at Edinburgh Academy and Balliol College, Oxford. He became a Fellow and tutor in classics at Balliol from 1930 to 1933. From 1933 to 1936, he served as the director of the British School in Rome. In 1936 he returned to Oxford as Fellow and tutor in classics at Magdalen. Hardie spoke to the Socratic Club on May 26, 1947, on the topic of "The Oedipus Myth." Both Hardie and Lewis found a common interest in Dante, and both were members of the Oxford Dante Society. This was undoubtedly one of the reasons that Hardie also became an Inkling. *The Silver Chair* is dedicated to Hardie's son Nicholas. Later, Hardie became public orator of the university from 1967 until 1973. After 1971, he was

Honorary Professor of Ancient Literature at the Royal Academy of Arts. He retired with his wife to Sussex in 1973.

FRANK (WILLIAM FRANCIS ROSS) HARDIE (1902–1990), brother of Colin (see previous), was educated at Balliol College and became a Fellow by Examination[14] at Magdalen in 1925. He taught philosophy at the college for one year before becoming a Fellow and tutor in philosophy at Corpus Christi College, Oxford. He taught at Corpus Christi until 1950 when he became president of the college, serving in that capacity until 1969. Specializing in ancient philosophy and ethical studies, Hardie wrote *A Study in Plato* (1936) and *Aristotle's Ethical Theory* (1968). As a friend of Lewis, he is mentioned in Lewis's diary.[15]

KENNETH BRUCE MCFARLANE (1903–1966). "There are a few historians, not more than a handful, to whom it is given not only to arrive at new insights upon a hitherto obscure period and misunderstood society but also to pioneer the methods and collect the neglected sources by which these insights are gained and the foundations of further research securely laid. Bruce McFarlane was such a historian."[16] So begins Karl Leyser's memoir of Bruce McFarlane, one of Oxford's most gifted and beloved tutors.

McFarlane won a scholarship to read history at Exeter College in 1922, gaining a First in the History School in 1925. As an undergraduate, he won the Stanhope Essay Prize in 1924. He won the Bryce Research Studentship and a Senior Demyship (see Glossary) at Magdalen in 1926. In 1927 McFarlane was elected to the college's Fellowship by Examination. In 1928 McFarlane was elected to a tutorial fellowship upon Murray Wrong's retirement. He served as vice president in 1942 and 1943 and as acting president in 1942. During the Second World War, McFarlane wrote hundreds of letters to students serving in the war and sent numerous parcels of books as well.

McFarlane studied English political society in the later Middle Ages with a focus on social, literary, and economic history, especially "The English Nobility, 1290–1536," which he prepared for the Ford Lectures. He authored *The Lollard Knights* (1952) and, with the help of much posthumous editorial work, *Hans Memling* (1971), *Lancastrian Kings and Lollard Knights* (1972), and *The Nobility of Later Medieval England, The Ford Lectures for 1953 and Related Studies* (Oxford, 1973). McFarlane also wrote reviews and articles and read papers for international conferences, such as the 1960 Anglo-Russian conference of historians at Moscow and the Twelfth International Historical Congress at Vienna in 1965. McFarlane moved to the left in the 1920s, enamored with a Marxist perspective while attempting to maintain what is valuable in cultural tradition. He later retreated from that Marxist viewpoint but remained opposed to the governing class and its suburban supporters. He was in favor of social reform, supporting trade unions and reading the publications of the Fabian Society. Before World War II, both A. J. P. Taylor and McFarlane were members of the Pink Lunch Club, a group that brought together various left-wing Fellows at Oxford, including Isaiah Berlin and A. J. Ayer.

McFarlane mentioned Lewis in passing several times. Together Lewis and McFarlane founded the Michaelmas Club in 1927, a student literary society, probably because of their common interest in the medieval period. On at least one occasion in 1929 they went for a long walk together in the Oxford countryside.[17] In a letter dated June 7, 1954, McFarlane wrote to Gerald Harriss, McFarlane's former pupil and successor at Magdalen: "C. S. Lewis has been persuaded to accept the new chair at Cambridge . . . and all the good men in college are in mourning. Of course the ruling clique is delighted."[18]

C. T. (CHARLES TALBUT) ONIONS (1873–1965) earned his B.A. from Mason College, Birmingham, in 1892 with a Third Class in French. He received the M.A. in 1895. In September 1895, J. A. H. Murray invited Onions to join the staff of the English dictionary at Oxford, and he lived in Oxford for most of the rest of his life. Onions prepared various portions of the dictionary from 1906 to 1913. He became a university lecturer (see Glossary) in English at Oxford in 1920 and a Reader (see Glossary) in English philology (1927–1949). Upon the death of Henry Bradley, Onions was elected a Fellow of Magdalen in 1923 and filled that position until 1965 in English and English philology. He was president of the Philological Society from 1929 to 1933 and was appointed CBE in 1934 and elected FBA in 1938. Because of his skill as a lexicographer and grammarian, Onions was involved in the preparation of various English dictionaries. In 1940 he was appointed librarian of Magdalen and served in that capacity until 1955. A member of the Coalbiters (see Glossary), Onions is best known for the *Oxford Dictionary of English Etymology* (1966).[19] Until 1956 he was the founder and editor of *Medium Aevum*, the journal of the Society for the Study of Medieval Languages and Literature. His portrait hangs in the Magdalen College Senior Common Room (see Glossary).

J. A. (JOHN ALEXANDER) SMITH (1863–1939) was Ferguson Scholar in Classics at the Collegiate School, Edinburgh University, then went to Balliol College, Oxford, in 1884. He earned First Class in Classical Moderations and Literae Humaniores. He later served from 1888 to 1891 as assistant to S. H. Butcher, professor of Greek at Edinburgh University. In 1891 Smith returned to Balliol as a Fellow and tutor in philosophy. He was the Waynflete Professor of Moral and Metaphysical Philosophy, a Fellow of Magdalen from 1910 until his retirement in 1935, and the perennial vice president of Magdalen. He was known as the foremost scholar of Aristotle at Oxford and, according to philosopher H. J. Paton, "the best teacher I have ever known."[20] Smith was editor of the *Oxford Aristotle*, president of the Oxford Aristotelian Society (1908), defender of philosophic idealism in the tradition of T. H. Green and Edward Caird, advocate of the views of Benedetto Croce, and catalyst for renewed interest in medieval history and literature. He was joint editor of *The Works of Aristotle* (1908–1912), and his translation of Aristotle's *De Anima* appeared in 1931.

Smith was a Scotsman and a friend of Lewis but an agnostic who did not think that there could be final answers in religious matters. The two men became acquainted over breakfast and frequently enjoyed each other's company.[21] Smith may have been put off by Lewis's apparent acceptance of Carritt's realism during Lewis's 1922 application for a fellowship in philosophy at Magdalen, but by the time Lewis applied for the English language and literature position at Magdalen in 1925, he had moved to idealism, which Smith espoused.[22] As noted in the preface, Lewis's *The Allegory of Love* owed much to Smith, who may be Lewis's model for the Socratic, unbelieving MacPhee in *That Hideous Strength*[23] (though some claim that Kirkpatrick served as the model). Smith died, unmarried, in 1939.

C. E. (COURTNEY EDWARD, "TOM BROWN") STEVENS (1905–1976), M.A., was educated at Winchester and at New College, Oxford, and became a Robinson Exhibitioner (see Glossary) at Oriel College, Oxford, in 1929. He came to Magdalen in 1933 as Fellow by Special Election,[24] leaving in 1940 for service in the Foreign Office. Stevens returned in 1946 as a Fellow and tutor in ancient history. He was invited to join the Inklings and came for the first time on November 27, 1947. Stevens became vice president of Magdalen in 1950. He was especially known for the effectiveness of his tutorials, earning the undergraduates of Magdalen a disproportionate number of the Firsts awarded.[25] He published two books: *Sidonius Apollinaris and His Age* (1933, his B.Litt. thesis) and *The Building of Hadrian's Wall* (1966). Stevens retired in 1972.[26]

A. J. P. (Alan John Percivale) Taylor (1906–1990), M.A., Ph.D., matriculated to Oriel College, Oxford, in 1924, winning the college essay prize in his first year[27] and graduating with a First Class in 1927. In 1930 he became assistant lecturer in modern history at the University of Manchester.[28] Taylor was a Fellow and tutor at Magdalen from 1938 until 1978. He was vice president of Magdalen from 1958 to 1960. He was elected FBA in 1938. After moving to London in 1963, Taylor began lecturing at the University of London and the Polytechnic of North London (now the University of North London) and was appointed a special lecturer of University College in 1965. He also became a visiting professor at the University of Bristol. Taylor continued at Magdalen as a Senior Research Fellow and was made Honorary Fellow in 1977.[29] During the war, Taylor and Lewis were founding members of the Home Guard, and both apparently agreed not to profit from their wartime work speaking to military and civilian groups about the war. The two men also both appeared on the BBC during World War II.[30] Taylor gave the 1956 Ford Lectures on English History, the Raleigh Lecture in History to the British Academy (1959), the Leslie Stephen Lecture (1961) in Cambridge, and the Romanes Lecture (Oxford, 1982).[31]

Taylor focused on European diplomatic history, serving alongside McFarlane in the History Department. Taylor was known for a dynamic lecturing style that used no notes, his radio and television appearances (he delivered the first television lectures in 1956[32]), a strong pro-Soviet stance, and involvement in the late-1950s in the Campaign for Nuclear Disarmament. Taylor authored twenty-three books, including the controversial *The Origins of the Second World War* (1961), which claimed that everything the English nation told him up until 1939 was a lie and that Hitler had not planned to go to war but merely reacted to events as they unfolded. Taylor wrote more than six hundred essays and articles and nearly sixteen hundred book reviews. Among others, he also wrote *The Struggle for Mastery in Europe 1848–1918* (1954, named in 1995 as one of the hundred most influential books published since 1945); *English History 1914–1945* (1965); *Bismarck: The Man and the Statesman* (1955); *The Troublemakers: Dissent over British Foreign Policy 1792–1939* (1957); and histories of Russia, Germany, Italy, and Austria.³³ Taylor once described Lewis as intellectually destructive with "an urgent Low Church piety which he preached everywhere except in the college common room,"³⁴ hardly an accurate portrayal of a man whose tutorial students heard nothing about his faith.

THOMAS HERBERT WARREN (1853–1930), M.A., Hon. DCL, professor of poetry, attended Balliol College on a Classical Scholarship in 1872, earning Firsts in Classical Moderations and Literae Humaniores, the Hertford and Craven Scholarships,³⁵ the Gaisford Prize for Greek Verse,³⁶ occasionally representing the university at rugby football, and graduating in 1876.³⁷ In 1877 he was elected to a prize fellowship in classics at Magdalen, and in 1878 he was appointed to a classical tutorship at Magdalen. Warren was elected master (see Glossary) of Magdalen on October 13, 1885, only eight days before he turned 32, and he held the office until October 1928. Warren presided over a revival of the fortunes of Magdalen, both demonstrating scholarship and gathering distinguished scholars around himself. He served as vice chancellor of the university from 1906 until 1910. Warren held numerous honorary degrees and wrote two volumes of verse: *By Severn Sea* and *The Death of Virgil*. In 1922 Warren wrote to Lewis, who had applied for a fellowship in philosophy at Magdalen, stating, "I am afraid you cannot have done yourself full justice."³⁸ This caused Lewis to take up English language and literature, the field in which he eventually won a Magdalen fellowship.

C. C. J. (CLEMENT CHARLES JULIAN) WEBB (1865–1954), FBA, D.Litt., was educated at Westminster School and later attended Christ Church as a Westminster Scholar. He earned a First in Literae Humaniores in 1888 and came to Magdalen as a Fellow and tutor in philosophy and medieval history in 1889, holding the position until 1922 and from 1938 until his death, the latter period as an Honorary Fellow. Webb tutored in philosophy and maintained interests in medieval and modern history, the history of philosophy and theology, and the historical element in religion. He became Oxford's most important philosopher of religion. In 1911 Webb was appointed Wilde Lecturer in Natural and Comparative Religion. In 1922 he became a Fellow of Oriel as professor of the philosophy of the

Christian religion. In 1930 Webb retired from his professorship to spend more time lecturing and writing. When he began his Oxford career, modern history was a new discipline at the university. When Webb ended his career, history, especially medieval history, was part of the mainstream of English scholarship. Webb and J. A. Smith were members of the Aristotelian Society; the Synthetic Society, a London club that promoted the discussion of the relationship between faith, philosophy, and science; the Oxford Philosophical Society; and the Deipnosophic, a forum for the discussion of classical metaphysics.[39] Webb was one of five great Magdalen men whom Lewis admired, the person who provided an etymology for the term *oyarsa* in the Space Trilogy,[40] and who, with his wife Eleanor, probably served as the model for Professor and Mrs. Dimble in *That Hideous Strength*.[41]

THOMAS DEWAR ("HARRY") WELDON (1896–1958), M.A., earned a B.A. from Magdalen in 1921, and was Fellow and tutor in philosophy at Magdalen from 1923 to 1958. Later, Weldon served as dean (see Glossary). Weldon's specialty was the work of the German philosopher Immanuel Kant. His writings included *States and Morals* (1946) and *The Vocabulary of Politics* (1953). He has been described as "the most influential Fellow in the College . . . who fought hardest to raise Magdalen's academic standards."[42] Weldon had a temper, a penchant for argument, and an insolence, but he was capable of kindness. Lewis thought of Weldon as a man of great abilities and wrote about him frequently in his diary.[43] Weldon, allegedly an atheist, is apparently the man who shocked Lewis one day when he said that it almost looked as if the idea of a dying and rising god had happened once; he was referring to the New Testament Gospels. During a 1926 conversation between the two men, Weldon said he believed in the Hegelian doctrine of the Trinity and considered himself a Christian in some sense.[44] Although not appreciative of some of Lewis's writings, Weldon nevertheless appreciated the man Lewis. Weldon thought that *The Pilgrim's Regress* should not have been written, and he once said to an undergraduate, "The man is not as bad as his books."[45] Some think of Weldon as the model for Lord Feverstone in *That Hideous Strength* because Lord Feverstone taunted Mark Studdock with the same words that Weldon had used against Lewis twenty years previously: "Incurable romantic!"[46]

Weldon was a wing commander during the Second World War, serving at Bomber Command Headquarters during the height of the bombing offensive (he also served in World War I). Along with Archbishop of Canterbury William Temple and others, Weldon took the position that the bombing was necessary. Lewis, however, joined a group of clergy and laity that published a manifesto against the bombing. Lewis was one of many nationally known individuals invited by Chaplain John Collins to speak against the bombing at the Royal Air Force training center in Yatesbury. The bombing was considered inhumane because of the number of civilian casualties. In 1944 Collins was transferred to Bomber Command Headquarters, High Wycombe. It was there that the personal assistant of Sir Arthur Harris, "T. D. Weldon, a tutor in Moral Philosophy at Magdalen College, Oxford," was invited by Harris to speak on the bombing. Weldon praised the work of the Bomber Command, concluding that the bombing was strategically justified because it shortened the war and kept the loss of life to a minimum.[47]

THE ENGLISH FELLOWS OF OXFORD UNIVERSITY

For an English Fellow at Magdalen College, the people with whom C. S. Lewis had the most in common were the English Faculty of Oxford University. The English Fellows determined the English curriculum across the university, set standards for the various examinations in English, and conducted the *viva voces* at the end of the testing period.

LASCELLES ABERCROMBIE (1881–1938), M.A., attended Malvern College and Manchester University, beginning to write poetry at Manchester University at the age of 20. He was one of the six Dymock Poets, so-called because of their proximity to the village of Dymock. He attempted to develop the idea of realism in poetry. Abercrombie authored *Interludes and Poems* (1908); *The Sale of Saint Thomas* for an anthology of Georgian Poetry (1912); *The End of the World* for the second issue of *New Numbers* (a quarterly magazine begun by Abercrombie and his wife, Catherine, in 1914); *The Idea of Great Poetry* (1926, a work read by Lewis); and *Poems* (1930, his collected poems and plays). After World War I, Abercrombie became professor of poetry at Liverpool University, Leeds University, Bedford College in London, and Merton College, Oxford (from 1929). He was Goldsmiths' Professor of English Literature from 1935 to 1938. Abercrombie became a

Fellow of the Royal Academy in 1937. Abercrombie wrote Georgian poetry, much liked by Lewis, and was attacked for his poetic style by Ezra Pound, a poet Lewis disliked. Abercrombie was a friend of Robert Frost, writing a review (June 13, 1914) for Frost's *North of Boston* that first gained Frost acclaim in the United States. Lewis mentioned Abercrombie in his essay "What Chaucer Really Did to Il Filostrato," hoping that he was not guilty of Abercrombie's criticism of turning from the known effect of an ancient poem to speculation about the poet's intent. Lewis also credited Abercrombie in his preface to *The Allegory of Love* for help with his appendix on *Danger*. Lewis once complimented Abercrombie for understanding poetry, especially the long poem.[48]

F. W. (Frederick Noel Wilse) Bateson (1901–1978), B.A., B.Litt., M.A., attended Trinity College, Oxford, graduating with a B.A. in English in 1924. He was Commonwealth Fellow at Harvard (1927–1929). Bateson served as visiting professor at the University of Minnesota; Cornell University; the University of California, Berkeley; and Penn State. He was lecturer (see Glossary) in English at Corpus Christi College, Oxford (1946–1963); Fellow and lecturer, Corpus Christi (1963–1969); and emeritus Fellow (1969–1978). Bateson was a frequent reviewer for the *New York Review of Books*; founder in 1951 and editor until 1971 of *Essays in Criticism*, which was Oxford's answer to *Scrutiny*; editor of the *Cambridge Bibliography of English Literature* (1940); and a poet. He wrote about eighteenth-century comedy, Wordsworth, Blake, Pope, Matthew Arnold, and others. Bateson authored *English Comic Drama: 1700–1750*; *English Poetry and the English Language* (1934); *Wordsworth: A Reinterpretation* (1954); and many other books. He edited *The Works of Congreve: Comedies, Incognita, Poems* (1930) and *The Poems of Matthew Arnold* (1965).

John Bayley (1925–), FBA, CBE, was educated at Eton and matriculated to St. Antony's and Magdalen Colleges, Oxford (1951–1955). He was tutor in English at New College (1955–1974) and later Warton Professor of English Literature and Fellow of St. Catherine's College (1974–1992). He is a critic and novelist and the author of more than two dozen books, including *Tolstoy and the Novel* (1967) and *Russian Short Stories* (1992). Bayley received the PEN Stern Prize for *Iris: A Memoir of Iris Murdoch* (1998), an account of his marriage. A. N. Wilson, the controversial biographer of C. S. Lewis, was one of Bayley's pupils at New College.[49]

PETER BAYLEY (1921–) matriculated to University College in 1940 and, after service in the army, earned a First in English in 1947. He took some tutorials in his first three terms with Lewis because at the time University College had no Fellow in English.[50] Bayley became a Fellow of University College and a university lecturer in English, after serving at Collingwood College, Durham University, and the University of St. Andrews. Bayley wrote especially on Spenser and Milton and once wrote an article on "The Martlets" for the *University College Record* (1949–1950). Bayley wrote of *The Allegory of Love*: "I doubt if any other scholar of this century could have brought a survey of such magnitude to such triumphant fruition or have written with such transcendent and illuminating power—and yet so engagingly—about so much almost lost or unknown medieval literature."[51] He is currently emeritus professor at the University of St. Andrews and emeritus Fellow of University College, Oxford. Bayley lives in Oxfordshire.

J. A. W. BENNETT (1911–1981) (see pp. 179, 200).

CECIL MAURICE BOWRA (1898–1971) was Fellow of New College and later professor of poetry (1946–1951). He was known especially for his expertise in ancient Greek poetry and culture. He became the Charles Eliot Norton Professor (1948–1949, in honor of Harvard's first professor of the history of art), vice chancellor (1951–1954), warden (see Glossary) of Wadham College (1938–1971, some sources say 1922–1971), and president of the British Academy (1958–1962). Bowra was knighted in 1951. He was the author of *The Oxford Book of Greek Verse* (1938, with T. F. Higham), *The Heritage of Symbolism* (1943), *The Creative Experiment* (1949), *Ancient Greek Literature* (1960), and *Greek Lyric Poetry from Alcman to Simonides* (1961).

H. F. B. (HERBERT FRANCIS BRETT) BRETT-SMITH (1884–1951), B.A., M.A., matriculated to Corpus Christi College in 1903 and earned a Fourth Class in Classical Moderations in 1905 and a Second Class in the Final Honour School of English in 1907. He earned his M.A. in 1910. He was lecturer and tutor in English at Queen's, Brasenose, Jesus, Pembroke, and Hertford Colleges; Oxford University Reader (see Glossary) in English (1926–1939); and Goldsmiths' Reader in English (1939–1947).[52] Brett-Smith was an ally of Tolkien in the exclusion of literature after 1800 from the modern literature course.[53]

JOHN BUXTON (1912–1989) matriculated to New College in 1931, read Honour Moderations and Greats, and participated in the Oxford University Dramatic Society. He was elected lecturer in English literature in 1946 at New College and Fellow in 1949. He was appointed Reader in English literature in 1972. He wrote *Sir Philip Sidney and the English Renaissance* (1965) and edited *New College Oxford 1379–1979*.[54] Among his poems are *Westward* (1942) and *Such Liberty* (1944). With Norman Davis, Buxton was the editor of part 1 of vol. 11 of the Oxford History of English Literature.

DAVID CECIL (LORD EDWARD CHRISTIAN DAVID GASCOYNE CECIL) (1902–1986), Goldsmiths' Professor of English Literature from 1948 to 1970, was a biographer and a member of the Inklings (see Glossary). He was a Fellow and lecturer in modern history and English literature at Wadham College (1924–1930) and later a Fellow of English at New College (1939–1948). He published a masterful two-volume life of Lord Melbourne in *The Young Melbourne* (1939) and *Lord Melbourne* (1954), as well as books on Sir Walter Scott, Jane Austen, Walter Pater, and Max Beerbohm.

NEVILL COGHILL (1899–1980), like Lewis, was born in Ireland. He was educated at Bilton and Haileybury Colleges, then at Exeter College, Oxford, beginning in 1919 (after a tour in World War I), reading history and English. He earned a First in English in 1923, the same year Lewis first mentioned him in his diary. In *Surprised by Joy*, Lewis described Coghill as both intelligent and Christian, a combination he hardly thought possible. Coghill became a Research Fellow (see Glossary) at Exeter College in 1924, and served as a Fellow of English and librarian at Exeter College from 1925 to 1957. In 1957 Coghill was elected Merton Professor of English Literature in Oxford and held that position until his retirement in 1966. He worked to get a theater for Oxford and produced brilliant plays for the Oxford University Dramatic Society, once casting Richard Burton as Angelo in *Measure for Measure*. In 1966, the year he retired, Coghill directed Richard Burton and Elizabeth Taylor in *Dr. Faustus*. Coghill was a close friend of Lewis, whom he met in a discussion class of George Gordon. Later, they were both Inklings.[55] Coghill is well known for his translation of Chaucer's *The Canterbury Tales* (1951), which Lewis praised highly. He also translated *Piers Plowman* as *Visions from Piers Plowman* (1949).

Helen Darbishire (1881–1961), D.Litt., CBE, a Wordsworth and Milton scholar, earned First Class at Somerville in 1903. Founded in 1879, Somerville was one of the first women's colleges and only began to admit men in 1994. Darbishire became an English tutor at Somerville College (1908–1931); a member of council, Somerville (1913–1945); Fellow (1923–1931); university lecturer (1926–1931); principal (1931–1945; see Glossary); and Honorary Fellow (1946–1961). Her conscientious duties as principal, an office she did not seek, and her stature as a Wordsworth scholar especially marked her career. She published *Wordsworth's Poems Published in 1807* (1914); *The Manuscript of Paradise Lost, Book I* (1931); *The Early Lives of Milton* (1932); and edited the five-volume *Poetical Works of William Wordsworth* with her former teacher Ernest de Selincourt (1940–1949), as well as *The Poetical Works, Volume II* (1963).[56] Lewis mentioned favorably her work on Milton, alongside that of Tillyard, in chapter 1 of *A Preface to Paradise Lost*.[57]

H. V. D. (Henry Victor Dyson, nicknamed Hugo) Dyson (1896–1975), B.A., B.Litt., M.A., was educated at Brighton College and the Royal Military College at Sandhurst (where Warren Lewis attended).[58] Dyson fought in the Battle of the Somme, the Battle of Arras, and the Battle of Passchendaele in World War I. He matriculated at Exeter College, Oxford, in October 1919 to read English, earning the B.A. in 1921. After earning the B.Litt. in 1924, he became lecturer and tutor in English in 1924 at Reading University. Dyson was known as a scholar with a rare ability for quoting Shakespeare. In 1945 he was elected Fellow and tutor in English literature at Merton College, Oxford. A frequent participant at meetings of the Inklings and, earlier, the Coalbiters (see Glossary), Dyson retired from Merton in 1963.[59] Dyson wrote *Pope* (1933), *The Emergence of Shakespeare's Tragedy* (1950), and articles for *Essays on the Eighteenth Century Presented to David Nichol Smith* (1945). He met Lewis in 1930 through Nevill Coghill. Dyson is most noted for his midnight conversation with Lewis and Tolkien on September 19, 1931, on the subject of myth, a conversation that led to the conversion of Lewis to Christianity. From this time on, Dyson regularly participated in the meetings of the Inklings.

DAME HELEN LOUISE GARDNER (1908–1986), D.Litt., Hon. CBE, DBE, FRSL, attended St. Hilda's College, Oxford, obtaining First Class in English language and literature in 1929. After teaching at the University of Birmingham and the Royal Holloway College, London (1931–1934), she returned to Birmingham in the English Department (1934–1941). She became tutor (1941–1954) and later Fellow (1942–1966) of St. Hilda's College, Oxford. In 1966 she was elected Merton Professor of English Language and Literature at Lady Margaret Hall, the first woman to hold this chair. She was a medieval and Renaissance scholar who once turned down the Cambridge position that Lewis held. She edited *The New Oxford Book of English Verse, 1250–1950* (1972) and John Donne's *Elegies and Songs and Sonnets* in the Oxford Scholarly Classics series (1965). Among her other works are *The Art of T. S. Eliot* (1949); *The Metaphysical Poets* (1969); an anthology of the poetry of John Milton, John Donne, and other seventeenth-century poets; and *In Defence of the Imagination* (1982). Gardner won the academic book prize for women writers from the British Academy in 1980. She is remembered especially for her work on T. S. Eliot and John Donne.[60]

H. W. (HEATHCOTE WILLIAM) GARROD (1878–1960), M.A., became professor of poetry at Merton College in 1923; authored *Q. Horati Flacci Opera, Wordsworth*, and *Jane Austen: A Depreciation*; edited *The Poems of John Keats*; and wrote various essays and book chapters, such as the chapter on Merton College in *The Victorian History of the County of Oxford*.

GEORGE STUART GORDON (1881–1942), M.A., Hon. LL.D., attended Glasgow University and Oriel College, Oxford. He was a Fellow of Magdalen from 1907 to 1915; tutor and university lecturer in English literature from 1908 to 1913; professor of English language and literature at Leeds University from 1913 to 1922; and Merton Professor of English Literature from 1922 to 1928, following Sir Walter A. Raleigh. Gordon supported the practice of maintaining an English curriculum that ended with literature up to 1830. He was professor of poetry from 1933 to 1938, publishing his lectures as *The Discipline of Letters* (1946). Gordon continued Raleigh's practice of holding a discussion class for those who read English literature. He became president of Magdalen in 1928 and served in that capacity until his death in 1942. As an undergraduate, Lewis studied English literature with Gordon.

Mary Madge Lascelles (1900–1995), B.A., B.Litt., M.A., attended Lady Margaret Hall, earning a First Class in English in 1922. After serving as an assistant lecturer at Royal Holloway College (1926–1928), Lascelles excelled as tutor in English at Somerville (1931–1960), vice principal (1947–1960), Fellow (1932–1960), university lecturer in English literature (1960), Additional Fellow (1960–1966), Professorial Fellow (1966–1967; see Glossary), university Reader in English literature since 1966, and Honorary Fellow since 1967. She authored *Jane Austen and Her Art* (1939), *Shakespeare's "Measure for Measure"* (1953), an edition of Johnson's *Journey to the Western Islands* (1971), and numerous articles and essays. Lascelles was appointed FBA in 1962.[61]

Cecil Day Lewis (1904–1972) (no relation to C. S. Lewis), professor of poetry (1951–1956), attended Sherborne College and graduated from Wadham College, Oxford, in 1927. In Oxford, he became part of a circle of leftist poets that gathered around W. H. Auden. Lewis was also a member of the Communist Party from 1935 until 1938, though he retreated from that position later in life. His first collection of poems, *Beechen Virgil*, appeared in 1925, and Lewis joined Auden to edit *Oxford Poetry* (1927). In 1937 Cecil Day Lewis edited a socialist symposium, *The Mind in Chains*. During the 1930s, he wrote detective novels under the pseudonym Nicholas Blake, as well as three autobiographical novels. Lewis delivered the Clark Lectures at Cambridge in 1946 and strengthened his literary reputation with translations of Virgil, collections of original verse, and a translation of *Valéry* (1946). In 1951 he was elected to the professorship of poetry, a position that many felt C. S. Lewis should have received. Cecil Day Lewis was named British poet laureate in 1968, succeeding John Masefield. He also wrote several collections of poetry, including *Collected Poems* (1935), *A Time to Dance and Other Poems* (1935), *Word Over All* (1943), and many novels, including *A Question of Proof* (1935).[62]

Gervase Mathew (1905–1976), O.P., taught English at Oxford University. He entered the Order of Preachers in 1928 and later became a scholar in patristics and Byzantine art, medieval English literature, and the archaeology of East Africa. He was also an Inkling. Among his books were *Byzantine Painting, The Reformation and the Contemplative Life*, and *The Court of Richard II*.

W. W. (WILLIAM WALLACE) ROBSON (1923–1993) was a Fellow of Lincoln College at Oxford University; Masson Professor of English Literature, University of Edinburgh (1972–1990); and emeritus professor. He edited *The Case-Book of Sherlock Holmes by Arthur Conan Doyle*, *The Hound of the Baskervilles*, and *The Oxford Sherlock Holmes*. He wrote *Critical Essays* (1966), *Modern English Literature* (1984), and other works. He later taught English at the University of Leeds.

ELEANOR WILLOUGHBY ROOKE (1888–1952) earned her B.A. from the Final Honours School in English at Lady Margaret Hall, Oxford, in 1908 (First Class) and her M.A. in 1921. She was English mistress at Cheltenham Ladies' College (1911–1917), taught at Sheffield Central School for Girls (1917–1920), and was tutor in English at St. Hilda's College (1920–1941), Fellow (1926–1941), vice principal (1933–1941), and Honorary Fellow (1947–1952).[63]

ERNEST DE SELINCOURT (1870–1943), FBA, LL.D., attended Dulwich and University Colleges, Oxford. As an undergraduate he earned a Second Class in Literae Humaniores. He was appointed lecturer in English language and literature at University College (1896) and university lecturer (1899). In 1908 he was elected professor of English language and literature at the University of Birmingham (1919–1935). He was also professor of poetry at Oxford from 1928 until 1933 and Honorary Fellow of University College, Oxford, in 1930, thereby holding two positions simultaneously. His lectures were published in 1934 as *Oxford Lectures on Poetry*. With Helen Darbishire, he edited *The Poetical Works of William Wordsworth* (1940–1949, 5 vols.). He was especially known for his definitive editions of William and Dorothy Wordsworth, including the *Letters of William and Dorothy Wordsworth* (1935–1939).[64]

PERCY SIMPSON (1865–1962) attended Denstone and Selwyn Colleges, Cambridge, later teaching at Selwyn. At Cambridge he became known for his knowledge of Elizabethan literature, especially drama. In 1914 Walter Raleigh had him appointed as the first librarian of the English Faculty Library in Oxford. He became a Fellow of Oriel College in 1921, university Reader in English textual criticism in 1927, and he succeeded David Nichol Smith as Goldsmiths' Professor of English Literature (1930–1935). He became Honorary Fellow of Oriel in 1943. With C. H. Hertford and his wife, Evelyn, he painstakingly edited an eleven-volume work on Ben Jonson (1925–1952).[65] He also wrote *Shakespearian Punctuation* (1911) and *Proof-Reading in the Sixteenth, Seventeenth and Eighteenth Centuries* (1935). In 1951 Simpson became Honorary Fellow of Selwyn College.

DAVID NICHOL SMITH (1875–1962), M.A., was Goldsmiths' Professor of English Literature (1908–1929) and Merton Professor of English Literature (1929–1946), succeeding George Gordon. His emphasis was in eighteenth-century studies. He was Goldsmiths' Reader in English and author of chapter 8, "Johnson and Boswell," in volume 10 of The Cambridge History of English and American Literature. Many consider this encyclopedia to be the most important work of literary history and criticism ever published. Smith also edited *Letters of Jonathan Swift to Charles Ford* (Oxford, 1935).

JANET SPENS (1876–1963), Hon. LL.D. (Glasgow, 1944), was a Fellow and tutor of English at Lady Margaret Hall (1911–1936) after some years as co-headmistress of Laurel Bank School and as assistant tutor in English at the University of Glasgow. She had studied at Glasgow under A. C. Bradley and Gilbert Murray. She was an air raid warden during World War II and took in evacuee children. She was a specialist in Elizabethan drama, acquainted with Greek and French, and the author of *Spenser's Faerie Queen* (1934) and several essays in *Review of English Studies* and *Essays and Studies*.[66]

J. R. R. (JOHN RONALD REUEL) TOLKIEN (1892–1973), CBE, was born in South Africa and raised in Birmingham. He studied at King Edward's School, Birmingham, then entered Exeter College, Oxford, in 1911, reading Honour Moderations and studying comparative philology under Joseph Wright. He took a First in English language and literature in 1915. During his service in World War I, which included the Battle of the Somme, Tolkien began writing *The Silmarillion*. He became Reader in English language at the University of Leeds (1920–1924) and professor of English language at Leeds in 1924. In 1925 he became Rawlinson and Bosworth Professor of Anglo-Saxon at Oxford, a fellowship attached to Pembroke College, and in 1945 Merton Professor of English Language and Literature. Although never realized, he had a dream that he and Lewis might one day become the two Merton Professors of English. Merton College had the only two full professorships in the English School at Oxford. Tolkien met Lewis in 1926. That same year, he founded the Coalbiters, considered by some a forerunner of the Inklings. Tolkien quickly became one of Lewis's closest friends. Lewis's encouragement was important for the authoring of *The Hobbit* (1937) and *The Lord of the Rings* (1954–1955), the latter named the most important book of the twentieth century in four separate polls. Tolkien read these books to the Inklings while they were in progress. Tolkien was also extremely influential in Lewis's spiritual pilgrimage. Tolkien retired in 1959 and became a Resident Honorary Fellow at Merton College after the death of his wife, Edith, in 1971. Oxford conferred upon him an honorary Doctor of Letters in 1972.

RACHEL TRICKETT (1923–1999) was English tutor at St. Hugh's College from 1954 and later principal of St. Hugh's (from 1973). She was educated at Lady Margaret Hall, Oxford.

JOAN ELIZABETH TURVILLE-PETRE (nee BLOMFIELD) (1911–), B.A., B.Litt., Dipl., M.A., attended Somerville College (1930–1934) and studied English as an exhibitioner (see Glossary), earning a Second Class. Later she became lecturer in English language at Somerville College (1936–1938), assistant tutor (1938), tutor and Fellow (1941–1946), and lecturer in English language (1946–1955). She served as editor of *The Old English "Exodus"* (1981) in collaboration with J. R. R. Tolkien, published *Translation of The Story of Raud and His Sons* (1947), and wrote numerous articles for *Review of English Studies, Saga Book of the Viking Society, Journal of English and Germanic Philology, Traditio, Arkiv*, and *Studia Neophilologica.*

DOROTHY WHITELOCK (1901–82), M.A., D.Litt., FSA, FBA, CBE, doyenne of Anglo-Saxon studies at St. Hilda's College (1930–1957), was educated at Leeds High School for Girls and Newnham College, Cambridge (1921–1924), where she read for the English Tripos under Henry Chadwick especially on the Anglo-Saxon period. She came to St. Hilda's in 1930 as lecturer in English language, becoming a tutor in 1936, a Fellow in 1937, and an Honorary Fellow in 1957. She served on the governing body and for seven years as vice principal. She was known for her gracious treatment of undergraduates, offering polite criticism with "Perhaps you remember . . ." or "Have you forgotten . . . ?" In 1957 she returned to Cambridge as professor. She revised Sweet's *Anglo-Saxon Reader in Prose and Verse* (1967) and wrote *Anglo-Saxon Wills* (1930), *The Audience of Beowulf* (1951), *The Beginnings of English Society* (Pelican History of England, vol.

2, 1952), and many other works. She was elected to the British Academy in 1956.[67]

JOHN BARRINGTON WAIN (1925–1994) earned the B.A. (1946) and the M.A. (1950) from St. John's College, Oxford, where he became a Fellow upon graduation (1946–1949). He was appointed lecturer in English at Reading University (1949–1955), then became a freelance writer. He eventually returned to Oxford University to become professor of poetry (1973–1978). His writings included an early novel, *Hurry on Down* (1953); *Sprightly Running: Part of an Autobiography* (1962); a book of poetry and lectures, *Professing Poetry* (1977); *Young Shoulders* (1982, for which he won the Whitbread Award);[68] *Where the Rivers Meet* (1988); and many other works. Wain occasionally attended meetings of the Inklings, though he did not share many of their views other than a love of literature.[69]

EDITH E. (ELIZABETH) WARDALE (1863–1943) matriculated at Lady Margaret Hall in 1887, then moved to St. Hugh's College in 1888. She earned a First Class in Modern Languages and became vice principal and tutor, and later a Fellow, at St. Hugh's, as well as tutor for the Association for the Higher Education of Women. She tutored in English at St. Hugh's until 1923. She is the author of *An Old English Grammar* (1922), *Introduction to Middle English* (1927), and other books. She tutored Lewis on Old English, sometimes prompting Lewis to complain about having to study Old English. He once wrote in his diary that he saw little use in phonology and the theory of language,[70] but he later came to appreciate Wardale's expertise, stating that phonology was giving him new insights all the time.[71] Lewis also spoke favorably of Wardale's support for classical education.[72]

CYRIL H. WILKINSON (1888–1960) attended Worcester College, Oxford, graduating in 1910, and later became a Fellow in the English School at Worcester. He edited *The Poems of Richard Lovelace* (1925) and wrote *Diversions* and *More Diversions*. After service in World War I, he returned to Worcester in 1919 as dean (serving until 1953). He served as assistant secretary and then secretary of the Oxford and Cambridge Examination Board, treasurer of the University Carlton Club, and commander of the Oxford University Officers Training Corps.[73] He was known as one of Oxford's most legendary book collectors.[74]

F. P. (FRANK PERCY) WILSON (1889–1963) earned a B.A. in English from the University of Birmingham and a B.Litt. at Lincoln College, Oxford. After serving in World War I, he returned to Oxford in 1920 as a university lecturer and became Reader in 1927. He became Merton Professor of English Literature at Merton College (1947–1957) when David Nichol Smith retired and Lewis was passed over for the position. Wilson had been a tutor to Lewis in English during Lewis's University College undergraduate days. Later, Wilson authored volume 5 of the Oxford History of the English Language, entitled *English Drama 1485–1585* (later completed by G. K. Hunter); *The Plague in Shakespeare's London* (1927); and other works. He also served as editor of *The Oxford Dictionary of English Proverbs* and *The Works of Thomas Nashe* (1958). He was the general editor of the Oxford History of the English Language and invited Lewis to write volume 3, *English Literature in the Sixteenth Century, excluding Drama.*

CHARLES LESLIE WRENN (1895–1969) was educated at Queen's College, Oxford. After lecturing at Durham, Madras, Dacca, and Leeds (1917–1930), he returned to Oxford in 1930 as lecturer in Anglo-Saxon. He was professor at King's College, London (1939–1946), and later became Rawlinson and Bosworth Professor of Anglo-Saxon (1946–1963), succeeding J. R. R. Tolkien in that position. Wrenn was an Inkling.[75]

HENRY CECIL KENNEDY WYLD (1870–1945) earned a B.A. from Oxford in 1899. He was a philologist and lexicographer, studying philology, phonetics, and linguistics at Corpus Christi, Oxford. After some years as lecturer in the Baines Chair of English Language (1899–1904) and professor of English language and literature at University College, Liverpool (1904–1920), he came to Oxford in 1920 as Merton Professor of English Language and Literature (1920–1945). He wrote *Studies in English Rhymes* (1923) and the *Universal Dictionary of the English Language* (1932).

THE FELLOWS OF MAGDALENE COLLEGE, CAMBRIDGE

In 1956 there were only nine Fellows at Magdalene College, Cambridge, who could be considered full-time teaching officers. The number of Fellows at Magdalene College grew to thirty over the next twenty-five years. The first Fellow in law was elected in 1955, and by 1963 fellowships had been added in engineering, architecture, zoology, botany, and history.

Lewis's arrival in 1955 coincided with the first award being offered in English. Among Lewis's colleagues for at least part of his tenure in Cambridge were the following.

SIMON BARRINGTON-WARD (1930–) became chaplain at Magdalene in 1956 after undergraduate studies at the college from 1950 to 1953. In 1960 he went to teach in Nigeria as a lecturer (see Glossary) in the Religious Studies Department at the University of Ibadan, returning only months before Lewis's death in September 1963. From 1963 to 1969 Barrington-Ward was a Fellow and Director of Studies in Theology, teaching church history, giving lectures in Divinity Faculty, and Dean of Chapel. He ran the Church Missionary Society Training Center at Selly Oak (1969–1975) and became general secretary of the society (1975–1985). He was bishop of Coventry from 1985 to 1997, returning to Magdalene in 1997 in retirement as an Honorary Fellow.

J. A. W. (JACK ARTHUR WALTER) BENNETT (1911–1981), discussed earlier concerning his Oxford career, became professor of medieval and Renaissance literature, succeeding Lewis at Cambridge in 1964. Therefore he was not a colleague of Lewis during Lewis's years at Magdalene, but he was a close friend. He wrote volume 1, *Middle English Literature 1100–1400*, of the Oxford History of English Literature. Bennett retired in 1978.

RONALD HYAM, Ph.D., D.Litt., came to Magdalene in 1960 as Fellow and Reader (see Glossary) in British Imperial history. He served as college librarian (1963–1993), president (1996–1998), and now serves as emeritus Fellow of Magdalene. He is an editor for the British Documents on the End of Empire Project. He co-authored *A History of Magdalene College, Cambridge, 1428–1988* and wrote many other works, including *Britain's Imperial Century* (1976); *Empire and Sexuality*; *The Labour Government and the End of Empire, 1945–1951*; *The Conservative Government and the End of Empire, 1957–1964* (with William Roger Louis); and *The Failure of South African Expansion, 1908–1948* (1972).

RICHARD W. (WILLIAM) LADBOROUGH (1908–1972) came to Magdalene as an undergraduate in 1927 and in 1954 returned as a Fellow and Director of Studies to serve as dean and librarian of the Pepys Library, as well as lecturer in French. He held a lectureship in French (1954–1969), leading the modern language division of the college until his retirement in 1969.

When Lewis came in 1955, Ladborough became his closest friend. His article on Lewis, "In Cambridge," appeared first in *CSL: The Bulletin of the New York C. S. Lewis Society* (July 1975) and later in James Como's *C. S. Lewis at the Breakfast Table*. In the essay, Ladborough wrote: "It is now common knowledge that his memory was prodigious and that he seemed to have read everything."[76] Ladborough authored numerous articles for the *Journal of the Warburg Institute, French Studies, Modern Language Review*, and other publications.[77]

ARTHUR SALE (1912–2000) in the 1950s and 1960s worked with John Stevens to develop English as a major subject for undergraduates. He did undergraduate work at the University of Nottingham, earning a First Class B.A. in 1932 and the M.A. in 1934, a First with distinction. He moved to Cambridge in 1936, teaching correspondence courses for the University Correspondence College. During this time, Sale edited introductions and notes on several important works, including John Dryden's play *All for Love* (1938), Jonathan Swift's satirical *A Tale of a Tub* (1939), and Ben Jonson's play *Every Man in His Humour* (1941). In 1956 a meeting with John Stevens brought Sale to Magdalene to supervise for the college. He became a lecturer in English in 1965 and a Fellow Commoner (see Glossary) in 1980. His special emphases were on American writing and on the novel, and he was known for his powerful memory that enabled him to quote extensive sections of verse or recall many plot details of minor fiction. Although Sale began writing poetry in the 1930s, the first of his three collections of poetry did not appear until 1975 under the title *Under the War*. He retired in 1980.[78]

JOHN EDGAR STEVENS (1921–2002) came to Magdalene as an undergraduate, matriculating in 1940 and reading classics. He joined the Royal Navy during the Second World War, serving in minesweepers and advancing to the rank of lieutenant. He became a Fellow at Magdalene in 1950 and university lecturer in English in 1953, followed by a lectureship in English in 1958. He was made Reader in English and musical history in 1974 and professor of medieval and Renaissance English in 1978 (the third person to hold this position after Lewis and Bennett). Stevens was elected FBA in 1975 and was appointed CBE in 1980.

Stevens worked with Arthur Sale in the 1950s and 1960s to develop the study of English for undergraduates. When he was Director of Studies at

Magdalene, he brought Sale on staff to supervise for the college. Stevens greatly admired Lewis and based his notion of the courtly poets on Lewis's *The Allegory of Love*. Stevens's doctoral work was published in 1961 as *Music and Poetry in the Early Tudor Court*. Stevens lectured especially on medieval drama, lyrics, romance, and George Herbert. At one point he decided to study Anglo-Saxon with Lewis during Lewis's fellowship in Cambridge. Writing about this experience, Stevens stated, "Nothing, I think, better illustrates Lewis's extraordinary generosity than his sustained kindness."[79] From 1988 until his death, Stevens was emeritus professor of medieval and Renaissance literature. A distinguished musicologist and active musician, he occasionally combined the two disciplines with his work on late medieval song.[80]

HENRY URMSTON WILLINK (1894–1973) was master (see Glossary) of Magdalene (1948–1966) and subsequently elected to an honorary fellowship. Educated at Eton and Trinity College, Cambridge, he earned his B.A. in classics in 1919 and took his M.A. in 1933. He was vice chancellor of Cambridge from 1953 to 1955. Having served as a member of the bar, a member of Parliament (1940–1948), and the Minister of Health (1943–1945, appointed by Prime Minister Winston Churchill), Willink seemed prepared to become a High Court judge and possibly Lord Chancellor. He surprised many when he rejected such prospects to become the master of Magdalene. His primary contributions to the college were the friendly atmosphere he helped to maintain and the improvements of both buildings and finances. After his death, a memorial service was held in Westminster Abbey, with the archbishop of Canterbury speaking.[81]

THE ENGLISH FELLOWS OF CAMBRIDGE UNIVERSITY

MURIEL CLARA BRADBROOK (1909–1993), mistress of Girton College (1968–1976), her alma mater, and lecturer in English, was the first woman to hold a chair (see Glossary) on the English Faculty of Cambridge. She held a faculty assistant lectureship in English (1945–1948), a lectureship in English (1948–1962), a readership beginning in 1962, and a professorship of English beginning in 1966. Her interests lay in drama, Ibsen, and Shakespeare, and though her writings do not reflect it, she was a deeply committed Christian.[82] Bradbrook wrote *Themes and Conventions in Elizabethan Tragedy* (1935); *The Rise of the Common Player* (1962); *Malcolm*

Lowry, His Art and Early Life (1974); and other publications, including works on Virginia Woolf, Joseph Conrad, and T. S. Eliot. Bradbrook retired in 1985. Lewis wrote to her on April 18, 1958, regarding words that have two or more meanings, such as the word *simple* in the phrase "simple meal."[83] In the appendix on George Chapman and Christopher Marlow in *English Literature in the Sixteenth Century*, Lewis mentioned Bradbrook's *The School of Night* (1936).[84] Early in her acquaintance with Lewis, when Lewis was confidently and outrageously using the breadth of his knowledge to shred an argument by a student during a meeting of the English Club, which everyone present felt was wrong, she interrupted him, saying, "Really, Professor, I cannot allow you to continue being so outrageous." Nor did she that evening.[85]

T. R. (THOMAS RICE) HENN (1901–1974), CBE, M.A., FRSL, matriculated to St. Catherine's College in 1920, earned First Class English Tripos in 1922, and became a Fellow of St. Catherine's College and lecturer (see Glossary) in English in 1926. He was praelector (1927–1934); tutor until 1939, when he entered the army; senior tutor (1945–1957); and president (1958–1962, 1968–1969). He was also Wilson Lecturer in Poetry and Drama and Reader in Anglo-Irish Literature (1964–1969). Henn wrote *Longinus and English Criticism* (1934), *The Lonely Tower: Studies in the Poetry of W. B. Yeats* (1950), *The Harvest of Tragedy* (1956), *Selected Poems* (1958), *Kipling* (1967), and many other works.[86]

L. C. KNIGHTS (1925–1998), Queens' College, was in charge of the English Faculty. Originally of the Leavis school and a contributor to *Scrutiny*, Knights was a socialist who specialized in Shakespeare but who also wrote broadly on many subjects, including George Herbert. Knights's works have been collected into two volumes. He wrote *Drama and Society in the Age of Jonson* (1937), *Essays in Criticism* in the Further Explorations Series (1965), *'Hamlet' and other Shakespearean Essays* (1979), and many other works.

F. R. (FRANK RAYMOND) LEAVIS (1895–1978), probationary faculty lecturer (1927–1931), a Fellow of Downing College, Cambridge (1936–1962), and assistant university lecturer, was the most influential literary critic of his time after T. S. Eliot. Leavis's first major book, *New Bearings in English Poetry* (1932), argued that Eliot, G. M. Hopkins, Ezra Pound, and W. B. Yeats were the more important and creative of the modern writers. Leavis was co-founder and editor of *Scrutiny*, a quarterly journal of literature and cultural criticism (1932–1953), in which Leavis described literature as a moral resource to address the problems of everyday life. Leavis also used the pages of *Scrutiny* to provide a canon of worthwhile English literature and to criticize mass culture, especially politics, commercialism, technology, and science. Leavis described the university as a place where human responsibility and courage should be developed and warned against turning the university into a business enterprise.[87] His standards were egalitarian, anti-capitalistic, and moral, though he was not a Christian. Leavis viewed English as the new classics, and he used his platform to criticize the culture and its media environment in the hope of bringing about change.[88] Leavis claimed to be able to reveal both the meaning of literature and the meaning of life.[89] He also authored *Revaluation* (1936), *Education and the University* (1943), *The Great Tradition* (1948), *D. H. Lawrence: Novelist* (1955), *English Literature in Our Time and the University* (1969), and other works.[90]

F. L. LUCAS (1894–1967) won the Pitt University scholarship in 1914 and later the Porson Prize for Greek Iambics at Trinity College, Cambridge. After service in World War I on the western front, he returned to Cambridge in 1920 and won the Chancellor's Medal for Classics and a Browne Medal in Latin, a First Class in the Classical Tripos, and a fellowship in classics at King's College, Cambridge. Lucas became known both for his studies of English literature and his studies of the classics. After publishing works in classics, he joined the English faculty. In the field of poetry, Lucas wrote *Time and Memory* (1920), *Marionettes* (1930), and *Poems 1935* (1935). Among his novels were *The River Flows* (1926), *Cécile* (1930), and *Dr. Dido* (1938). Among his works of criticism were *Studies French and English* (1934) and *The Decline and Fall of the Romantic Ideal* (1936). Lucas's outspoken opposition to totalitarianism resulted in *Delights of Dictatorship* (1938) and *Journal under the Terror 1938* (1938). During World War II, he worked in intelligence at Bletchley Park decoding German messages. During the years of the ascendancy of F. R. Leavis, when he was a Reader (see Glossary) in the English Faculty (1947–1962), Lucas considered that movement to be an aberration, a position reflected in his chapter on English literature in Harold Wright's *Cambridge University Studies* (1933).[91]

ARTHUR QUILLER-COUCH (1863–1944) was named the first King Edward VII Professor of English Literature at Cambridge in 1912. His inaugural lectures were published under the title *On the Art of Writing*, and he was an editor of the *New Cambridge Shakespeare* beginning in 1921. He was influential in the development of the English Tripos,[92] leading to the course of study in English at Cambridge about the same time that it was introduced at Oxford. In 1917 an English Tripos was agreed upon, but it was followed by what some called the Golden Age of Cambridge English. I. A. Richards, William Empson, and F. R. Leavis were major figures in this period of the 1920s and 1930s. Quiller-Couch wrote novels about his native Cornwall (*Dead Man's Rock* [1887], *Troy Towers* [1888], *Hetty Wesley* [1903]), and he edited the *Oxford Book of English Verse* (1900) and the *Oxford Book of English Prose* (1923). Quiller-Couch once praised *Spirits in Bondage* (1919), Lewis's lyric cycle of poems, for its rich metaphor,[93] though Lewis did not return the favor, once describing Quiller-Couch's opinion as "valueless."[94] Quiller-Couch was knighted in 1910.

I. A. (IVOR ARMSTRONG) RICHARDS (1893–1979) matriculated at Magdalene in 1911. In 1915 he earned a First Class in part one of the Tripos, graduating in moral sciences (philosophy). He was appointed college lecturer in English and moral sciences at Magdalene in 1919. In 1926 he was elected to the Millington Fellowship at Magdalene, the first Fellow in English at Cambridge and therefore a founding father of the English faculty. F. R. Leavis was one of Richards's most famous pupils. Richards received the D.Litt. degree in 1932 from Cambridge. He became professor at Harvard University in the United States in 1944 but returned to Cambridge annually. Therefore he did not serve on the English faculty during Lewis's years at Cambridge, though he exerted a significant influence. Richards retired from Harvard in 1963 and was made an Honorary Fellow of Magdalene in 1964. His practice of "practical criticism," claiming that literary language was crammed with meaning, is said to have revolutionized the teaching of English literature around the world. Richards was a literary critic and poet. He authored *The Principles of Literary Criticism* (1926) and co-authored *The Meaning of Meaning* (1926) with C. K. Ogden. He also wrote *Science and Poetry* (1926), *Practical Criticism* (1929), *Basic in Teaching: East and West* (1935), *How to Read a Page* (1942), *Basic English and Its Uses*

(1943), and many other books. The word *Basic* stood for British, American, Scientific, Industrial, and Commercial.

Arthur Sale, Magdalene College. See p. 201.

Hugh Sykes Davies (1909–1984), St. John's College, specialized in Wordsworth, Trollope, Lamb, De Quincey, and the English language. He wrote *Petron* (a prose-poem written in his surrealist period, 1935), *The Papers of Andrew Melmoth, The English Mind* (editor, 1964), *Wordsworth and the Worth of Words* (posthumously, 1986), biographies on Trollope and De Quincey, and numerous articles and reviews. A devout atheist but son of a Yorkshire clergyman, he was a Communist during the 1930s and 1940s and also for a time a structural linguist. Davies enjoyed discussing the Italian comic epics with Lewis, though he found Lewis too argumentative at times.[95]

John E. Stevens, Magdalene College. See p. 201–202.

E. M. W. (Eustace Mandeville Wetenhall) Tillyard (1889–1962), Jesus College, was a Fellow in English (1926–1954) and master (see Glossary) of Jesus College (1945–1959). He authored *The Elizabethan World Picture* (1943), a work still read in many schools; *Milton* (1930); *The Miltonic Setting: Past and Present* (1938); and many other works. His historical scholarship and contextual analysis informed the study of sixteenth-century literature and became the foundation for much of what Cambridge undergraduates would study to succeed in their examinations. He is best known to students of Lewis as the man who joined Lewis in the point-counterpoint essays that later comprised *The Personal Heresy.*

George Watson (1927–) came to St. John's College in 1959 as a Fellow in English. He had attended Lewis's lectures in Oxford after he matriculated at Trinity College in 1948. Watson was greatly influenced by Lewis's concept of the Tao and his defense of objective value in *The Abolition of Man.* Watson is the author of *The Literary Critics* (1962), *The Lost Literature of Socialism* (1998), *Never Ones for Theory?* (2000), and general editor of the *New Cambridge Bibliography of English Literature.* He retired in 1991 and continues to live and write at St. John's College.

Basil Willey (1897–1978), professor of English literature, came to Magdalene with a faculty assistant lectureship in English in 1926. He was elected to a lectureship in English in 1934 and the King Edward VII Professorship of English Literature in 1946. He wrote *The Seventeenth Century Background: Studies in the Thought of the Age in Relation to Poetry and Religion* (1934) and *The Eighteenth Century Background: Studies on the Idea of Nature in the Thought of the Period* (1940).

RAYMOND WILLIAMS (1921–1988), a Welshman, read English at Cambridge in the 1930s. He joined the Communist Party during his undergraduate years. He later brought a Marxist interest in literature to his work in English criticism, adopting the approach of F. R. Leavis in reading a text as a tool for social criticism. The author of *The Long Revolution* (1961) and *The Country and the City* (1973), Williams was appointed to a lectureship in English in 1961 as a Fellow of Jesus College, a lectureship in poetry and drama in 1966, a readership in drama in 1967, and a professorship of drama in 1974. In 1952 his *Drama from Ibsen to Eliot* criticized English theater for failing to communicate to modern society. He established his reputation with *Culture and Society: 1780–1950* (1958), a work that portrayed industrial society as the enemy of culture and democracy as in danger. Later, during the 1970s and 1980s, Williams earned a reputation for his support of feminism, ecology, Welsh nationalism, and the armed struggle against imperialism. He retired in 1983.[96]

OTHER FELLOWS OF OXFORD AND CAMBRIDGE UNIVERSITIES

The English Faculty at both Oxford and Cambridge decided upon the English Syllabus as the course of studies in English that undergraduates would follow. They determined the content of the syllabus, including the extent to which the linguistic side of the curriculum was emphasized compared with the literature side. At Cambridge, Arthur Sale and John Stevens laid the foundation that made it possible for Lewis to be offered a position at Cambridge. Both inside and outside the English Faculty, at least eleven of these Fellows attended various meetings of the Inklings (see Glossary) and became close friends of Lewis: Bennett, David Cecil, Coghill, Dyson, Fox, Hardie, Mathew, Stevens, Tolkien, Wain, and Wrenn. Because the Inklings only met in Oxford, some of Lewis's closest friends in Cambridge would never have had the opportunity to meet with them, though they would have, if given the opportunity (e.g., Barrington-Ward, Ladborough).

Other faculty were occasional walking partners or conversation partners of Lewis (e.g., Hyam, McFarlane, Smith), taught the undergraduate Lewis (e.g., Gordon, Wardale, Wyld), shaped the young scholar Lewis (Brightman, Smith, Benecke, Onions, and Webb), held views that Lewis affirmed or opposed (e.g., Leavis, Weldon), wrote works that influenced Lewis's thinking (e.g., Onions, Richards, Tillyard, Tolkien), studied under Lewis (e.g., Bayley, Mathew), or met with him in various settings (e.g., Bradbrook). These individuals were a part of Lewis's academic world and have given us a clearer understanding of Lewis, the educator.

The following section lists those colleagues of Lewis who were not mentioned in his writings or who apparently played only a minor role in his career.

MAGDALEN COLLEGE, OXFORD

ARTHUR WHITE ADAMS (1912–1997), M.A., graduated from Sheffield University, becoming Dean of Divinity and chaplain at Magdalen (1949–1975), Fellow (1949–1979), and emeritus Fellow (1979–1997). He became university lecturer (see Glossary) in theology in 1950 and Grinfield Lecturer from 1953 to 1959.

JOHN LANGSHAW AUSTIN (1911–1960), M.A., OBE, was Fellow and tutor of moral philosophy at Magdalen (1935–1952). He left the college in 1952 to become White's Professor of Moral Philosophy and Fellow of Corpus Christi, Oxford.

JOHN ALFRED BARLTROP (1920–?), M.A., was Fellow and university demonstrator (see Glossary) of chemistry at Magdalen (1946–1948).

MICHAEL GEORGE BARRAT (1927–?), M.A., D.Phil., became a Fellow by Examination (see Glossary) and Hulme Lecturer in Mathematics in 1954.

CHARLES ERNEST BAZELL, M.A., was a Magdalen Fellow in general linguistics (1934–1942). In 1942 he became professor of general linguistics in Istanbul, and he accepted the same position at London University in 1957.

THOMAS SHEERER ROSS BOASE (1898–1974), M.A., became president of Magdalen in 1947 after serving as professor of the history of art for London University (1937–1947). He taught English art and the history of art.

H. L. (HERBERT LISTER) BOWMAN (1874–1942), M.A., D.Sc., Waynflete Professor of Mineralogy.

DONALD GEORGE BROWN (1926–?), became a Magdalen Fellow by Examination in philosophy in 1952 and served at the college until 1955, when he left to become assistant professor of philosophy at British Columbia University.

FRANK ADOLF BURCHARDT (1902–1958) became lecturer in economics at Magdalen in 1941, Fellow in 1948, and Reader (see Glossary) in economics and social statistics in 1950. He left in 1954 to become a Faculty Fellow at Nuffield College.

JOHN HARRISON BURNETTE (1922–?), M.A., FRSE, became Fellow by Examination and university demonstrator in botany (1949–1953). In 1954 he left Oxford to become lecturer at the University of Liverpool.

CYRIL ROBERT CARTER (1863–1930) was Dean of Divinity (1896–1902) and bursar (see Glossary) of Magdalen (1910–30).[97]

ROBERT WILLIAM CHAPMAN (1881–1960), M.A., became a Fellow of Magdalen in 1931, serving until 1947, when he became Clark Lecturer at Trinity College, Cambridge. He was a member of the Friends of the Bodleian and the Oxford Bibliography Society.

CHRISTOPHER ROBERT CHENEY (1906–1987), M.A., FBA, was a Fellow in history at Magdalen (1938–1945), specializing in medieval history. He became professor of medieval history at Manchester University in 1945.

J. T. (JOHN TRAILL) CHRISTIE (1899–1980) graduated from Trinity College, Oxford, and served as Fellow and classical tutor of Magdalen (1928–1932). He left Magdalen to become headmaster at Repton School. He later became principal (see Glossary) of Jesus College, Oxford (1950–1967).[98]

ANTHONY WILLIAM CHUTE (1884–1958) graduated from Winchester College and became a Fellow of Magdalen and Dean of Divinity (1925–1929). He left Magdalen to become vicar of Highfield, Southampton.

KENNETH MCKENZIE CLARK (1903–1983), M.A., FBA, read Greats at Trinity College, Oxford, and was later a Fellow of Magdalen (1933–1937). He served as director of the National Gallery (1934–1945) during this same period and later became Slade Professor of Art at Oxford University

(1947–1950). Clark began to help at the Ashmolean Museum during his undergraduate years and in 1930 was offered the position of keeper. He held such appointments as surveyor of the King's pictures, chairman of the War Artists' Advisory Committee, and chairman of the Arts Council (1953–1960). Clark was well known for his work in television, especially for the 1969 series *Civilisation,* and he authored *Another Part of the Wood* (1974) and *The Other Half* (1977).

COLIN ARTHUR COOKE (1903–2002), M.A., was senior bursar and Fellow (1944–1970).

EDWIN STEWART CRAIG (1865–1939), M.A., matriculated to University College, Oxford, and was later a demonstrator in the electrical laboratory of Oxford (1905–1913). Born in Belfast, Craig was a Fellow of Magdalen (1918–1930), during which time he was vice president of the college (1926–1928), assistant registrar to the Board of Faculties (1907–1924), and registrar of the university (1924–1930). Craig was the parliamentarian among the Magdalen faculty.

ALFRED RUPERT NEALE CROSS (1912–1980), FBA, M.A., was Fellow and tutor in law at Magdalen (1948–1964) and was elected Honorary Fellow of Magdalen in 1975.

CYRIL DEAN DARLINGTON (1903–1981), B.Sc., Ph.D., was Fellow and Sheridan Professor of Botany at Magdalen (1953–1971), where he also became the keeper of the Botanic Garden. He was director of the John Innes Horticultural Institution (1939–1943) and contributed to our knowledge of chromosomes, the gene, and meiosis. In 1947 he founded the journal *Heredity.*

NOEL DENHOLM-YOUNG (1904–?), B.Litt., M.A., D.Litt., became Fellow by Examination (1931–1933) and Fellow by Special Election (1933–1946). He wrote *Handwriting in England and Wales* and *History and Heraldry 1254 to 1310: A Study of the Historical Value of the Rolls of Arms* (1965).

ALEXANDER PASSERIN D'ENTREVES (1902–?), D.Phil., was Serena Professor of Italian Studies and Fellow of Magdalen (1946–1957). He wrote *Natural Law: An Historical Survey* (1965) and *The Notion of the State: An Introduction to Political Theory* (1967).

JOHN CAREW ECCLES (1903–1997), M.A., D.Phil., earned a First Class in medicine in 1925 at Melbourne University, entering Magdalen College, Oxford, in 1925 to study under Sir Charles Sherrington. He earned a First Class in natural sciences from Magdalen in 1927, and he served as research assistant to Sherrington from 1928 to 1931. He was awarded the D.Phil. from Oxford in 1929 for a thesis on excitation and inhibition. He was appointed to an Exeter College Fellowship in 1932, became Fellow and tutor at Magdalen (1934–1937), and became the director of the Kanematsu Institute of Pathology in Sydney, Australia, in 1937. He was professor of physiology of the Australian National University. Eccles continued his research at the Institute of Biomedical Research at Chicago (from 1966) and at the State University of New York at Buffalo (from 1968). He published much of his work, including *The Physiology of Nerve Cells* (1957), *The Physiology of Synapses* (1964), and *Facing Reality* (1970). Eccles became a Fellow of the Royal Society, London, in 1941; a Fellow of the Royal Society of New Zealand; a Fellow of the Australian Academy of Science; was made an Honorary Fellow of Exeter College and Magdalen; and was awarded nine honorary doctorates. He won the Nobel Prize for medicine in 1963 for his work at the Canberra Laboratory and at the Australian National University.[99]

ARTHUR LEE DIXON (1867–1955) was educated at Kingswood School in Bath (1879–1885). He graduated from Worcester College, Oxford, in 1889 with a degree in mathematics. He won a prize fellowship and was appointed a Fellow of Merton College (1891–1922) and Fellow of Magdalen and Waynflete Professor of Pure Mathematics (1922–1945). He was friendly, able to get along with almost anyone, and humble, though not spiritual. Dixon had once been employed by Lewis Carroll (C. L. Dodgson), author of *Alice's Adventures in Wonderland*, as a temporary tutor in mathematics at Christ Church.[100] Dixon was able to speak on a wide variety of topics beyond his field of mathematics.[101] He enjoyed hockey, tennis, squash, and croquet, and he played the flute in an orchestra.[102] In 1912 Dixon was elected FRS, and he served the London Mathematical Society as president from 1924 until 1926. He retired in 1945.

GODFREY R. DRIVER (1892–1975) was professor of Semitic philology (1938–1962) and senior tutor and Fellow of Magdalen (1919–1962). His father, Samuel Rolles Driver, D.D., had been Regius Professor of Hebrew and canon of Christ Church, Oxford. With Alfred Plummer and Charles Augustus Briggs, the elder Driver was editor of the International Critical Commentary on the Holy Scriptures of the Old and New Testaments (ICC). The elder Driver also authored the ICC volume on Deuteronomy and co-authored the ICC volume on Job. The younger Driver graduated from New College, Oxford, becoming a Fellow and classical tutor at Magdalen in 1919. He became university lecturer in comparative Semitic philology in 1927 and Reader in 1928. He was editor of *The New English Bible* and authored *The Hebrew Scrolls from the Neighborhood of Jericho and the Dead Sea* (1951), *Inspiration: Poetical* (1954), *Aramaic Documents of the Fifth Century BC* (1957), as well as many other works.

C. (CESARE) C. FOLIGNO (1878–1963), became a Fellow of Magdalen and professor of Italian in 1926 after serving as Taylorian Lecturer in Italian and Serena Professor of Italian Studies for Queen's College, Oxford (1912–1926).

ARNOLD JOHN FORSTER (1885–?), M.A., LSE, MBE, was Fellow and estates bursar at Magdalen (1930–1940).

J. F. (JOHN FARQUHAR) FULTON (1899–1960), M.A., D.Phil., M.D., attended Harvard University, becoming a Fellow of Magdalen in 1928. He returned to the United States in 1930 to become the Sterling Professor of Physiology at Yale University.

AUSTIN GILL (1906–?), M.A., was Fellow and tutor in modern languages (French) at Magdalen (1945–1950, 1954–1966), and vice president of the college (1960–1962), with an intervening stint as the director of the British Institute in Paris from 1950 to 1954. He wrote *The Early Mallarme* (1988).

JACOB HOWARD EAGLE GRIFFITHS (1908–?), M.A., D.Phil., OBE, was Fellow of Magdalen in physics (1934–1968). He served as university demonstrator and lecturer in physics (1945–1966) and Reader (1966). He was president of Magdalen from 1934 to 1968.

VICTOR KURT ALFRED MORRIS GUGENHEIM (1923–?), M.A., D.Phil., became Magdalen Fellow by Examination in mathematics (1950–1954).

ROBERT W. T. GUNTHER (1869–1940), M.A., Hon. D.Litt., was a Fellow of Magdalen (1897–1928), lecturer (1894–1995), tutor in natural sciences

(1896–1921), librarian (1920–1923), and lecturer in comparative anatomy (1900–1918).

JOHN ALAN HARGREAVES (1929–?), M.A., was a Fellow at Magdalen (1948–1950), leaving Magdalen to serve as a foreign officer for the Economic Intelligence Department.

DAVID GEORGE HOGARTH (1861–1927), M.A., D.Litt., was a Fellow of Magdalen (1886–1927). He was an archaeologist, conducting excavations in Asia Minor, Syria, Cyprus, Crete, Melos, and Egypt. He was also the keeper of the Ashmolean Museum and Antiquarium from 1908 until 1927.

EDWARD HOPE (1886–1953), D.Sc., M.A., was educated at Manchester University and Magdalen. He was a Fellow and tutor in chemistry at Magdalen from 1919 until his retirement, junior Dean of Arts (1926–1928), vice president (1929–1930), and demonstrator in chemistry from 1926. He was quiet, friendly, unassuming, and scholarly.[103]

ALBERT HABIB HOURANI (1915–1993), M.A., was Fellow and university lecturer of modern history of the Near and Middle East at Magdalen (1948–1959). He wrote *History of the Arab Peoples* (1991) and *Arabic Thought in the Liberal Age: 1798–1939* (1983).

WILLIAM HUME-ROTHERY (1899–1968), M.A., D.Sc., OBE, was a Fellow and lecturer in metallurgical chemistry at Magdalen (1938–1943).

GEORGE HUMPHREY (1889–1966), M.A., was a professor of psychology and Fellow at Magdalen in 1947. He left Oxford for St. John's College, Cambridge.

DAVID WALTER STATHER HUNT (1913–1998), M.A., earned a First in classics at Oxford in 1936 and became a Fellow in history at Magdalen (1937–1947). He served as British high commissioner to Cyprus (1965–1967) and ambassador to Brazil (1969–1973). He authored *A Don at War* (1966) and *An Ambassador Remembered* (1975).

PATRICK JOHNSON (1904–1996), M.A., OBE, became a lecturer in physics at Magdalen in 1927 after a demyship (1923–1927; see Glossary). He also was a Fellow (1928–1947), junior Dean of Arts (1932–1934), senior Dean of Arts (1934–1938), and vice president (1946–1947).

Frederick G. Keeble (1870–1952), CBE, Sc.D., M.A., graduated from Caius College, Cambridge. He was the Sherardian Professor of Botany and Fellow (1920–1927). Before coming to Oxford, he was controller of horticulture for the Ministry of Agriculture (1916–1919) and assistant secretary for the Board of Agriculture (1919–1920). He left Magdalen in 1927 to work for Imperial Chemical Industries Ltd.

David George Kendall (1918–?), FRS, matriculated to Queen's College, Oxford, took his M.A. in 1943, and was a Fellow and lecturer in mathematics at Magdalen (1946–1962). During World War II, he worked as an experimental officer with the Ministry of Supply beginning in 1940. In 1962 Kendall was appointed as professor of mathematical statistics at Cambridge. He became emeritus Fellow at Magdalen in 1989. Kendall was a leading authority on applied probability and data analysis. He was awarded the Weldon Memorial Prize and Medal for Biometric Science from Oxford University in 1974, and Princeton University awarded him the Wilks Prize in 1980.[104]

N. R. (Neil Ripley) Ker (1908–1982), M.A., CBE, Hon. D.Litt., was educated at Eton and later took tutorials in English from Lewis as a Magdalen undergraduate from 1929 to 1932. As a postgraduate student, he studied Aelfric's *Catholic Homilies* and completed the B.Litt. thesis. He became lecturer (1936–1946), then a Fellow and Reader in paleography from 1946 until his retirement in 1968. He also served as librarian (1956–1968). Ker wrote *Medieval Libraries in Great Britain: A List of the Surviving Books* (1941, rev. ed. 1964); *A Catalogue of Manuscripts containing Anglo-Saxon* (1957); and contributed to *Medieval Manuscripts in British Libraries*. He was made FBA in 1958, won the 1959 Sir Israel Gollancz Prize (won by Lewis in 1937), was Gold Medalist of the Bibliographical Society in 1975, and received honorary doctorates from Reading University (1964), Leyden (1972), and Cambridge (1975). Ker was appointed CBE for services to paleography in 1979.[105]

Stephen Grosvenor Lee (1889–1962), M.A., was an undergraduate at Magdalen (1908–1912), where he read history. He was assistant master (see Glossary) at King's School, Worchester (1912–1913) and a lecturer at Magdalen (1913–1914). During the First World War, Lee was a captain in the 6th Rifle Brigade (1914–1918), followed by two years as assistant master at Cheltenham College (1919–1920). Lee was a Fellow and tutor in modern history, specializing in the Tudor and Stuart periods, and senior Dean of Arts at Magdalen (1920–1947), as well as vice president (1933–1934). He wrote *A Cromwellian Major-General: The Career of Colonel James Berry* (1938).[106]

KARL JOSEPH LEYSER (1920–1992), M.A., took tutorials at Magdalen with A. J. P. Taylor, graduating with First Class Honors in modern history (1947). In 1948 he became a Fellow and tutor in modern history at Magdalen, where he remained until 1974.

EDWARD GEORGE TANDY LIDDEL (1895–?), M.A., B.Ch., was Fellow and Waynflete Professor of Physiology (1940–1960) after serving twenty years at Trinity College.

R. P. (ROBERT PATON) LONGDEN (1903–?), M.A., attended Trinity College, Oxford, graduating in 1926. He became a Fellow of Magdalen in 1926 before moving to Christ Church to become a lecturer there in 1928.

BRIAN BEYNON LLOYD (1920–?), M.A., was made Fellow by Examination in 1948, Fellow by Special Election and lecturer in physiology in 1952, senior tutor in 1963, and emeritus Fellow in 1970.

MALCOLM HENRY MACKEITH (1895–1942), B.M., B.Ch., M.A., D.M., was Fellow and tutor of Magdalen (1922–1933), demonstrator in the university Department of Human Anatomy (1921–1923), university demonstrator in pharmacology (1922–1933), and dean of the Medical School (1930–1933). He was instrumental in the founding of the British Pharmacological Society in 1931 and served as its first secretary.

WILLIAM JAMES MILLAR MACKENZIE (1909–1996), M.A., CBE, was Fellow and tutor at Magdalen (1933–1948). In 1949 he became professor of government and administration at Manchester University and emeritus Fellow of Magdalen.

JOHN JOB MANLEY (1863–1946), M.A., formerly an undergraduate at Magdalen, was elected a Fellow in 1917. He was also the curator of the Daubenay Laboratory from 1888 until 1929 and science master from 1889 to 1918.

PETER BRIAN MEDAWAR (1915–1987), M.A., CBE, was Fellow at Magdalen (1938–1944), and university demonstrator in zoology (1940–1947). He came to Magdalen as an undergraduate in 1935. In 1938 Medawar received the Edward Chapman Research Prize and was named a Fellow by Examination for his work on organic growth and transformation in animal organs. After becoming Fellow at Magdalen in 1938, Medawar left the college in 1944 to become assistant professor of zoology at St. John's, Oxford. While at St. John's, Medawar worked on penicillin and received the Nobel Prize with Sir Howard Florey in 1945 for his work on the immunology of transplantation.[107] In 1951 Medawar became a Jodrell Professor of Zoology and Comparative Anatomy at University College, London. He also won the Nobel Prize for medicine in 1960 with Sir MacFarlene Burnet for discoveries in the field of immunity. He wrote *The Future of Man* (1959). In 1962 Medawar became the director of the National Institute for Medical Research.

JOHN MELLANBY (1878–1939), M.A., M.D., was Fellow and Waynflete Professor in Physiology in 1936. He later became medical senior professor of physiology at London University.

NICHOLAS AVRION MITCHISON (1928–?), M.A., FRS, was made Fellow by Examination (1950–1954). He left Oxford for the Department of Zoology at Edinburgh University in 1954 and in 1987 become professor of University College of London. He was the founding director of the German Research Center for Rheumatism, established in 1988 in Berlin.

JOHN HUMPHREY CARLILE MORRIS (1910–1984), M.A., DCL, was Fellow, tutor, and, later, university Reader in law at Magdalen (1936–1977).

ERIC BALLIOL MOULLIN (1893–1963), M.A., became a member of Magdalen College and university Reader in engineering and science in 1930 and a Fellow in 1932.

REDVERS OPIE (1900–?), M.A., D.Phil., was Fellow and tutor at Magdalen (1931–1945) and home bursar (1935–1939). Previously he had been lecturer in economy at Durham University (1919–1923) and at Harvard (1924–1930).

LESLIE ELEAZER ORGEL (1912–) earned the B.A. with a First Class in 1949 from Oxford, the M.A., the D.Phil. (1951), and was made Fellow by Examination (1951–1954). He left to become Noyes Research Fellow at California Institute of Technology and later a Fellow of Peterhouse, Cambridge (1956). He was awarded the Harrison Prize in 1957 for his work in inorganic chemistry and was elected a Fellow of the Royal Society in 1962. In the United States, Orgel received a Guggenheim Fellowship in 1971, the Evans Award from Ohio State University in 1975, and the H. C. Urey Medal from the International Society for the Study of the Origin of Life. In 1964 Orgel was appointed Senior Fellow and Research Professor at the Salk Institute for Biological Studies. He is an adjunct professor in the Department of Chemistry and Biochemistry at the University of California, San Diego, and one of five principal investigators in the NASA-sponsored NSCORT program in exobiology. He was elected a member of the National Academy of Sciences in 1990. Orgel wrote *The Origins of Life: Molecules and Natural Selection* (1970) and co-authored with Stanley Miller *The Origins of Life on the Earth* (1974). He has published more than three hundred articles in his research areas.[108]

THEODORE GEORGE BENTLY OSBOURN (1887–1987), B.Sc., M.Sc., D.Sc., was Fellow and Sherardian Professor of Botany at Magdalen (1937–1950) after serving as professor of botany at Sydney University.

JOHN OWEL (ORWELL?) (1925–?), M.A., D.Phil., was made Fellow by Examination (1953–1955).

H. M. D. (HENRY MICHAEL DENNE) PARKER (1894–1972), M.A., graduated from Hertford College, Oxford. He was tutor of Keble College (1921–1923) and a Fellow and tutor in ancient history at Magdalen (1926–1945). He became university lecturer in Roman history in 1928. Lewis usually referred to him as the "Wounded Buffalo" or "Wounded Bison." He was a plain, no-nonsense man with much common sense that he was always willing to share. He lacked appreciation of the arts, read nothing but detective stories, and was not considered by Lewis to be a man of intellect.

W. H. (WILLIAM HENRY) PERKIN (1860–1929), M.A., Waynflete Professor of Chemistry.

ERIC GEORGE PHILLIPS (1909–?), M.A., D.Phil., was a Fellow of Magdalen (1933–1939) and was made university lecturer in mathematics in 1950.

R. L. (REGINALD LANE) POOLE (1857–1939) was a lecturer in history at Jesus College (1886–1910), a research Fellow (1898–1933), and Honorary Fellow (from 1933). He did editorial work for the *English Historical Review* from 1886 to 1920. Elected FBA in 1904, he received honorary doctorates from Oxford, Cambridge, Louvain, and Leipzig.[109]

J. O. (JOHN OSWALD) PRESTWICH (1914–2003), M.A., was appointed to a Junior Research Fellowship by Examination in modern history at Magdalen (1936–1937). He won the Lothian Historical Essay Prize and the Amy Mary Preston Read Scholarship. During World War II, Prestwich served as an intelligence officer at both Bletchley Park and the Pentagon. He was Fellow of Queen's College, Oxford (1937–1981), focusing primarily on Anglo-Norman and medieval history.

ALAN G. RAITT (1930–), M.A., D.Phil., was Fellow by Examination at Magdalen (1953–1955) and became Fellow and tutor in French in 1966. He wrote *The Originality of Madame Bovary* (2002). He is emeritus Fellow of Magdalen and emeritus professor of French literature at Oxford University.

JOHN MORRIS ROBERTS (1928–), M.A., D.Phil., was made Fellow by Examination at Magdalen (1951–1953). He became a Fellow and tutor at Merton College, Oxford, in 1953; Commonwealth Fund Fellow, Princeton and Yale (1953–1954); Fellow and tutor at Merton College, Oxford (1953–1979); acting warden (see Glossary) of Merton College (1969–1970, 1977–1979); senior proctor, Oxford (1967–1968); vice chancellor and professor, University of Southampton (1979–1985); and warden of Merton College, Oxford (1984–1994).

ROBERT ROBINSON (1886–1975), M.A., Hon. LL.D., was Waynflete Professor of Chemistry, succeeding W. H. Perkin, and Fellow of Magdalen (1929–1955) after teaching in Sydney, Liverpool, St. Andrews, Manchester, and London. He was made honorary FRSE and won the Nobel Prize for chemistry in 1947.

GILBERT RYLE (1900–1976), M.A., was a Fellow and Waynflete Professor of Metaphysical Philosophy at Magdalen (1945–1968). He spoke at the Socratic Club on May 26, 1952, on the topic "Subjective and Objective Language." He embraced linguistic philosophy, following the approach of Ludwig Wittgenstein, and was a proponent of philosophical behaviorism, a philosophical development of the work begun by Pavlov. Ryle was the author of *The Concept of Mind* (1949), *Dilemmas* (1954), and *Plato's Progress* (1966).

HERBERT EDWARD SALTER (1863–1951), M.A., Hon. D.Litt., attended New College, graduating in 1887. He became a Fellow of Magdalen in history in 1918 after serving the church as a curate of Sandhurst, vice principal of Leeds Clergy School, vicar of Mattingley, and vicar of Shirburn, Oxon.

ERWIN R. J. A. SCHRÖDINGER (1887–1961), M.A., Hon. D.Sc., was professor of theoretical physics in Stuttgart (1920–1921), Breslau (1921), Zurich (1921–1927), and Berlin (1927–1933). He was a Fellow at Magdalen (1933–1938). He won the Nobel Prize for physics in 1933 and the Matteuci Medal in 1927. He was a member of the Academy of Science of Berlin, Vienna, Leningrad, Dublin, and six other cities.

ROBERT SEGAR (1879–1961) was educated at Stonyhurst and Liverpool University. He became a barrister of the Middle Temple in 1903, and during the First World War, he served as a captain in the Worcestershire Regiment in France. At the age of 40 he became a Commoner (see Glossary) at Magdalen, and after taking his B.A., Segar was lecturer in jurisprudence at Wadham College and tutor in law at Magdalen (1919–1921). He was a Fellow of Magdalen (1921–1935).

CHARLES SCOTT SHERRINGTON (1857–1952), M.A., M.D., Sc.D., became Fellow and Waynflete Professor of Physiology in 1913. In 1932 he was awarded the Nobel Prize in physiology or medicine for his contributions to the understanding of the functions of the central nervous system. Sherrington obtained his degree in medicine from Cambridge in 1885. From early studies of the nervous systems and reflexes of higher mammals, he proved that the stimulation of one set of muscles causes the simultaneous inhibition of the opposing set of muscles. Sherrington originated the words *synapse* and *neuron*. He was knighted in 1922.[110]

HUGH MCDONALD SINCLAIR (1910–1990), B.Sc., M.A., was Fellow and tutor at Magdalen beginning in 1937. His rooms in New Building were close to those of Lewis.[111] Educated at Oriel College, Oxford, Sinclair taught in the life sciences, later becoming a visiting professor in food science for Reading University.

G. R. S. (GEORGE ROBERT SABINUS) SNOW (1897–1969), B.Sc., M.A., attended New College, Oxford, graduating in 1921. He became a Fellow of Magdalen in 1922, publishing papers in various journals on plant sensitivity and correlations between growing parts.

H. C. Stewart (1928–?).

John Walter Stoye (1917–?), M.A., D. Phil., became Fellow and tutor in history at Magdalen in 1948 and vice president in 1969.

Leslie Earnest Sutton (1906–?), M.A., D.Phil., was a Fellow at Magdalen from 1932 until 1973. He became Reader in physics and chemistry (1962–1973).

Arthur George Tansley (1871–1955), M.A., attended University College, London, and Trinity College, Cambridge. He taught botany at University College, London (1893–1906), and at Cambridge (1906–1923). He was a Fellow of Magdalen and the Sherardian Professor of Botany (1927–1937). He was elected an Honorary Fellow in 1944 and was knighted in 1950.

James Matthew Thompson (1878–1956) was Dean of Divinity (1906–1915), home bursar (1920–1927), and Fellow in history (1904–1938). He was especially known for his historical work on the French Revolution. He expressed some of his doubts about his faith in his book *Miracles in the New Testament* (1911).[112]

Patrick John Thompson (1907–1978) attended Malvern and Balliol Colleges, Oxford. He became Fellow and Dean of Divinity at Magdalen (1942–1949).

E. C. (Edward Carol) Titchmarsh (1899–1962), M.A., was lecturer and Reader of pure mathematics at University College, London (1924–1929); professor of pure mathematics at Liverpool University (1929–1931); and a Fellow in mathematics at Magdalen (1923–1930). He later became a Fellow of New College. Titchmarsh was a pupil of G. H. Hardy, Savilian Professor of Geometry at New College, Oxford. Titchmarsh succeeded Hardy as Savilian Professor of Geometry in 1931, carrying on Hardy's work in the school of analysis that Hardy established.[113]

Kenneth Tite (1918–?), M.A., was Fellow and tutor in politics at Magdalen from 1949.

Henry Thomas Tizzard (1885–1959) was made an Honorary Fellow and president of Magdalen (1942–1946).

Gunther Heinz Treital (1928–?), M.A., was Fellow and tutor in law at Magdalen (1954–1979).

C. H. (CUTHBERT HAMILTON) TURNER (1860–1930), M.A., was lecturer in church history, New Testament, and the literature of the early Christian centuries. He became a Fellow of Magdalen in 1889.

MARK DUNBAR VAN OSS (1909–?), M.A., was Fellow and estates bursar (1940–1944).

GEOFFREY JAMES WARNOCK (1923–1995), M.A., was made Fellow by Examination in moral philosophy at Magdalen in 1949 and Fellow and tutor from 1953 to 1971. He also served as principal of Hertford College (1971–1988) and vice chancellor (1981–1985).

ELLIS KIRKHAM WATERHOUSE (1905–1985), M.A., CBE, FBA, MBE, was a Fellow in art history at Magdalen (1938–1947). He became Reader in art history at Manchester University in 1947. In 1949 he became director of the National Galleries of Scotland.

JOHN HENRY C. WHITEHEAD (1904–1960), M.A., FRS, was the son of the Rev. Henry Whitehead, bishop of Madras, India. The famous mathematician and philosopher Alfred North Whitehead was his uncle. After specializing in mathematics at Eton, John Whitehead won a scholarship in March 1923 to study at Balliol College, Oxford, earning a First in 1927. After a year with the stockbrokerage Buckmaster and Moore, Whitehead returned to Oxford and applied for a Commonwealth Fellowship to study for a doctorate at Princeton. After three years at Princeton, Whitehead was awarded his doctorate in 1932, writing a dissertation on "The Representation of Projective Spaces." Whitehead and his doctoral supervisor Veblen co-authored *The Foundations of Differential Geometry* (1932), which is considered a classic in the field. Whitehead was elected to a fellowship at Balliol College in 1933 and became Fellow and Waynflete Professor of Pure Mathematics in 1947 at Magdalen. During World War II, he assisted several Jewish mathematicians in escaping the Nazi purge, and Erwin Schrödinger (see p. 219) lived in Whitehead's home after his escape from Austria. Whitehead was elected FRS in 1944 and served as president of the London Math Society (1953–1955).[114]

DAVID WHITTERIDGE (1912–1994), M.A., FRS, Hon. D.Sc., was Fellow at Magdalen (1945–1950, 1968–1970), the latter period in the Waynflete Chair of Physiology. He held the Chair of Physiology in Edinburgh (1950–1968), bringing that department to a point of international renown. At the Edinburgh Medical School, Whitteridge developed the intercalated science degree for medical students. He was elected to the Royal Society of Edinburgh in 1951 and of London in 1953. Upon his retirement, Magdalen elected Whitteridge to an honorary fellowship, and in 1993 the University of Edinburgh conferred on him the Hon. D.Sc.

LESLIE JOHN WITTS (1898–1982), CBE, was Fellow at Magdalen in the field of physics (1938–1965). As a postgraduate student, he worked with Lord Florey, who discovered penicillin.

JOHN FREDERICK WOLFENSEN (1906–?), M.A., CBE, was Fellow and tutor (1929–1934) and became headmaster of Uppingham.

OSCAR PATRICK WOOD (1924–1994), M.A., was Fellow by Examination (1948–1952) and lecturer in philosophy (1952–1955).

GEORGE DAVID NORMAN WORSWICK (1916–2001), M.A., CBE, FBA, was Fellow and tutor in economics (1945–1965), vice president (1963–1965) and became emeritus Fellow in 1969.

EDWARD MURRAY WRONG (1889–1928), M.A., taught at the University of Toronto and at Balliol College, Oxford (1910–1914). He came to Magdalen as Fellow and tutor in history (1914–1928). He authored a *History of England 1688–1815*. His son Charles took tutorials with Lewis in political science.

JOHN ZACHARIUS YOUNG (1907–?), M.A., FRS, was a Fellow at Magdalen (1931–1945), leaving Oxford in 1945 to become professor of anatomy at University College, London.

MAGDALENE COLLEGE, CAMBRIDGE

D. W. (DENNIS WILLIAM) BABBAGE (1909–1991), OBE, B.A. (1927), was a mathematician and wartime cryptographer at Bletchley Park. He returned to his alma mater as a tutor. He had a faculty assistant lectureship in mathematics (1934–1935) and a lectureship in mathematics (1935–1976). He eventually became president of Magdalene.

R. F. (RALPH FRANCIS) BENNETT (1912–2002), M.A., D.Litt., who became a Magdalene undergraduate in 1929, later became a Fellow in 1938. He held a faculty assistant lectureship in history (1946–1947) and a lectureship in history (1947–1979). During his career, he translated numerous works from German and Latin into English.

J. F. (JOHN "JOCK" FORBES) BURNET (1910–1989) was educated at Christ's College, Cambridge, in Historical Tripos. He became a Fellow of Magdalene and bursar in 1949 after serving as bursar of St. George's Choir School, Windsor; in the Air Ministry during World War II; and as a director of the publisher A. & C. Black. He was a friendly, hospitable man, a devout Anglican, and an expert in the Victorian period, reviewing books on that subject for the *English Historical Review*. His management of the college's funds helped improve the institution's financial standing during his long tenure as bursar.[115]

R. W. M. (REGINALD WALTER MICHAEL) DIAS, M.A., LL.D., originally from Sri Lanka, attended Trinity Hall, Cambridge, as an undergraduate in 1939 to read law. He assumed a lectureship in law in 1951, which he maintained until 1987. He became a Fellow in 1955, serving as Director of Studies in Law and later as president. Derek Brewer mentioned him as a friend of Lewis.[116]

J. B. (JOHN BARTOW) DWIGHT, M.A., M.Sc., matriculated at Corpus Christi College, Cambridge, and read mechanical sciences. After spending ten years in the aluminum industry, he joined Birmingham University in 1958 and came to Magdalene in 1960, when he accepted a lectureship in structural engineering. He accepted a readership in structural engineering in 1973. Dwight is also a Fellow of the Institution of Structural Engineers and a chartered engineer. His research at Cambridge was in structural steel, particularly the problems of buckling and the effects of welding, and he wrote *Aluminum Design and Construction* (1999). He retired in 1984.

STEPHEN GARRETT (1906–1989), professor of mycology, became a Fellow of Magdalene in 1962, holding that fellowship until his death. He was educated at Eastbourne College, Magdalene (1926), and Imperial College, London.

P. J. (PETER JOHN) GRUBB, Sc.D., professor of investigative plant ecology in the Department of Plant Sciences, came to Magdalene in 1961 with a demonstratorship in botany. In 1964 he was elevated to a lectureship in botany. He formerly served as president of the British Ecological Society, did ecological work in Ecuador and the Sahara, and co-authored *Toward a More Exact Ecology* (1989), as well as writing many articles, reports, and research papers. He retired in 2001.

DAVID WYN-ROBERTS was appointed to a faculty assistant lectureship in architecture in 1946, promoted to an assistant lectureship in fine arts in 1949, and in 1950 was made university lecturer in architecture. He became a Fellow in 1958.

F. R. F. (FRANCIS REGINALD FAIRFAX) SCOTT (1897–1969) was educated at Lancing College and Magdalene College, Cambridge. He matriculated in 1919 and earned First Class Classical Tripos, Part I, in 1921 and Part II in 1923. He was Charles Kingsley Bye-Fellow (see Glossary) in 1923 and assistant university printer (1923–1927). He became a Magdalene Fellow and tutor in 1927, proctor (1933), senior tutor (1945–1964), and president (1962–1967).

F. McD. C. (FRANCIS MCDOUGALL CHARLEWOOD) TURNER (1897–1982) was educated at Marlborough College and at Magdalene College, where he read history. His flying career during World War I earned him the M.C. and D.F.C. He became a Bye-Fellow of Magdalene in 1923, a Fellow in 1926, and president (1957–1962). He retired in 1962. He served as college and Pepysian Librarian, precentor, tutor, and Fellows' steward.[117] He wrote *The Element of Irony in English Literature: An Essay.*

JOHN (J. D.) WALSH, history, joined the Magdalene faculty in 1952 as a Bye-Fellow.[118] He later became a Fellow at Jesus College, Oxford. His impression of Lewis as the best-read man he had ever met appears in the first chapter of this book.[119]

An Educational Timeline of C. S. Lewis

Birth: November 29, 1898

Wynyard School: September 18, 1908–July 12, 1910

Campbell College, Belfast: September 1910–November 15, 1910

Cherbourg House: January 1911–July 1913

Malvern College: September 18, 1913–July 1914

Studied under Kirkpatrick: September 19, 1914–April 25, 1917

Scholarship Exam at Oxford: December 5–9, 1916

Scholarship awarded to University College, Oxford: December 13, 1916

Sat for Responsions: March 20, 1917

Enrolled at University College, Oxford: April 29, 1917

Joined Officers' Training Corps: May 1917

Crossed over to France in World War I: November 17, 1917

Arrived back in Oxford: January 13, 1919

Joined the Martlet Society at Oxford University: February 1919

First Class Honours, Classical Honour Moderations: March 31, 1920

Won Chancellor's English Essay Prize: May 24, 1921

First Class, Literae Humaniores: August 4, 1922

Began degree in English language and literature: October 1922

Exams, English language and literature: June 14–19, 1923

Oral Exam (*viva*) for English language and literature: July 10, 1923

First Class, English language and literature: July 16, 1923

Offered one-year appointment at University College for E. F. Carritt, Philosophy: May 1924

First lecture at University College, Oxford, "The Good, Its Position among Values": October 14, 1924

Elected Fellow, Magdalen College, Oxford: May 20, 1925

The Times announcement of Lewis's appointment: May 22, 1925

Beginning of the fellowship: June 25, 1925

First lecture as a Fellow, "Some Eighteenth-Century Precursors of the Romantic Movement": January 23, 1926

Met J. R. R. Tolkien: May 11, 1926

Joined the Coalbiters: Spring 1927

Began lecture series "The Romance of the Rose and Its Successors": October 17, 1928

Exams in Cambridge: August 8–10, 1929

Read paper to Oxford Junior Linguistic Society: January 27, 1930

Late night conversation with Dyson and Tolkien: September 19, 1931

Conversion to Christianity: September 28, 1931

Began lecture series "Prolegomena to Medieval Poetry": January 18, 1932

First meeting of the Inklings: fall 1933

Vice president of Magdalen College: Michaelmas term 1940–1941

First RAF talk: April 1941

Preached "The Weight of Glory" at St. Mary's, Oxford: June 8, 1941

First meeting of the Oxford Socratic Club: January 26, 1942

Delivered the Riddell Memorial Lectures, University of Durham: February 24–26, 1943

Received honorary Doctor of Divinity, University of St. Andrews: June 28, 1946

Lewis on cover of *Time* magazine: September 8, 1947

Anscombe-Lewis debate at the Oxford Socratic Club: February 2, 1948

P. J. Fitzgerald and C. S. Lewis at the Oxford Socratic Club on the topic "Are Tautologies Really Necessary?": October 10, 1949

Last meeting of the Inklings: October 20, 1949

Archibald Robertson and C. S. Lewis at the Oxford Socratic Club on the topic "Grounds for Disbelief in God": February 13, 1950

Michael Foster and C. S. Lewis at the Oxford Socratic Club on the topic "God and History": October 16, 1950

Received honorary Doctor of Letters, L'université Laval, Quebec: 1952

D. E. Harding and C. S. Lewis at the Oxford Socratic Club on the topic "A Living Universe": November 3, 1952

Accepted Chair of Medieval and Renaissance Literature, Magdalene College, Cambridge University: June 4, 1954

Effective date of Cambridge appointment, postponed: October 1, 1954

Inaugural lecture at Cambridge: November 29, 1954

Last tutorial at Oxford: December 3, 1954

Cambridge appointment after dispensation: January 1, 1955

Took up residence at Magdalene College, Cambridge: January 7, 1955

Elected to the British Academy: July 1955

Elected Honorary Fellow, University College, Oxford: March 26, 1959

Received the Doctor of Letters, Manchester University, Manchester, England: May 13, 1959

Received honorary doctorate from the University of Dijon, Dijon, France: 1962

Received honorary doctorate from the University of Lyon, Lyon, France: 1963

Resigned chair at Magdalene College, Cambridge: August 1963

Death: November 22, 1963

GLOSSARY

bursar: the chief financial officer of a college. Some colleges have a senior bursar who handles the overall finances of the college, in particular its estates and investments, and a home bursar who deals with domestic matters, such as the appointment of staff.

Bye-Fellow: a fellowship that carries a year's privilege, allowing the individual to complete a doctorate and remain at the college.

chair: the equivalent of the position held by a full professor in the U. S. system, a luminary in a particular subject who is offered this position at the university level. Those who hold a chair in the British system need not do tutorials.

Coalbiters (or Kolbitar Club): an Oxford club, founded by J. R. R. Tolkien, for dons who wanted to read Icelandic and Norse sagas.

Collections: examinations taken by students at the start of a term to determine their knowledge of the previous term's work and work done during vacation.

Commoner: an undergraduate scholarship won by many.

dean: the head position at Christ Church, Oxford. Also known as senior censor.

demonstrator: "One who exhibits and describes specimens, or performs experiments, as a method of teaching a science; an assistant to a professor of science, who does the practical work with the students" (*Oxford English Dictionary*). In the sciences, the greater part of teaching depends on experimental work; therefore scientists probably spend more of their working lives in the various science faculty buildings than in their colleges. The various science faculties also need members of the staff who will be employed directly by them and have nothing to do with a college. Many demonstrators fall into this category, so one could have the phenomenon of a well-respected scientist enjoying a position of some respect because of his skill as a demonstrator. However, this individual may have no attachment to a college. Thus a university demonstrator would work in one of the central science blocks and might be attached to a college.

demyship: the highest undergraduate scholarship.

don: a Fellow or tutor in a college of Oxford or Cambridge University, derived from the Latin *dominus*, which means master.

exhibitioner: another category of undergraduate scholarship.

Fellow: a professor.

Fellowship by Examination: a fixed-term appointment, usually three years, intended for younger scholars who have been working on or who have just completed their doctoral theses and want to pursue an academic career. Previously awarded by taking an examination, such fellowships now are awarded on the basis of an application, references, and examples of work.

Fellowship by Special Election: special appointments for a variety of reasons, such as the need to keep someone when there are no vacancies or as a tactful way of easing someone out. May also be given for an approved research program.[1] These fellowships offered no fixed salary, unlike normal fellowships, but if such a Fellow taught, he or she would be paid for the number of hours taught.

head: the top position at an Oxbridge college, the equivalent of a president in the U. S. system.

Hilary term: the winter term at Oxford, beginning after Christmas and ending around Easter (January to March); *see* Lent term.

The Inklings: a group of Oxford Fellows and their friends who met weekly during the 1930s and 1940s to read works they were in the process of writing.

Junior Common Room: Similar to the Senior Common Room (see p. 231), the Junior Common Room was an independent club for the undergraduates. Sometimes it included more than one room with fine silver and servants. It always included a dining room. The concerns of those who came to the JCR were food, drink, periodicals, sporting facilities, domestic comforts, and conversations about those topics.[2]

junior student: a student who does not already hold a degree.

lecturer: the rank above Research Fellow, a full member of the college and automatically a part of the faculty.

Lent term: The Cambridge term for Hilary term. *See* Hilary term.

master: the head of Balliol College, Oxford, and all Cambridge colleges, the equivalent of a president in the U. S. system.

Michaelmas term: the fall term (October to December).

neo-scholasticism: a renewal of the study of Thomas Aquinas and other medieval writers, spurred by Pope Leo XIII's 1879 recommendation. The movement centered at the University of Louvain and, by 1920, in the writings of Jacques Maritain and Etienne Gilson.

Oxbridge: Oxford and Cambridge Universities.

president: the second position of authority in an Oxford or Cambridge college but the head of Magdalen College and Trinity College, Oxford.

principal: the term for the head of Jesus College and the head of five former women's colleges.

Professorial Fellow: a Fellow attached to a particular college who has rooms at that college for living accommodations and for research.

Reader: a special title given by a faculty to honor a lecturer of distinction; the grade below professor.

Research Fellow: a Fellow who has a doctorate and may give some lectures in the college while preparing for a lectureship.

senior censor: the head of Christ Church, Oxford.

Senior Common Room: "like an officers' mess, was a club within a club";[3] the place where the dons drank port after dinner while the undergraduates retired to the Junior Common Room (see p. 230). Here the dons conducted meetings about employees, ate, drank, and participated in ceremonial functions. Sometimes called Senior Combination Room in Cambridge.

senior student: a student taking an undergraduate degree who already holds one degree, either from another university or in another subject from the same university.

Trinity term: the spring term, beginning around Easter and ending with summer vacation (April to June/July).

vice president: Fellows were elected to this position at Magdalen College for two years in order of seniority. The position included the duties of presiding after dinner in the Senior Common Room and assigning guest rooms.[4] Lewis served his term in 1940–1941.

warden: another term for the heads of some Oxford colleges, notably New College, Merton, Nuffield, and All Souls; the equivalent of a president in the U. S. system.

Notes

Introduction

1. Lewis, *Studies in Words*, 1.
2. Lewis, *Lion, the Witch, and the Wardrobe*, 47 (*emphasis original*). Professor Kirke spoke almost exactly the same words at the end of the book; see Lewis, *Lion, the Witch, and the Wardrobe*, 186.
3. Lewis, *Lion, the Witch, and the Wardrobe*, 45. He also said much the same at the end of *The Last Battle*; see Lewis, *Last Battle*, 170.
4. Lewis, *Horse and His Boy*, 201.
5. Lewis, *Out of the Silent Planet*, 7.
6. Lewis, *Abolition of Man*, 27.
7. John Wain, review of *English Literature in the Sixteenth Century*, by C. S. Lewis, *Spectator* (October 1, 1954): 403.

Chapter One

1. Lewis is quoting Augustine in this extract from *Preface to Paradise Lost*, 117.
2. Vanauken, *Severe Mercy*, 85.
3. From *Jack: A Life of C. S. Lewis* by George Sayer, copyright 1994, p. 204.
4. Ladborough, "In Cambridge," 100.
5. See Lewis, *All My Road before Me*, 197–200. See also Lewis, *All My Road before Me*, 370f.
6. See Lewis's notes on Herodotus from April 24, 1922, in *All My Road before Me*, 24. A couple of weeks later, Lewis memorized his notes on Immanuel Kant and Greek history. See entry dated May 8, 1922, in Lewis, *All My Road before Me*, 32.
7. Brewer, "The Tutor," 47.
8. Barfield, "In Conversation," 100.
9. Havard, "Philia," 219.
10. Schofield, *In Search of C. S. Lewis*, 6f. See also Musacchio, *Lewis: Man and Writer*, 13.

11. Griffin, *Clive Staples Lewis*, 359f. Only the portions in quotation marks are actually quoted from Griffin.

12. See Fowler, "C. S. Lewis: Supervisor," 73.

13. From an entry dated May 29, 1951, in the unpublished diary of J. O. Reed. Reed won a demyship to Magdalen College and took tutorials with Lewis from 1949 to 1952. Nicholas Mikhailovich Zernov (1898–1980) is the author of *Three Russian Prophets: Khomiakov, Dostoevsky, Soloviev* (London: SCM, 1944).

14. Green and Hooper, *Lewis: A Biography*, 42.

15. Green and Hooper, *Lewis: A Biography*, 141.

16. "Reminiscences" (1) Magdalene, 1948–58, *Magdalene College Magazine and Record*, n. s. 34 (1989–1990): 45–49, in Hooper, *Lewis: A Companion and Guide*, 76.

17. Personal correspondence with Ronald Hyam, June 27, 2002. Used by permission of Ronald Hyam.

18. Personal correspondence with Ronald Hyam, June 27, 2002. Used by permission of Ronald Hyam.

19. Kilby, "Creative Logician Speaking," 19.

20. Lewis, *Surprised by Joy*, 170.

CHAPTER TWO

1. Lewis, *Abolition of Man*, 27.

2. Lewis, *Abolition of Man*, 27.

3. Lewis, *Experiment in Criticism*, 112.

4. Lewis, *Surprised by Joy*, 217.

5. Lewis, "Weight of Glory," 26.

6. Lewis, *Last Battle*, 148.

7. Edmonds, "I Was There," 12.

8. See F. R. Leavis, *Education and the University: A Sketch for an "English School* (London: Chatto & Windus, 1943).

9. Personal correspondence with Geoffrey Stone, March 27, 2003.

10. See Lewis's inaugural address at Cambridge University, "De Descriptione Temporum."

11. Carpenter, *Inklings*, 26f.

12. While most would dispute this contrast, I am using the idea of romanticism as a concept closely related to the imaginative because it is less rational and more intuitive.

13. See Lewis, *Surprised by Joy*, 114. See also his November 17, 1922, entry on Wagner in Lewis, *All My Road before Me*, 138.

14. This book is subtitled *An Allegorical Apology for Christianity, Reason and Romanticism.*

15. Lewis, *Allegory of Love*, 222, cited in Peter Bayley, "From Master to Colleague," 66.

16. From a 1954 letter to the Milton Society of America in Lewis, ed., *Letters of C. S. Lewis* (London: Geoffrey Bles, 1966), 260, cited in Stevens and Lyne, *Centenary Readings from C. S. Lewis*, 19. This letter does not appear in the American edition of *Letters of C. S. Lewis*.

17. Stevens and Lyne, *Centenary Readings from C. S. Lewis*, 20.

18. Stevens and Lyne, *Centenary Readings from C. S. Lewis*, 20.

19. Lewis, "Bluspels and Flalanferes," 157f. See especially Peter Schakel, *Imagination and the Arts in C. S. Lewis* (Columbia, Mo.: University of Missouri Press, 2002).

20. Lewis writes: "Now I tasted the classics as poetry, Euripides' picture of Dionysus was closely linked in my mind with the whole mood of Mr. Stephens' *Crock of Gold*, which I had lately read for the first time with great excitement. Here was something very different from the Northernness. Pan and Dionysus lacked the cold, piercing appeal of Odin and Frey. A new quality entered my imagination . . ." (Lewis, *Surprised by Joy*, 113.).

21. See Lewis, "On Stories," 17, where Lewis talks about how the story can communicate the imaginative life to people.

22. Hooper, "Life of C. S. Lewis," in *Lewis: A Companion and Guide*, 43–44.

23. "Reason," in Lewis, *Poems, 81*, cited in Schultz and West, *Lewis Readers' Encyclopedia*, 65.

24. See Appendix III. The actual title of the book was *The Control of Language* by Alec King and Martin Ketley.

25. Lewis, *Abolition of Man*, 27.

26. *Ethica nichomachea (Nichomachean Ethic)* 1104 B; quoted in Lewis, *Abolition of Man*, 29.

27. Lewis, "Our English Syllabus," 84.

28. Lewis, "Our English Syllabus," 81–82. Cf. Lewis's reflections on Aristotle's views of education in *Abolition of Man*, 10.

29. Lewis, "Our English Syllabus," 85.

30. Lewis, "Our English Syllabus," 84, 86.

31. Lewis, "Our English Syllabus," 86.

32. Ransom, thinking about Hyoi, the hrossa, in Lewis, *Out of the Silent Planet*, 55.

33. Newman, *Idea of a University* (London: Longmans, Green, & Co., 1858).

34. Lewis, "Christianity and Culture," 35.

35. Lewis, "Parthenon and the Optative," 109. The *optative* is a verbal mood in the Greek language that is similar to the subjunctive.

36. The actual title of this report was *Curriculum and Examinations in Secondary Schools: Report of the Committee of the Secondary School Examinations Council Appointed by the President of the Board of Education in 1941*, a report prepared by a committee chaired by Sir Cyril Norwood. See Appendix II.

37. See the September 14, 1923, entry in Lewis, *All My Road before Me*, 268.

38. Lewis also writes about the first type of education in "Lilies That Fester," 36f.

39. Lewis, "Parthenon and the Optative," 111.

40. Lewis, "Is English Doomed?" 28.
41. Lewis, "Is English Doomed?" 29.
42. Lewis, "Is English Doomed?" 30.
43. These are enumerated by Lewis in *Studies in Words*, 130. Music would include the theory of sound, especially physics (Egan, "Prolegomena to Medieval English Literature," 18). Sometimes a fifth discipline—medicine—was added to the medieval educational system (Everest, "Prolegomena to Medieval Poetry," 40).
44. See Everest, "Prolegomena to Medieval Poetry," 29.
45. Lewis, *Discarded Image*, 187.
46. "Grammar meant all about a text—grammar, syntax, etymology, explanation of allusions, metrics, textual criticism—in fact scholarship or learning" (Egan, "Prolegomena to Medieval English Literature," 14; and Everest, "Prolegomena to Medieval Poetry," 29f.).
47. "Out of dialectic came therefore the whole of medieval philosophy" (Egan, "Prolegomena to Medieval English Literature," 14).
48. Rhetoric included poetry and especially consisted of five parts: invention, disposition, elocution, pronunciation, and memory, with elocution the most important of the parts (Egan, "Prolegomena to Medieval English Literature," 16f.; and Everest, "Prolegomena to Medieval Poetry," 34).
49. Lewis, *Surprised by Joy*, 148, where Lewis mentions grammar, dialectic (logic), and rhetoric.
50. Lewis, *Discarded Image*, 185ff.
51. Lewis, *Experiment in Criticism*, 9.
52. Lewis, *Experiment in Criticism*, 82–83.
53. Lewis, *Surprised by Joy*, 231.
54. Lewis, *All My Road before Me*, 236f.
55. Lewis, *Experiment in Criticism*, 129. See also Lewis, "On the Reading of Old Books," 200.
56. Email correspondence with Paul Piehler, June 2002.
57. Brewer, "The Tutor," 45.
58. Paraphrased from correspondence with J. O. Reed, August 2003.
59. Lewis, *English Literature*, 275.
60. Lewis, preface to *Rehabilitations*, vii.
61. Lewis, *English Literature*, 275.
62. Lewis, *Experiment in Criticism*, 30.
63. See Appendices III and IV.
64. Kort, *Lewis Then and Now*, 107. This is what Lewis called "an unregenerate little bundle of appetites" ("Our English Syllabus," 83–84).
65. "Oxford discouraged any narrowly vocational approach to study" (Harrison, "College Life, 1918–1939," 90).
66. Lewis, *Perelandra*, 89.

67. See chapter 4, "Reading and Rereading Books," pp. 59–63.

68. Lewis, "Our English Syllabus," 87. See also Lewis, preface to *Rehabilitations*, vii.

69. Lewis, "Rejoinder to Dr. Pittenger," in *God in the Dock*, 181.

70. Lewis, "Is Theology Poetry?" 106. My thanks to Margaret Humphreys for suggesting this quotation here.

71. This word is borrowed from Taoism and Confucianism, both Chinese religions. It refers to the creative principle that orders the universe.

72. Lewis, *Discarded Image*, 74f. Lewis's precise image is that of a stairway, with God at the top in the medieval model and man at the top in the modern model.

73. Lewis, *Abolition of Man*, 31. See also Lewis, "The Poison of Subjectivism," in *Christian Reflections*, pp. 72–81.

74. Keefe, "Education," 149.

75. Lewis, *Abolition of Man*, 35.

76. Patrick, *Magdalen Metaphysicals*, 126.

77. See Appendix III.

78. Lewis, *Abolition of Man*, 74.

79. Lewis, *Abolition of Man*, 41.

80. Lewis, *Studies in Medieval and Renaissance Literature*, 38.

81. Lewis, *Silver Chair*, 5.

82. Lewis, *Magician's Nephew*, 159.

83. Lewis, "On the Transmission of Christianity," 115.

84. Lewis, "Answers to Questions on Christianity," 61.

85. See Lewis, "If We Have Christ's Ethics, Does the Rest of the Christian Faith Matter?" a presentation by Lewis to the Socratic Club on February 8, 1943, in Hooper, "Oxford's Bonny Fighter," 143f.

86. Kreeft, *Lewis for the Third Millennium*, 95f.

87. Lewis, "Membership," 126.

88. Lewis, "Membership," 127.

89. Lewis, "Membership," 123.

90. See Anne Morse, copyright 2002, www.boundless.org/2001/features/a0000593.html

91. Lewis, "Equality," 17f.

92. Lewis, *Screwtape Letters with Screwtape Proposes a Toast*, 204.

93. Lewis, "Democratic Education," 34.

94. Lewis, "Democratic Education," 33.

95. Lewis, "Democratic Education," 34.

96. Lewis, "Democratic Education," 34.

97. Lewis, "Democratic Education," 34.

98. Lewis, "Democratic Education," 34.

99. Lewis, letter dated August 11, 1959, in *Letters to Children*, 88.

100. Lewis, *Screwtape Letters with Screwtape Proposes a Toast*, 203ff.

101. For example, Screwtape advises Wormwood to attempt to level the playing field by allowing no one to be better than any other; Lewis, *Screwtape Letters with Screwtape Proposes a Toast*, 203. See also, Lewis, *Four Loves*, 47f.

102. Lewis, "Democratic Education," 32.

103. Lewis, "Democratic Education," 32f.

104. Lewis, "Democratic Education," 33.

105. Lewis, "Our English Syllabus," 81f.

106. Lewis wrote about the lack of one joint in his thumbs; see *Surprised by Joy*, 12. He had the joint just below the nail but lacked the joint at the connection to the hand, so he could not fully oppose his thumbs.

107. See a letter dated May 18, 1922, in *Letters of C. S. Lewis*, 161. See also Lewis, *Surprised by Joy*, 90, where he complains about his clumsiness and lack of training in athletics.

108. Lewis, *English Literature*, 275.

109. See Lewis, *Letters to Malcolm*, 3.

110. Although not the same as model schools, the English public schools exhibited many of the same characteristics.

111. Letter dated November 3, 1929, in *Letters of C. S. Lewis*, 261.

112. Lewis, *Voyage of the 'Dawn Treader,'* 2.

113. Lewis, *Voyage of the 'Dawn Treader,'* 28. See also Lewis, *Lion, Witch and the Wardrobe*, 177, where Lewis states that school is where Edmund began to go wrong.

114. See Lewis, *Silver Chair*, 214f.

115. In a January 1963 letter quoted in Green and Hooper, *Lewis: A Biography*, Lewis wrote to *Encounter*: "The whole picture of myself as one forming a cabinet, or cell, or coven, is erroneous. Mr. Wain has mistaken purely personal relationships for alliances. He was surprised that these friends were 'so different from one another.' But were they more different from one another than he is from all of them? Aren't we always surprised at our friend's other friendships? As at all his tastes?" (154).

116. Lewis, *Four Loves*, 30.

117. Lewis, *Surprised by Joy*, 83.

118. From his diary at 28 Warneford Road, entry dated October 16, 1922, in *All My Road before Me*, 120.

119. See the letter to Albert Lewis dated July 10, 1928, in Hooper, ed., *Collected Letters*, 1:767. The word *back-scratching* is correct; it is not *back-stabbing*.

120. Griffin, *Clive Staples Lewis*, 196.

121. For Lewis's thorough description of the inner ring, see "Inner Ring," 107–18.

122. Ladborough, "In Cambridge," 101.

123. Lewis, "Inner Ring," 112.

124. Lewis, "Inner Ring," 117.

125. See John Stormer, *None Dare Call It Education* (Florissant, Mo.: Liberty Bell Press, 1998), with its critique of John Dewey's anti-God views, outcome-based education, and other methods of social reengineering.

126. Lewis, *Abolition of Man*, 26.

127. Lewis, *Abolition of Man*, 20.

128. Lewis also opposed the amateur philosophy of Sigmund Freud when Freud spoke outside of his specialty of psychoanalysis. See "Morality and Psychoanalysis," chapter 4 of Book 3 in *Mere Christianity*, especially p. 89.

129. Lewis, "Historicism," 44. Lewis also writes about the difficulty of achieving a philosophy of history; see "Historicism," 59. See also Lewis, "De Descriptione Temporum," 3.

130. See Lewis, *Discarded Image*, 174.

131. See a letter to Warren Lewis dated December 12, 1927, and written from Magdalen College, Oxford, in *Letters of C. S. Lewis*, 249.

132. Lewis, "Reply to Professor Haldane," 77.

133. Lewis, "Modern Man and His Categories of Thought," 63.

134. Howard, *Lewis: Man of Letters*, 99.

135. Lewis, *That Hideous Strength*, 87, cited in Howard, *Lewis: Man of Letters*, 176.

136. Lewis, *That Hideous Strength*, 185. See also Lewis, "Reply to Professor Haldane," 78.

Chapter Three

1. Lewis, *Lion, the Witch, and the Wardrobe*, 47.

2. Lewis, "Our English Syllabus," 79–93.

3. A September 29, 1958, letter to Martin, in *Letters to Children*, 83. Lewis said the same thing in *Surprised by Joy*, stating his preference for fewer subjects (112f.).

4. Lewis, *Surprised by Joy*, 112–13.

5. Lewis, "Idea of an English School," 75.

6. Lewis, *English Literature*, 275.

7. Lewis wrote about the medieval student in *English Literature*, 61f.

8. Lewis, "Our English Syllabus," 88.

9. A May 18, 1922, letter to Albert Lewis written from University College, in *Letters of C. S. Lewis*, 161.

10. Grammar, logic, and rhetoric are the three subjects of the medieval Trivium. Rhetoric was among the subjects that Prince Caspian was taught by Doctor Cornelius, as was history (see Lewis, *Prince Caspian*, 52f.). See also Lewis, *Discarded Image*, 193, which speaks of the study of rhetoric.

11. Lewis, *Silver Chair*, 8, speaks favorably of French, Latin, and mathematics.

12. Miss Prizzle, the teacher in a modern school in *Prince Caspian*, taught a reconstructed history that excluded the true history of Narnia (see Lewis, *Prince Caspian*, 194). See also a December 12, 1927, letter, in which Lewis wrote about the value of history and the challenge of the historian (*Letters of C. S. Lewis*, 249f.).

13. Lewis's debt to Plato and Aristotle, cited earlier, appears in "Idea of an English School," 64.

14. Lewis, "Learning in War-Time," 42.

15. Music was one of the subjects Cor said he would be learning in Lewis, *Horse and His Boy*, 201. Although Lewis disliked congregational singing, he loved classical music, especially the music of Wagner.

16. Lewis, *Discarded Image*, 185f., cited in note 9 above. Notice the presence of the medieval Quadrivium—arithmetic, music, geometry, and astronomy—in this list of subjects.

17. Lewis wrote about a person who thought that science and education would soon solve the problem of death in "Revival or Decay?" 252.

18. Lewis, "Learning in War-Time," 28.

19. In *That Hideous Strength*, 185, Lewis wrote disparagingly of Mark Studdock that he was unable to appreciate the importance of abstraction and high human tradition.

20. See Lewis, *Out of the Silent Planet*, 27. Cf. Howard, *Lewis: Man of Letters*, 99.

21. Lewis, "Modern Man," 62.

22. Lewis, "Modern Man," 62.

23. Email correspondence with Paul Piehler, June 28, 2002.

24. Lewis mentioned many of the Greek and Roman authors he held in high regard. Among the Romans, Lewis named Boethius, Ovid, Virgil, Juvenal, Cicero, Seneca, Horace, Statius, Claudian, Apuleius, and Pliny the Elder. Among the Greeks, Lewis identified Plutarch, Diogenes Laertius, Theocritus, Longus, and Heliodorus. See Lewis, "Idea of an English School," 65f.

25. Letter 182, written December 17, 1932, in Hooper, *They Stand Together*, 447.

26. Lewis, *Pilgrim's Regress*, Book Ten, Chapter VI, Ignorantia, 185. Used by permission of Eerdmans Publishing Company.

27. Lewis, "Idea of an English School," 69.

28. Lewis, "Idea of an English School," 64.

29. Lewis, "Modern Man," 65.

30. Lewis, *Lion, the Witch, and the Wardrobe*, 45.

31. Lewis, *Mere Christianity*, 52.

32. I am indebted to Angus J. L. Menuge, a former colleague, for this explanation of the disjunctive syllogism. Menuge edited C. S. Lewis, *Lightbearer in the Shadowlands*, a study of Lewis's work as a literary evangelist.

33. Lewis, *Allegory of Love*, 66.

34. See Patrick, *Magdalen Metaphysicals*, 42.

35. Lewis, "Learning in War-Time," 35.

36. Letter XXVII in Lewis, *Screwtape Letters*, 147.

37. Lewis, *Pilgrim's Regress*, 143–45, cited in Patrick, *Magdalen Metaphysicals*, 128. Used by permission of Eerdmans Publishing Company.

38. Lewis, "De Descriptione Temporum," 12–13.

39. See Lewis, "Learning in War-Time," 42.

40. Brewer, "The Tutor," 41, 50.

41. A May 18, 1922, letter to Albert Lewis written from University College, in *Letters of C. S. Lewis*, 161.

42. Carpenter, *Inklings*, 55.

43. See Wain, "Great Clerke," 71.

44. See Carpenter, *Inklings*, 230; and Fowler, "C. S. Lewis: Supervisor," 77.

45. Sayer, *Jack*, 357f.

46. Lewis, "Our English Syllabus," 91.

47. Lewis, "Our English Syllabus," 91. See also Green and Hooper, *Lewis: A Biography*, 150f.

48. Letter 36, dated June 28, 1916, in Lewis, *They Stand Together*, 116.

49. Lewis, "Idea of an English School," 73.

50. Lewis, "Our English Syllabus," 92.

51. Lewis wrote in favor of Old French in "Idea of an English School," 70.

52. Diary entry dated November 2, 1922, in Lewis, *All My Road before Me*, 177.

53. A May 18, 1922, letter to Albert Lewis written from University College, in Letters of C. S. Lewis, 161.

54. Sayer, *Jack*, 260. See also Lewis, "Our English Syllabus," 92f.

55. Lewis, preface of *Essays Presented to Charles Williams* (London: Oxford University Press, 1947), xi.

56. "Letters to Derek Brewer," in Brewer, "The Tutor," 44f.

57. Although he later wrote that English students should know Greek and Latin before they go to university; see Lewis, "Idea of an English School," 77.

58. Brewer, "The Tutor," 45.

CHAPTER FOUR

1. Lewis, *They Stand Together*, 435.

2. Bailey, "In the University," 91.

3. See Martin, *Reading the Classics with C. S. Lewis*.

4. Lewis, *Experiment in Criticism*, 2. See also Lewis, "On Stories," 17.

5. Lewis, *Experiment in Criticism*, 2–3.

6. Lewis, *Experiment in Criticism*, 12.

7. Lewis, *Surprised by Joy*, 199.

8. Lewis, *Surprised by Joy*, 146.

9. Lewis, *Surprised by Joy*, 184.

10. Lewis, *Experiment in Criticism*, 137, 139.

11. Lewis, *Experiment in Criticism*, 85.

12. Lewis, *Experiment in Criticism*, 128.

13. Lewis, *Experiment in Criticism*, 93.

14. Lewis, *Experiment in Criticism*, 106. This is also the proper posture of the creature toward the Creator, according to Lewis. We should submit ourselves to whatever presents itself to us in the moment. See Meilaender, *Taste for the Other*, 18, 33; Lewis, *Letters to Malcolm*, 28.

15. Lewis, *Experiment in Criticism*, 28–30.

16. Lewis, *Experiment in Criticism*, 19.

17. Lewis, "On the Reading of Old Books," 201f.

18. Lewis would include Athanasius in this category, having argued in this fashion in an introduction to Athanasius's work *The Incarnation of the Word of God*. See Lewis, "On the Reading of Old Books," 200.

19. Green and Hooper quote Lewis, who apparently preferred to concentrate on "actual texts and their historical meaning, rather than on modern critical books" (*Lewis: A Biography*, 143).

20. Watson, *Never Ones for Theory?* 93.

21. Lewis, "Is English Doomed," 29. See also Lewis, *Screwtape Letters*, 151, on cutting each generation off from other generations, thus ruining the study of history.

22. Lewis, "On the Reading of Old Books," 202f.

23. Lewis, "Modern Man," 62.

24. Lewis, "Modern Man," 62.

25. Lewis, "Learning in War-Time," 35.

26. Lewis, *Screwtape Letters*, 150.

27. Lewis, *Studies in Medieval and Renaissance Literature*, 2.

28. In the entry dated May 9, 1926, in Lewis, *All My Road before Me*, 390.

CHAPTER FIVE

1. Lewis, *Surprised by Joy*, 184.

2. Sayer, *Jack*, 25.

3. There are two kinds of lawyers in the United Kingdom. A solicitor serves as an intermediary agent between a barrister and his client, whereas a barrister argues a case before a judge.

4. Bresland, *Backward Glance*, 2.

5. Sayer, *Jack*, 29f.; Bresland, *Backward Glance*, 19.

6. Sayer, *Jack*, 43.

7. Lewis, *Surprised by Joy*, 10.

8. See *Lewis Papers*, 3:102.

9. Boxen is an invented country about which Lewis wrote as a boy. The stories featured talking animals and military and political struggles.

10. Lewis attended Wynyard School from September 18, 1908, to July 1910. He attended Campbell College from September 1910 to November 15, 1910. See

Appendix VI.

11. Lewis, *Surprised by Joy*, 23.

12. Robert Capron was declared insane by the authorities two years after C. S. Lewis left Wynyard School. Capron died in 1911 while a resident of Camberwell House Asylum, Peckham, South London. See Hooper, *Lewis: A Companion and Guide*, 797.

13. Lewis, "My First School," 26.

14. Williams and Nicholls, *Dictionary of National Biography*, 1961–1970, 651; Bresland, Backward Glance, 27.

15. Lewis, *Surprised by Joy*, 130.

16. Lewis attended Cherbourg House from January 1911 to July 1913 and Malvern College from September 13, 1913, to July 28, 1914.

17. Lewis calls it "Chartres" in *Surprised by Joy*, 56.

18. Lewis calls it "Wyvern College" in *Surprised by Joy*, apparently under the equation Why did I have to go to Malvern? = Wyvern.

19. Cunich et al., *History of Magdalene College*, 210.

20. Lewis, *Surprised by Joy*, 118.

21. Lewis, *Surprised by Joy*, 112.

22. Lewis, *Surprised by Joy*, 151.

23. Lewis studied with Kirkpatrick from September 19, 1914, to April 25, 1917.

24. Lewis, *Surprised by Joy*, 128.

25. Lewis, *Surprised by Joy*, 135. See the later discussion of the role of logical positivism in Oxford in the 1930s and thereafter (pp. 106ff.).

26. Lewis, *Surprised by Joy*, 135.

27. Lewis, Surprised by Joy, 136.

28. Lewis, Surprised by Joy, 137.

29. In 1935, Oxford removed Cicero and Demosthenes from the requirements of Classical Honour Moderations. See Harrison, *History of the University of Oxford*, 8:116.

30. Lewis, *Surprised by Joy*, 144–45.

31. A January 1915 letter in *Lewis Papers*, 4:131, cited in Hooper and Green, *Lewis: A Biography*, 45f.

32. Personal correspondence from J. O. Reed, May 2003.

33. *Lewis Papers*, 5:74.

34. An entry dated June 28, 1923, in Lewis, *All My Road before Me*, 249.

35. Entry from March 28, 1921, in *Lewis Papers*, 6:269–70.

CHAPTER SIX

1. Lewis, *They Stand Together*, 172.

2. Harrison, "College Life, 1918–1939," 93.

3. *Lewis Papers*, 5:183.

4. *Oxford University Handbook*, 100. "Deemed to have passed" are the exact words that Lewis wrote to his father on January 27, 1919, his first letter to his father after arriving in Oxford after the war; see Lewis, *Letters of C. S. Lewis*, 100.

5. *Lewis Papers*, 6:189.

6. Lewis, *Surprised by Joy*, 137.

7. *Oxford University Handbook*, 18.

8. *Oxford University Handbook*, 102. The Latin means "in Greek and Latin texts."

9. Personal correspondence from P. C. Bayley, April 19, 2003. Daniel Greenstein charts the percentage in the early 1920s, however at about 10 percent; see Daniel I. Greenstein, "The Junior Members, 1900–1990: A Profile," Fig. 3.5 (p. 63).

10. Personal correspondence from Geoffrey Stone, March 27, 2003.

11. *Oxford University Handbook*, 135.

12. For Greek history, students could choose from 776–403 B.C. or 478–322 B.C.

13. For Roman history, students could choose from the First Punic War to the Battle of Actium, the Third Punic War to the accession of Vespasian, or 43 b.c. to the death of Trajan.

14. *Oxford University Handbook*, 132–40.

15. For example, in 1935 Oxford removed Cicero and Demosthenes from the requirements of Classical Honour Moderations; see Harrison, *History of the University of Oxford*, 8:116.

16. *Handbook to the University of Oxford*, 253f.

17. I am indebted to Bishop Simon Barrington-Ward, Honorary Fellow in Residence of Magdalene College, Cambridge, and Honorary Assistant Chaplain, for this description of the tutorial system. This description is based on a personal interview conducted with Barrington-Ward in his rooms at Magdalene College, January 10, 2003. His rooms are a portion of those in which Lewis lived during his tenure at Cambridge.

18. Lewis, *All My Road before Me*, 126, 131, 147, 196.

19. Graham, *We Remember C. S. Lewis*.

20. A. Flexner, *Universities, American, English, German*, 275.

21. Lewis, *All My Road before Me*, 120.

22. Lewis, *Letters to an American Lady*, 35. Used by permission of Eerdmans Publishing Company.

23. The English School was the collective English faculty across Oxford University. The English School set the course of study in English for undergraduates in all of the colleges.

24. Bell, "Oxford's Contribution to Modern Studies in the Arts," 211f.

25. In this context, the word *syllabus* means what some would indicate by the word *curriculum*. Thus the syllabus is a collection of courses, or subjects, that must be studied in the pursuit of an academic degree.

26. A course is an entire three- or four-year course of study rather than what Americans would call a single three-credit semester-long class. What is described as a paper in the English School is much closer to a semester-long course in the U.S. higher educational system.

27. Currie, "Arts and Social Studies," 114.

28. Unpublished letter of C. S. Lewis to J. O. Reed, July 8, 1947.

29. Entry dated March 8, 1950, in the unpublished diary of J. O. Reed.

30. Currie, "Arts and Social Studies," 121f.

31. Cunningham, "Literary Culture," 437.

32. Lewis attended from April 26, 1917, to June 8, 1917, and from January 13, 1919, to July 10, 1923.

33. Lewis, *All My Road before Me*, 55.

34. The title "master" refers to the number one position at University College, while the title "president" refers to the number two position. The terms differ from college to college within the Oxbridge system. See also the Glossary.

35. Green and Hooper, *Lewis: A Biography*, 47.

36. Bramlett and Higdon, *Touring C. S. Lewis' Ireland and England*, 25.

37. *Oxford University Handbook*, 230.

38. Sayer, *Jack*, 116, 118.

39. Lewis, *Surprised by Joy*, 187.

40. Writing to Albert Lewis on June 8, 1917, the younger Lewis stated that six months of service would exempt him from Responsions; see *Letters of C. S. Lewis*, 59.

41. Arthur Blackburne Poynton (1867–1944) took a First in Classics at Balliol College in 1889, was elected to a fellowship at Hertford College in 1890, and went to University College in 1894 as Fellow and praelector in Greek and tutor in classical scholarship. He was a brilliant classical teacher, an expert especially in Greek oratory. He was master of University College from 1935 to 1937. See Lewis, *All My Road before Me*, 468.

42. Hooper, *Collected Letters*, 1:444.

43. E. F. (Edgar Frederick) Carritt (1876–1964) was a Fellow and praelector in philosophy at University College from 1898 to 1941. He was Lewis's tutor in philosophy. Carritt was an excellent lecturer and a devoted socialist, publishing *Theory of Beauty* (1914), *Philosophies of Beauty* (1931), and *Ethical and Political Thinking* (1947). See Lewis, *All My Road before Me*, 461. See also a letter in which Lewis mentions having two tutors at this time (Hooper, *Collected Letters*, 1:485). According to Walter Hooper, in 1906 George Hope Stevenson was elected to a fellowship at University College as praelector in ancient history, remaining there until he retired in 1949. See Lewis, *All My Road before Me*, 470.

44. Patrick, *Magdalen Metaphysicals*, 2. Moral science is philosophy.

45. Como, *Lewis at the Breakfast Table*, xxiiif.

46. Patrick, *Magdalen Metaphyiscals*, 2.

47. *Handbook to the University of Oxford,* 135–37.

48. Lewis, *Surprised by Joy,* 167.

49. Lewis, *All My Road before Me,* 184, which refers to M. C. Gordon, *The Life of George S. Gordon 1881–1942* (Oxford: Oxford University Press, 1945).

50. Green and Hooper, *Lewis: A Biography,* 75.

51. Carpenter, *Inklings,* 13.

52. Personal correspondence from Hugh Whitney Morrison, April 9, 2003. Morrison attended Oxford on a Rhodes Scholarship, reading the Honours School of English Language and Literature and gaining Second Class in 1932. His tutors were Percy Simpson and Edmund Blunden. His examiners were C. S. Lewis, J. R. R. Tolkien, E. V. Gordon, and Percy Simpson. He received his master's degree from Oxford in 1964.

53. Annan, *The Dons,* 25.

54. Described as "The Chancellor's Prize for an English Essay" in *Oxford University Handbook,* 215.

55. A June 17, 1921, letter to Albert Lewis, in Hooper, *Lewis: Collected Letters,* 1:551f.

56. Patrick, *Magdalen Metaphysicals,* 117. Only the outline of this essay remains: "1. Introduction, 2. Objectivity of Value, 3. Statement of Problems, 4. Same Continued, 5. Philebus and Republic, 6. Critique, 7. Utilitarian Ethics, 8. Critique, 9. Kantian Ethics, 10. Critique, 11. Fundamental Errors of both these theories, 12. Practical Hegemony of the Moral Value, 13. Basis of Obligation, 14. Summary" (Patrick, *Magdalen Metaphysicals,* 127n).

Chapter Seven

1. Lewis, *Out of the Silent Planet,* 7.

2. A reading of *Pilgrim's Regress* will demonstrate those influences that Lewis saw in Oxford during the 1920s, many of them described below.

3. Musacchio, "Exorcising the Zeitgeist," 213–34.

4. Sayer, *Jack,* 176.

5. Patrick, *Magdalen Metaphysicals,* 60.

6. See Appendix VI.

7. *The Times,* May 22, 1925, cited in Hooper, *Collected Letters,* 1:642.

8. Makin, "Magdalene College Cambridge," 2.

9. According to Bishop Simon Barrington-Ward, those who give this extra tuition (extra to the university lectures, that is) are called tutors at Oxford University, and their periods of tuition are called tutorials. Lewis served in this function in addition to lecturing. At Magdalene College, Cambridge, the role is called supervisor and the periods of tuition on the side are called supervisions. The person in charge in a pastoral and legal capacity is called a tutor at Cambridge and a moral tutor at Oxford.

10. A May 10, 1921, letter to Warren Lewis, in *Letters of C. S. Lewis,* 131. See also chapter 1 and the Annexe, especially p. 9, in Annan, *The Dons.* Annan speaks of the dynasties and the aristocracy that the dons created.

11. Lewis, *Allegory of Love*, vii.

12. The Martyrs' Memorial on St. Giles, a street moving north from the center of town, was built in their remembrance in 1841 as a reaction to the Oxford Movement under John Cardinal Newman.

13. This, the oldest part of the library at Oxford, was built in 1488 and named after the Duke of Gloucester (1390–1447), who donated many manuscripts to the library in the fifteenth century. The duke is most famously portrayed in Shakespeare's *Henry IV*, Parts 1–2.

14. *The University City of Oxford* (Andover, Hampshire: Pitkin Pictorials, 1995), 17.

15. Magdalen College Archives: C. E. Saltzman, S. Weston, W. A. Breyfogle, R. McK. Campbell, E. L. Skinner, N. A. F. Williams, H. W. Piper, R. L. Gordon, R. W. Burchfield, W. C. Clemons, W. V. Whitehead, W. B. Patterson, and R. J. Selig.

16. Bramlett and Higdon, *Touring C. S. Lewis' Ireland and England*, 19.

17. Betjeman, *Oxford University Chest*, 148.

18. This would comprise the years 1925 to 1954.

19. Havard, "Philia," 217.

20. Lewis, *Surprised by Joy*, 208.

21. Como, *Lewis at the Breakfast Table*, xxxi.

22. Rowse, *Oxford in the History of England*, 221. Rowse was Fellow of All Souls College, Oxford.

23. Soddy worked on research that led to the splitting of the atom and the beginning of nuclear physics; see Rowse, *Oxford in the History of England*, 246.

24. Musacchio, "Exorcising the Zeitgeist," 222.

25. Musacchio, "Exorcising the Zeitgeist," 228.

26. Webster, "Medicine," 317–43.

27. Wain, *Sprightly Running*, cited in Harrison, 295.

28. Turner, "Religion," 295–316.

29. Cited in Kort, *Lewis Then and Now*, 19.

30. Cunningham, "Literary Culture," 413–50.

31. James Patrick uses the word *metaphysicals* because the philosophy of the four Magdalen metaphysicals tended toward poetry—similar to the achievement of the seventeenth-century metaphysical poets Donne, Cowley, Crashaw, and Herbert—and because they wrote as if philosophy were a literary genre. They saw language as a kind of truth, whereas many of their Oxford contemporaries thought of poetry and language as incapable of carrying truth. See Patrick, *Magdalen Metaphysicals*, xix.

32. Patrick, *Magdalen Metaphysicals*, xviii–xix.

33. Lewis, *Surprised by Joy*, 209.

34. Lewis, "Bluspels and Flalansferes," 157.

35. Lewis, *Surprised by Joy*, 209.

36. Patrick, *Magdalen Metaphysicals*, 4, 12–16.

37. Sayer, *Jack*, 219.

38. Patrick, *Magdalen Metaphysicals*, xix–xx.

39. Patrick, *Magdalen Metaphysicals*, 149.

40. Patrick, *Magdalen Metaphysicals*, 140–42.

41. Patrick, *Magdalen Metaphysicals*, xxvf.

42. Patrick, *Magdalen Metaphysicals*, 19.

43. Williams and Nicholls, *Dictionary of National Biography, 1961–1970*, 652. Lewis wrote in his diary on March 8, 1924, about Alexander's *Space, Time, and Deity*; see Lewis, *All My Road before Me*, 301.

44. See Appendix I for specific volumes.

45. Lewis, *All My Road before Me*, 138.

46. Mitchell, "Lewis and the Oxford University Socratic Club," 336.

47. Patrick, *Magdalen Metaphysicals*, 137.

48. Patrick, *Magdalen Metaphysicals*, 151. See the description of J. A. Smith in Appendix V.

49. Carpenter, *Inklings*, 207.

50. See "Adam Fox" in Appendix V.

51. Patrick, *Magdalen Metaphysicals*, 139.

52. See Appendix III and Appendix IV.

53. Morris, *Oxford Book of Oxford*, 374, 381.

54. Rowse, *Oxford in the History of England*, 223.

55. Rowse, *Oxford in the History of England*, 225, 236, 238, 240.

56. Betjeman, *Summoned by Bells*, 101–2.

57. Patrick, *Magdalen Metaphysicals*, 152.

58. Patrick, *Magdalen Metaphysicals*, 152f.

59. Turner, "Religion," 309.

60. Sir Israel Gollancz (1863–1930) lectured in English at University College, London, from 1892, at Cambridge from 1896, and at King's College, London, from 1905 until his death. He was one of the founders of the British Academy and its first secretary. The Sir Israel Gollancz Prize was established in 1924. It is awarded biennially for published work in Anglo-Saxon, early English language and literature, English philology, the history of English language, or for work done on the history of English literature (the category for which Lewis was selected) or on the works of English writers.

61. Griffin, *Clive Staples Lewis*, 83.

62. Bayley, "From Master to Colleague," 82.

63. Lawlor, *Lewis: Memories and Reflections*, 103.

64. Lewis, *All My Road before Me*, 321.

65. Tillyard's essay on Milton and T. S. Eliot's essay on Dante were offenders of the personal heresy. Green and Hooper, *Lewis: A Biography*, 125.

66. Lewis, "Christianity and Culture," 19. Used by permission of Eerdmans Publishing Company.

67. Email correspondence with Paul Piehler, October 31, 2002.

68. Hooper, "Oxford's Bonny Fighter," 174–85.

69. Hewish, "Radioastronomy in Cambridge," 48–57.

70. Griffin, *Clive Staples Lewis*, 215. The former was published on March 19, 1943, and the latter on March 26.

71. Lewis, "Dogma and the Universe," 42.

72. Lewis, *Surprised by Joy*, 203f.

73. Bramlett and Higdon, *Touring C. S. Lewis' Ireland and England*, 23f.

74. Morris, *Oxford Book of Oxford*, 376f.

75. Green and Hooper, *Lewis: A Biography*, 279.

76. Charles Wrong was Lewis's pupil briefly in political science for the obligatory exam known as Pass Moderations (1935–1936). After that exam, Wrong had a different tutor because his field was modern history. He graduated in 1938. He is the son of Edward Murray Wrong, mentioned in Appendix V.

77. Based on research done in the Magdalen College Archives, Dr. Robin Darwall-Smith, archivist. Records were unavailable for Michaelmas term, 1925; Trinity term, 1926; Michaelmas term, 1926; Hilary term, 1927; Trinity term, 1928; and Trinity term, 1929.

78. Griffin, *Clive Staples Lewis*, 243, 254.

79. The British Academy was established by royal charter in 1902 as the United Kingdom's national academy for the humanities and social sciences. It currently exists as a self-governing fellowship of approximately 750 scholars. Fellows are elected by the British Academy at the Annual General Meeting each year in July. Its counterpart is the Royal Society, which serves the natural sciences. See www.britac.ac.uk.

80. Williams and Nicholls, *Dictionary of National Biography, 1961–1970*, 653. The full name of the honor that Lewis was offered is "The Most Excellent Order of the British Empire." It was established in 1917 by King George V and has two divisions: a civil and a military division, each with five classes, one of which is Commander. It recognizes those who helped in the war effort, whether as a combatant or as a civilian. Since 1918, it has been used to reward service to the state through distinguished service to the arts and sciences, public service, and work with charitable and welfare organizations. It is an order of chivalry with more than 100,000 members. Its motto is "For God and the Empire," and St. Paul's Cathedral is the chapel of the Order. See www.royal.gov.uk/output/Page498.asp.

81. Griffin, *Clive Staples Lewis*, 326.

82. Hooper, "Oxford's Bonny Fighter," 168.

83. Lewis, *Experiment in Criticism*, 6.

84. Green and Hooper, *Lewis: A Biography*, 76. See also Lewis, *All My Road before Me*, 272.

85. Lewis, *All My Road before Me*, 294, 296. See also Hooper, *Collected Letters*,

1:623f.

86. Sayer, *Jack*, 329.

87. Burk, *Troublemaker*, 93.

88. *Handbook to the University of Oxford*, 399.

89. Hooper, *Collected Letters*, 1:642. The text from *The Times* read as follows: "NEW FELLOW OF MAGDALEN COLLEGE. The President and Fellows of Magdalen College have elected to an official Fellowship in the College as Tutor in English Language and Literature, for five years as from next June 15, Mr. Clive Staples Lewis M.A. (University College). Mr. Lewis was educated first at Malvern College. He won a scholarship in classics at University College in 1916, and, (after war service) a first class in Classical Moderations in 1920, the Chancellor's prize for an English essay in 1921, a first class in Literae Humaniores in 1922, and a first class in the Honour School of English Language and Literature in 1925" (May 22, 1925, cited in Hooper, *Collected Letters*, 1:642; permission to reprint granted by the President and Fellows of Magdalen College, Oxford).

90. See Appendix VI.

91. Bramlett and Higdon, *Touring C. S. Lewis' Ireland and England*, 81.

92. Hooper, *Lewis: A Companion and Guide*, 124–26.

CHAPTER EIGHT

1. Lewis, writing from Cambridge, "Interim Report," 93f.

2. Literally, "On a description of the times."

3. He wrote about this in jest, stating, "I shall haunt the place whence the most valued of my honours came" (Lewis, *Letters of C. S. Lewis*, 509).

4. Williams and Nicholls, *Dictionary of National Biography, 1961–1970*, 652. See also Green and Hooper, *Lewis: A Biography*, 281.

5. From a conversation with Dr. Richard Luckett at Magdalene College, Cambridge, January 10, 2003.

6. *Jarrold Guide to the University City of Cambridge* (Norwich: Jarrold, 1995).

7. Cunich et al., *History of Magdalene College*, 9.

8. Cunich et al., *History of Magdalene College*, 32.

9. Cunich et al., *History of Magdalene College*, 40.

10. Prothero, "Magdalene College, Cambridge," 5.

11. Cunich et al., *History of Magdalene College*, 22.

12. Cunich et al., *History of Magdalene College*, 222.

13. Cunich et al., *History of Magdalene College*, 225.

14. Cunich et al., *History of Magdalene College*, 252.

15. This would comprise the years 1955 to 1963.

16. Lewis, *Latin Letters of C. S. Lewis*, 95. G. E. Moore and Bertrand Russell represented the Cambridge phase of the realist and positivist movement; see Patrick, *Magdalen Metaphysicals*, 136.

17. A November 1, 1954, letter, in Lewis, *Letters to an American Lady*, 35.

18. Havard, "Philia," 224.

19. Catherwood, *Lewis: A Brief Life*, 12.

20. Watson, *Never Ones for Theory?* 53.

21. Hooper, "Oxford's Bonny Fighter," 168.

22. Robinson was the Anglican bishop of Woolwich (1919–1983). He served as bishop from 1959 to 1969. *Honest to God* was considered by many to deny the existence of a personal God. In a February 22, 1966, article in *Look* magazine, James A. Pike said that Robinson had set aside "the Trinity, the Virgin Birth and the Incarnation" (John Warwick, Montgomery, *Suicide of Christian Theology* [Minneapolis: Bethany Fellowship], 231).

23. John A. T. Robinson, *Honest to God*.

24. Lewis attacked Alec Vidler's Windsor Sermons, published in 1958, in the essay "Fern-Seed and Elephants," otherwise known as "Modern Theology and Biblical Criticism" (in Lewis, *Fern-Seed and Elephants*). In that essay Lewis challenged many of the assumptions of modern liberal theology.

25. Letter dated August 2, 1956, in *Letters of C. S. Lewis*, 458.

26. Lewis, "Parthenon and the Optative," 111f.

27. Dean, "Last Critic?" accessed at http://www.newcriterion.com/archive/14/jan96/dean.htm.

28. Mason, *Cambridge Minds*, 30f.

29. Mason, *Cambridge Minds*, 29–31.

30. Annan, *The Dons*, 58.

31. Lewis, "Interim Report," 93f.

32. Carpenter, *Inklings*, 63, 246.

33. Carpenter, *Inklings*, 246.

34. Annan, *The Dons*, 58.

35. Davie in Hayman, *My Cambridge*, cited in Watson, *Never Ones for Theory?* 74.

CHAPTER NINE

1. Lewis, commenting on the lectures of Gilbert Murray; *Preface to Paradise Lost*, 28. Murray (1866–1957) was Regius Professor of Greek at Oxford from 1908 to 1936.

2. Bailey, "In the University," 79.

3. Brewer, "The Tutor," 52.

4. Green and Hooper, *Lewis: A Biography*, 81.

5. Edmonds, "I Was There," 3.

6. "Harry Blamires," 82, 84.

7. Carpenter, *Inklings*, 20, 58.

8. Bailey, "In the University," 88.

9. Graham, *We Remember C. S. Lewis*, 7.

10. Personal correspondence with Charles Arnold-Baker, February 16, 2003.

11. Edmonds, "I Was There," 1f.

12. Email correspondence with Paul Piehler, October 31, 2002.

13. Email correspondence with Paul Piehler, June 24, 2002.

14. Graham, *We Remember C. S. Lewis*, 59f.

15. Graham, *We Remember C. S. Lewis*, 47.

16. Lewis mentions the later British poet laureate several times in *All My Road before Me* as being poorly prepared. See the entries on April 28, 1926; May 5, 1926; May 27, 1926; June 4, 1926; June 11, 1926; January 19, 1927; January 31, 1927; and February 5, 1927. However, on May 29, 1926; June 3, 1926; June 14, 1926; February 7, 1927; and February 11, 1927, Lewis speaks well of Betjeman's work.

17. Lawlor, *Lewis: Memories and Reflections*, 7.

18. Fowler, "C. S. Lewis: Supervisor," 69.

19. Bayley, "From Master to Colleague," 78, 80.

20. Brewer, "The Tutor," 64.

21. Rigby, "Solid Man," 39.

22. Stevens and Lyne, *Centenary Readings from C. S. Lewis*, 4.

23. Lawlor, *Lewis: Memories and Reflections*, 3, 9. Alastair Fowler writes that Lewis "generally followed the adversarial system" (Fowler, "C. S. Lewis: Supervisor," 68).

24. Edmonds, "I Was There," 11.

25. Graham, *We Remember C. S. Lewis*, 62.

26. Personal correspondence with F. L. Hunt, dated January 31, 2003. Hunt took tutorials from Lewis in Oxford during the early 1950s. This quotation comes from Keats's August 16, 1820, letter to Shelley, evidently alluding to the Mammon episode in Spenser's *Faerie Queene*, Book II, Canto VII, stanza xxviii: "Embost with massy gold of glorious gift, And with rich metall loaded every rift," with the idea that Keats wanted richly textured verse. Thanks to J. O Reed for this insight.

27. Personal correspondence with A. E. F. Davis, February 17, 2003.

28. Bayley, "From Master to Colleague," 77. Alastair Fowler claimed it was Botticelli's *Mars and Venus*, also from the National Gallery, London. Given Lewis's Space Trilogy, this version seems more likely.

29. Email correspondence with Donald Whittle, January 31, 2003. Whittle matriculated at Magdalen College, Oxford, in 1943. After war service, he took his degree in modern history (1947–1949) at a time when Lewis helped with tutorials for the History School. Whittle did a term with Lewis on the political science paper in the modern history degree that consisted of a study of Aristotle, Hobbes, and Rousseau. Edward L. Edmonds (University College, 1934–1937) described the tutorial differently: "Lewis' own ritual rarely changed. He would first scrutinize his vast array of pipes, some short, some long: one of them was an old church warden type of pipe, white with a long stem, of the kind familiar from the painting of the Wellers at the table in the yard of the hostelry. Lewis

usually chose a short, curvy stemmed, chubby rosewood one. He delved into his pouch of tobacco, or more rarely a tin ('Three Nuns,' he once archly told me), thumbed into place a nicely rounded wad, lighted up with a blue cloudy flourish, reclined back in his own easy chair on the right of the fire, and motioned me to begin. Whilst I read, he puffed away steadily at his pipe; and I should add that Lewis was no dilettante with his pipe. He loved a good cloud, including from time to time a few smoke rings of varied convolutions" ("I Was There," 1).

30. Graham, *We Remember C. S. Lewis*, 57.

31. Lawlor, *Lewis: Memories and Reflections*, 6.

32. "Harry Blamires," 84.

33. Edmonds, "I Was There," 1.

34. Personal correspondence with A. E. F. Davis, February 17, 2003.

35. Graham, *We Remember C. S. Lewis*, 42.

36. Entry dated February 8, 1950, in the unpublished diary of J. O. Reed. A copy of Reed's essay is part of the collection at the Wade Center, Wheaton College, Wheaton, Illinois.

37. Entry dated June 9, 1950, in the unpublished diary of J. O. Reed.

38. This poem is probably by Lewis, written in response to Reed's confusion of the spelling of *satire* with *satyr*.

39. The Minor Poems are *L'Allegro, Il Penseroso, Lycidas, Comus*, etc., by Milton.

40. The August Eclogue is a portion of Spenser's *Shepherd's Calendar*.

41. An entry dated October 16, 1950, in the unpublished diary of J. O. Reed.

42. Dr. J. Stanley Mattson is the president of the C. S. Lewis Foundation, Redlands, California, which owns The Kilns, conducts triennial Lewis conferences at Oxford and Cambridge, and seeks to connect with Christian higher education faculty throughout the world.

43. Lawlor, *Lewis: Memories and Reflections*, 116.

44. Schofield, *In Search of C. S. Lewis*, 7. See also Musacchio, *Lewis: Man and Writer*, 13.

45. See Hooper, *Lewis: A Companion and Guide*, 35.

46. The Clark Lectures at Trinity College were started in 1884 by Leslie Stephen. T. S. Eliot gave those lectures in 1926 on a new theory of poetry. See Watson, *Never Ones for Theory?* 36.

47. The introduction was entitled "Old Learning and New Ignorance." See Hooper, *Lewis: A Companion and Guide*, 73, 524f.; and Graham, *We Remember C. S. Lewis*, 67.

48. Bailey, "In the University," 82.

49. "Don v. Devil," *Time* (September 8, 1947).

50. Mathew, "Orator," 96.

51. Brewer, "The Tutor," 54.

52. Graham, *We Remember C. S. Lewis*, 50.

53. Graham, *We Remember C. S. Lewis*, 57. Edward Edmonds wrote of Lewis's lectures: "These were a joy! Lewis throve on large audiences (his own love of strong verbs will here be apparent!); and he could be heard even at the back of the room! He did not do too many, as I recall, and the series I best remember were Prolegomena to Medieval Literature. Strangely enough I don't remember much about the literature, but I do recall how he talked at length about such literary devices as circumlocutio and expolitio. He loved to 'expatiate and confer' about medieval cosmology, including the 'three times three' hierarchy of angels . . . . It was in this series of lectures that he emphasized the importance of medieval order. He alluded to the crucial importance of Lady Macbeth's request, 'stand not on the order of your going': the importance of that line, as a clue to the disintegration of Macbeth's power, has stayed with me ever since" ("I Was There," 4).

54. Graham, *We Remember C. S. Lewis*, 151.

55. Fowler, "C. S. Lewis: Supervisor," 74.

56. Hooper, *Lewis: A Companion and Guide*, 72.

57. Sayer, *Jack*, 358.

58. Mathew, "Orator," 96.

59. Graham, *We Remember C. S. Lewis*, 67.

60. Como, *Lewis at the Breakfast Table*, xxi; Brewer, "The Tutor," 54. Personal correspondence from Michael Figgis, who read English at Queen's College (1946–1948), and Hugh Whitney Morrison, who attended Merton College (1930–1934).

61. Graham, *We Remember C. S. Lewis*, 72.

62. Babbage, "To the Royal Air Force," 71.

63. Sayer, *Jack*, xviii.

64. Sayer, *Jack*, 177.

65. Graham, *We Remember C. S. Lewis*, 153.

66. Graham, *We Remember C. S. Lewis*, 71.

67. An August 28, 1924 entry in *Lewis Papers*, 8:260.

68. Personal correspondence with Charles Arnold-Baker, February 16, 2003.

69. Graham, *We Remember C. S. Lewis*, 7.

70. See Roger Lancelyn Green in *Lewis: A Biography*. Cited in Hooper, *Lewis: A Companion and Guide*, 525f., who calls it the "best description" of a Lewis lecture.

71. Graham, *We Remember C. S. Lewis*, 153.

72. Personal correspondence from D. M. Lewis, March 8, 2003.

73. Story related by Dr. Richard Luckett, Pepys Librarian at Magdalene College, Cambridge, January 10, 2003.

74. Email correspondence with Paul Piehler, June 2002.

75. Graham, *We Remember C. S. Lewis*, 152.

76. Personal correspondence with Charles Arnold-Baker, February 16, 2003.

CHAPTER TEN

1. The cat, marine officer Alexander Cottle, to the bear, second lieutenant James Bar, in Lewis, *Boxen*, 179.

2. Conversation with Dr. Richard Luckett, January 10, 2003, in the Pepys Library at Magdalene College, Cambridge.

3. Williams and Nicholls, *Dictionary of National Biography, 1961–1970*, 653.

APPENDIX II

1. The Norwood Report, 68.

2. The Norwood Report, 91–98.

3. The Norwood Report, 92.

4. The Norwood Report, 92.

5. The Norwood Report, 93.

6. The Norwood Report, 94.

APPENDIX III

1. King and Ketley, *Control of Language*, xi.

2. King and Ketley, *Control of Language*, 14.

3. www.aboutscotland.com/water/clyde.html.

4. Wordsworth, *Recollections of a Tour Made in Scotland*, 63f.

5. King and Ketley, *Control of Language*, 17–20.

APPENDIX IV

1. "The Abolition of Man," in Schultz and West, eds., *C. S. Lewis Reader's Encyclopedia*, 68.

2. Biaggini, *Reading and Writing of English*, x.

3. Biaggini, *Reading and Writing of English*, xiii.

4. Biaggini, *Reading and Writing of English*, xv.

5. Biaggini, *Reading and Writing of English*, xxi.

6. Biaggini, *Reading and Writing of English*, xxv.

7. Biaggini, *Reading and Writing of English*, 3.

8. Biaggini, *Reading and Writing of English*, 5–6.

9. Biaggini, *Reading and Writing of English*, 9–10.

APPENDIX V

1. The 1928 photo shows, in alphabetical order: P. V. M. Benecke, H. L. Bowman, F. E. Brightman, C. E. Brownrigg (headmaster of Magdalen College School, who also matriculated to Magdalen College in 1928), C. R. Carter, J. T. Christie, A. W. Chute, E. S. Craig, A. L. Dixon, G. R. Driver, C. C. Foligno, E. Hope, S. G. Lee, C. S. Lewis, R. P. Longden, M. H. MacKeith, J. J. Manley, K. B.

McFarlane, C. T. Onions, H. M. D. Parker, W. H. Perkin, H. E. Salter, R. Segar, Charles Sherrington, J. A. Smith, G. R. S. Snow, H. C. Stewart, A. G. Tansley, J. M. Thompson, E. C. Titchmarsh, C. H. Turner, Herbert Warren (president of Magdalen), and three unidentified Fellows, one of them probably Thomas Dewar Weldon. The photo can be found in Lewis, *All My Road before Me*, photograph section between 272–73.

2. See Lewis, *All My Road before Me*, 475–83, for more information written by Lewis concerning various faculty members. Also valuable for information about colleagues of Lewis is Hooper, *Lewis: A Companion and Guide*, the section entitled "Who's Who." See also Appendix A in Carpenter, *The Inklings*. Some information for this section came from Dr. Robin Darwall-Smith, archivist, Magdalen College.

3. Carpenter, *Inklings*, 205.

4. Hooper, *Lewis: A Companion and Guide*, 628.

5. Blake and Nicholls, *Dictionary of National Biography, 1981–1985*, 35.

6. Lewis, *Surprised by Joy*, 216.

7. For more information, see "Frank Edward Brightman; 1856–1932," *Journal of Theological Studies* 33 (1932): 336–39.

8. Patrick, *Magdalen Metaphysicals*, xv.

9. Patrick, *Magdalen Metaphysicals*, xvi.

10. Lewis, *Surprised by Joy*, 210f.

11. Patrick, *Magdalen Metaphysicals*, 78.

12. Harrison, "Government and Administration, 1914–1964," 689.

13. Fox, "At the Breakfast Table," 94f.

14. This is a fixed-term appointment, usually three years, intended for younger scholars who have been working on, or have just completed, their doctoral theses and want to pursue an academic career. Previously awarded by taking an examination, these fellowships are now awarded on the basis of applications, references, and examples of work, according to Dr. Robin Darwall-Smith, archivist for University and Magdalen Colleges, Oxford.

15. He is to be mentioned in the forthcoming *Dictionary of Twentieth-Century British Philosophers*, edited by Stuart Brown and published by Thoemmes Press.

16. Harriss, *McFarlane: Letters to Friends*, ix. For the remainder of this biographical sketch by Karl Leyser, I am dependent upon the entire memoir; Harris, *McFarlane: Letters to Friends*, ix–xxvii.

17. Lewis, *They Stand Together*, 315, 321.

18. Harriss, *McFarlane: Letters to Friends*, 104.

19. Lewis, *All My Road before Me*, 468.

20. Patrick, *Magdalen Metaphysicals*, 47.

21. Hooper, *Lewis: A Companion and Guide*, 658; Lewis, *All My Road before Me*, 470.

22. Patrick, *Magdalen Metaphysicals*, 60.

23. Patrick, *Magdalen Metaphysicals*, 65.

24. These fellowships are made by special appointment for a variety of reasons, such as the need to keep someone when there are no vacancies or as a tactful way to ease someone out. These fellowships had no salary attached, but if such a Fellow taught, he or she would be paid for the number of hours taught, according to Dr. Robin Darwall-Smith, archivist for University College and Magdalen College, Oxford.

25. Hooper, *Lewis: A Companion and Guide*, 726f.

26. See a rather lengthy biographical sketch of Stevens in Hooper, *Lewis: A Companion and Guide*, 726–28.

27. Burk, *Troublemaker*, 61.

28. Burk, *Troublemaker*, 88f.

29. Burk, *Troublemaker*, 337f.

30. Burk, *Troublemaker*, 171, 174f., 182, 311.

31. Burk, *Troublemaker*, 203, 301, 366.

32. Burk, *Troublemaker*, 204.

33. Burk, *Troublemaker*, 230, 277.

34. Burk, *Troublemaker*, 152.

35. The former worth £45 annually and the latter worth £40 annually; see *Oxford University Handbook*, 212f.

36. "One prize is given for a composition in Greek Verse, the metre as well as the subject being fixed from year to year; the other is given for a composition in Greek Prose" (*Oxford University Handbook*, 214). Named after Thomas Gaisford (1779–1855), Regius Professor of Greek at Christ Church from 1812 and later dean of Christ Church.

37. Magnus, *Herbert Warren of Magdalen*, 25.

38. Patrick, *Magdalen Metaphysicals*, 59.

39. Patrick, *Magdalen Metaphysicals*, xii–xiii.

40. Green and Hooper, *Lewis: A Biography*, 162.

41. Patrick, *Magdalen Metaphysicals*, 45.

42. Email correspondence from Dr. Robin Darwall-Smith, archivist Magdalen College, Oxford, June 26, 2002.

43. See, for example, Lewis, *All My Road before Me*, 483.

44. Entry dated April 27, 1926, in Lewis, *All My Road before Me*, 379.

45. Sayer, *Jack*, 286.

46. Lewis, *That Hideous Strength*, 112.

47. "Black, White and Grey: Wartime Arguments for and against the Strategic Bomber Offensive," David Ian Hall. www.wlu.ca/~wwwmsds/vol7n1hallbomber.

48. Entry dated June 6, 1926, in Lewis, *All My Road before Me*, 407, upon reading Abercrombie's *The Idea of Great Poetry*.

49. Harrison, *History of the University of Oxford*, 8:417.

50. Bayley, "From Master to Colleague," 78.

51. Bayley, "From Master to Colleague," 82.

52. N. A. Flanagan, ed., *Corpus Christi College, Oxford: Biographical Register, 1880–1974*, comp. by P. A. Hunt (Oxford: Corpus Christi College, 1988).

53. Harrison, *History of the University of Oxford*, 8:121.

54. Buxton, "Reflections on an Undergraduate Diary," 138–43.

55. Hooper, *Collected Letters*, 1:984.

56. Williams and Nicholls, *Dictionary of National Biography, 1961–1970*, 270f.

57. Lewis, *Preface to Paradise Lost*, 3.

58. For much of this biographical sketch, I am indebted to Hooper, *Collected Letters*, 1:988–90.

59. Carpenter, *Inklings*, 256.

60. Nicholls, *Dictionary of National Biography, 1986–1990*, 153f.

61. *Somerville College Report and Supplement 1995*, Margaret Kohl (nee Cook) 1944–49, 49–52.

62. See "Day-Lewis, Cecil" in www.xrefer.com.

63. *St. Hilda's College Chronicle of the Association of Senior Members, 1951–1952*, 20f.

64. Legg and Williams, *Dictionary of National Biography, 1941–1950*, 770.

65. Williams and Nicholls, *Dictionary of National Biography, 1961–1970*, 945ff.

66. K. M. L., *The Brown Book, Lady Margaret Hall, Oxford* (December 1963): 33–35.

67. *St. Hilda's College Report and Chronicle, 1981–1982*, 12–16.

68. home.freeuk.net/castlegates/wain.htm

69. www2002.stoke.gov.uk/council/libraries/infolink/wain-life.htm

70. Entry dated October 24, 1922, in Lewis, *All My Road before Me*, 125.

71. Entry dated November 20, 1922, in Lewis, *All My Road before Me*, 140.

72. Entry dated October 17, 1922, in Lewis, *All My Road before Me*, 121.

73. *C. H. Wilkinson, 1888–1960*, passim.

74. Harrison, *History of the University of Oxford*, 8:477.

75. Carpenter, *Inklings*, 117, 131, 185, 259.

76. Ladborough, "In Cambridge," 100.

77. *Magdalene College Magazine* 16 (1971–1972): 3–6.

78. See www.btinternet.com/~j1837c/jbc/sale.html.

79. Stevens and Lyne, *Centenary Readings from C. S. Lewis*, 2.

80. http://books.guardian.co.uk/news/articles/0,6109,653310,00.html

81. *In Memoriam: The Rt. Hon. Sir Henry Willink, BT. (1894–1973)*, passim.

82. I am indebted to Dr. Richard Luckett, Pepys Librarian at Magdalene College, for this insight. From a personal conversation January 10, 2003.

83. Lewis, *Letters of C. S. Lewis*, 473.

84. Lewis, *English Literature in the Sixteenth Century*, 633, 660.

85. *Magdalene College Magazine and Record*, 38, 36–37, cited in Stevens and Lyne, *Centenary Readings from C. S. Lewis*, 4.

86. Personal emails from Suzan Griffiths, assistant librarian of St. Catharine's College, July 20, 2003.

87. Dean, "Last Critic?" http://www.newcriterion.com/archive/14/jan96/dean.html

88. Dean, "Last Critic?" 29–31.

89. Anna, *The Dons*, 58.

90. http://www.press.jhu.edu/books/hopkins_guide_to_literary_theory/f._r_leavis.html. See also George Watson's chapter on Leavis in *Never Ones for Theory?* 71–83.

91. Williams and Nicholls, *Dictionary of National Biography, 1961–1970*, 682.

92. The word *tripos* comes from the three-legged stool that students sat upon to take their exams. Now the term refers to the final examinations in a course of study. See the July 21, 1958, letter Lewis wrote to Mary Willis Shelburne of Washington, D.C., in *Letters to an American Lady*, 77.

93. Como, *Lewis at the Breakfast Table*, xxix.

94. An unpublished 1926 letter to Owen Barfield located in the Bodleian Library, Oxford.

95. http://Jacketmagazine.com/20/hsd-watson.html

96. Cowling, "Williams in Retrospect." See http://www.newcriterion.com/archive/08/feb90/cowling.htm.

97. Lewis, *All My Road before Me*, 387n13.

98. For much of the information about Christie and for some information concerning other Magdalen Fellows, I am indebted to the archives of Magdalen College, Oxford, and Dr. Robin Darwall-Smith, archivist.

99. The Nobel Foundation, Nobel e-Museum, at http://nobelprize.org.

100. Hooper and Green, *Lewis: A Biography*, 148.

101. Lewis, *All My Road before Me*, 478

102. www-groups.dcs.st-and.ac.uk/history/Mathematicians/Dixon_Arthur.html

103. Lewis compliments Hope for his intelligence and character; see Lewis, *All My Road before Me*, 477.

104. http://www-gap.dcs.st-and.ac.uk/~history/Search/historysearch.cgi?SUGGESTION=Oxford&CONTEXT=1

105. Parts of this summary come from *Mediaeval English Studies Newsletter* 7 (December 1982).

106. Burk, *Troublemaker*, 153.

107. Annan, *The Dons*, 129, note.

108. http://orpheus.ucsd.edu/speccoll/testing/html/mss0176d.html.

109. Burk, *Troublemaker*, 434. See also the *Oxford Dictionary of National Biography*

at www.oxforddnb.com/view/article/35568?docPos=2.

110. "Sherrington, Sir Charles Scott." Microsoft® Encarta® Encyclopedia 2001. © 1993–2000 Microsoft Corporation.

111. Sayer, *Jack*, 188.

112. Burk, *Troublemaker*, 153.

113. See the following resource from the Mathematical Institute at Oxford University: www.crdc.gifu-u.ac.jp/cerd/scs/resume2k1/ scs011214gifu1_I2.doc.

114. J. J. O'Connor and E. F. Robertson, www-history.mcs.st-andrews.ac.uk/ history/References/Whitehead_Henry.html

115. *Magdalene College Magazine* 36 (1989–1990): 2–6.

116. Brewer, "The Tutor," 56.

117. *Magdalene College Magazine* 26 (1981–1982): 1–5.

118. Hooper, *Lewis: A Companion and Guide*, 75.

119. "Reminiscences" (1) Magdalene, 1948–58, *Magdalene College Magazine and Record*, n.s. 34 (1989–1990): 45–49, cited in Hooper, *Lewis: A Companion and Guide*, 76.

GLOSSARY

1. Burk, *Troublemaker*, 221.

2. Harrison, "College Life, 1918–1939," 95.

3. Harrison, "College Life, 1918–1939," 86.

4. Burk, *Troublemaker*, 218.

Bibliography

Babbage, Stuart Barton. "To the Royal Air Force." In *C. S. Lewis: Speaker and Teacher*, edited by Carolyn Keefe. Grand Rapids: Zondervan, 1971.

Annan, Noel. *The Dons: Mentors, Eccentrics, and Geniuses*. Chicago: University of Chicago Press, 1999.

Bailey, George. "In the University." In *C. S. Lewis: Speaker and Teacher*, edited by Carolyn Keefe. Grand Rapids: Zondervan, 1971.

Balsdon, Dacre. *Oxford Life*. London: Eyre & Spottiswoode, 1957.

Barfield, Owen. "In Conversation." In *C. S. Lewis: Speaker and Teacher*, edited by Carolyn Keefe. Grand Rapids: Zondervan, 1971.

Barrington-Ward, Simon. Personal interview with the author at Magdalene College, Cambridge. January 10, 2003.

Bayley, Peter. "From Master to Colleague." In *C. S. Lewis at the Breakfast Table and Other Reminiscences*, edited by James T. Como. San Diego: Harcourt Brace Jovanovich, 1992.

Bell, Alan. "Oxford's Contribution to Modern Studies in the Arts." In *The Illustrated History of Oxford University*, edited by John Prest. Oxford: Oxford University Press, 1993.

Betjeman, John. *An Oxford University Chest*. Oxford: Oxford University Press, 1979.

———. *Summoned by Bells*. London: John Murray, 1960.

Biaggini, E. G. *The Reading and Writing of English*. New York: Harcourt, Brace, 1936.

Blake, Lord, and C. S. Nicholls, eds. *The Dictionary of National Biography, 1981–1985*. Oxford: Oxford University Press, 1991.

Bramlett, Perry C., and Ronald W. Higdon. *Touring C. S. Lewis' Ireland and England.* Macon, Ga.: Smyth & Helwys, 1998.

Bresland, Ronald W. *The Backward Glance: C. S. Lewis and Ireland.* Belfast: Institute of Irish Studies, Queen's University of Belfast, 1999.

Brewer, Derek. "The Tutor: A Portrait." In *C. S. Lewis at the Breakfast Table and Other Reminiscences,* edited by James T. Como. San Diego: Harcourt Brace Jovanovich, 1992.

Burk, Kathleen. *Troublemaker: The Life and History of A. J. P. Taylor.* New Haven: Yale University Press, 2000.

Buxton, John. "Reflections on an Undergraduate Diary." In *New College, Oxford, 1379–1979,* edited by John Buxton and Penry Williams. Oxford: Warden and Fellows of New College, Oxford, 1979.

Carpenter, Humphrey. *The Inklings: C. S. Lewis, J. R. R. Tolkien, Charles Williams, and their Friends.* London: HarperCollins, 1997.

Catherwood, Christopher. *C. S. Lewis: A Brief Life.* Cambridge: Christian Heritage, 1998.

Como, James T., ed. *C. S. Lewis at the Breakfast Table and Other Reminiscences.* San Diego: Harcourt Brace Jovanovich, 1992.

Cowling, Maurice. "Raymond Williams in Retrospect." *The New Criterion Online* 8, no. 6 (February 1990).

Cunich, Peter, David Hoyle, Eamon Duffy, and Ronald Hyam. *A History of Magdalene College, Cambridge, 1428–1988.* Cambridge: Magdalene College, 1994.

Cunningham, Valentine. "Literary Culture." In *The Twentieth Century,* edited by Brian Harrison. Vol 8 of *The History of the University of Oxford.* Oxford: Oxford University Press, 1994.

Currie, Robert. "The Arts and Social Studies, 1914–1939." In *The Twentieth Century,* edited by Brian Harrison. Vol 8 of *The History of the University of Oxford.* Oxford: Oxford University Press, 1994.

Dean, Paul. "The Last Critic? The Importance of F. R. Leavis." *The New Criterion Online* 14, no. 5 (January 1996).

Edmonds, Edward L. "I Was There: Recollections of C. S. Lewis at Magdalen." Unpublished paper.

Egan, Pamela. "Prolegomena to Medieval English Literature." Notes of Lewis's lectures taken by Pamela Egan, Somerville College, 1952–1955. Used by permission.

Everest, Ursula K. "Prolegomena to Medieval Poetry." Notes of Lewis's lectures taken by Ursula K. Everest, Somerville College, 1941–1944. Used by permission.

Flexner, Abraham. *Universities, American, English, German.* New York: Oxford University Press, 1930.

Fowler, Alastair. "C. S. Lewis: Supervisor." *The Yale Review* 91, no. 4 (October 2003): 64–80.

Fox, Adam. "At the Breakfast Table." In *C. S. Lewis at the Breakfast Table and Other Reminiscences*, edited by James T. Como. San Diego: Harcourt Brace Jovanovich, 1992.

Fulford, Roger et al. *C. H. Wilkinson, 1888–1960.* Oxford: Oxford University Press, 1965.

Graham, David, ed. *We Remember C. S. Lewis: Essays and Memoirs.* Nashville: Broadman & Holman, 2001.

Green, Roger Lancelyn, and Walter Hooper. *C. S. Lewis: A Biography.* New York: Harcourt Brace Jovanovich, 1974.

Greenstein, Daniel I. "The Junior Members: A Profile." In *The Twentieth Century*, edited by Brian Harrison. Vol 8 of *The History of the University of Oxford.* Oxford: Oxford University Press, 1994.

Griffin, William. *Clive Staples Lewis: A Dramatic Life.* San Francisco: Harper & Row, 1986.

Handbook to the University of Oxford. Oxford: Clarendon Press, 1954.

Halls, W. D. "United Kingdom." *The Encyclopedia of Education*, edited by Lee C. Deighton. New York: Macmillan, 1971.

Harriss, Gerald, ed. *K. B. McFarlane: Letters to Friends, 1940–1966.* Oxford: Magdalen College, 1997.

Harrison, Brian, ed. *The Twentieth Century.* Vol 8 of *The History of the University of Oxford.* Oxford: Oxford University Press, 1994.

———. "College Life, 1918–1939." Pages 81–108 in *The Twentieth Century*, edited by Brian Harrison. Vol 8 of *The History of the University of Oxford.* Oxford: Oxford University Press, 1994.

———. "Government and Administration, 1914–1964." Pages 683–719 in *The Twentieth Century*, edited by Brian Harrison. Vol 8 of *The History of the University of Oxford.* Oxford: Oxford University Press, 1994.

"Harry Blamires: Oral History Interview, October 1983." Conducted by Lyle W. Dorsett. *Seven* 16 (1999): 79–94.

Havard, Robert E. "Philia: Jack at Ease." In *C. S. Lewis at the Breakfast Table and*

Other Reminiscences, edited by James T. Como. San Diego: Harcourt Brace Jovanovich, 1992.

Hewish, Antony. "Radioastronomy in Cambridge." In *Cambridge Minds*, edited by Richard Mason. Cambridge: Cambridge University Press, 1994.

Hooper, Walter. *C. S. Lewis: A Companion and Guide*. San Francisco: HarperSan-Francisco, 1996.

———, ed. *Collected Letters*. Vol. 1, *Family Letters 1905–1931*, and Vol. 2, *Books, Broadcasts and War 1931–1949*. London: HarperCollins, 2000, 2004.

———. "Oxford's Bonny Fighter." In *C. S. Lewis at the Breakfast Table and Other Reminiscences*, edited by James T. Como. San Diego: Harcourt Brace Jovanovich, 1992.

———. "The Life of C. S. Lewis." In *C. S. Lewis: A Companion and Guide*. San Francisco: HarperSanFrancisco, 1996.

Howard, Thomas. *C. S. Lewis: Man of Letters*. San Francisco: Ignatius Press, 1987.

Howarth, T. E. B. *Cambridge between Two Wars*. London: Collins, 1978.

Hyam, Ronald. Personal Interview with the author at Magdalene College, Cambridge. January 10, 2003.

In Memoriam. The Rt. Hon. Sir Henry Willink, BT. (1894–1973). Cambridge: Cambridge University Press, 1973.

Keefe, Carolyn, ed. *C. S. Lewis: Speaker and Teacher*. Grand Rapids: Zondervan, 1971.

———. "Education." In *The C. S. Lewis Readers' Encyclopedia*, edited by Jeffrey D. Schultz and John G. West Jr. Grand Rapids: Zondervan, 1998.

Kilby, Clyde S. "The Creative Logician Speaking." In *C. S. Lewis: Speaker and Teacher*, edited by Carolyn Keefe. Grand Rapids: Zondervan, 1971.

King, Alec, and Martin Ketley. *The Control of Language: A Critical Approach to Reading and Writing*. London: Longmans, Green, 1939.

Kort, Wesley A. *C. S. Lewis Then and Now*. New York: Oxford University Press, 2001.

Kreeft, Peter. *C. S. Lewis for the Third Millennium*. San Francisco: Ignatius Press, 1994.

Ladborough, Richard W. "In Cambridge." In *C. S. Lewis at the Breakfast Table and Other Reminiscences*, edited by James T. Como. San Diego: Harcourt Brace Jovanovich, 1992.

Lawlor, John. *C. S. Lewis: Memories and Reflections*. Dallas: Spence, 1998.

Legg, L. G. Wickham, and E. T. Williams. *The Dictionary of National Biography,*

1941–1950. London: Oxford University Press, 1959.

Lewis, C. S. *The Abolition of Man.* New York: Simon & Schuster, 1996

———. *All My Road before Me: The Diary of C. S. Lewis, 1922–1927.* New York: Harcourt Brace, 1991.

———. *The Allegory of Love.* Oxford: Oxford University Press, 1936.

———. "Answers to Questions on Christianity." In *God in the Dock*, edited by Walter Hooper. Grand Rapids: Eerdmans, 1970.

———. "Bluspels and Flalanferes: A Semantic Nightmare." In *Rehabilitations.* London: Oxford University Press, 1939.

———. *Boxen, The Imaginary World of the Young C. S. Lewis.* San Diego: Harcourt Brace Jovanovich, 1985.

———. "Christianity and Culture." In *Christian Reflections*, edited by Walter Hooper. Grand Rapids: Eerdmans, 1967.

———. "De Descriptione Temporum." In *Selected Literary Essays*, edited by Walter Hooper. London: Cambridge University Press, 1969.

———. "Democratic Education." In *Present Concerns*, edited by Walter Hooper. San Diego: Harcourt Brace Jovanovich, 1986.

———. *The Discarded Image.* Cambridge: Cambridge University Press, 1964.

———. "Dogma and the Universe." In *God in the Dock*, edited by Walter Hooper. Grand Rapids: Eerdmans, 1970.

———. *English Literature in the Sixteenth Century, excluding Drama.* Vol. 3 of Oxford History of English Literature. Oxford: Clarendon Press, 1954.

———. "Equality." In *Present Concerns*, edited by Walter Hooper. San Diego: Harcourt Brace Jovanovich, 1986.

———. *An Experiment in Criticism.* Cambridge: Cambridge University Press, 1961.

———. *The Four Loves.* New York: Harcourt Brace, 1988.

———. "Historicism." In *Fern-Seed and Elephants and Other Essays on Christianity*, edited by Walter Hooper. Glasgow: William Collins Sons, 1975.

———. *The Horse and His Boy.* New York: Macmillan, 1954.

———. "The Idea of an English School." In *Rehabilitations.* London: Oxford University Press, 1939.

———. "The Inner Ring." In *The Weight of Glory and Other Addresses*, edited by Walter Hooper. New York: Simon & Schuster, 1980.

———. "Interim Report." In *Present Concerns*, edited by Walter Hooper. San

Diego: Harcourt Brace Jovanovich, 1986.

———. "Is English Doomed?" In *Present Concerns*, edited by Walter Hooper. San Diego: Harcourt Brace Jovanovich, 1986.

———. "Is Theology Poetry?" In *The Weight of Glory and Other Addresses*, edited by Walter Hooper. New York: Simon & Schuster, 1980.

———. *The Last Battle.* New York: Macmillan, 1956.

———. *The Latin Letters of C. S. Lewis,* translated and edited by Martin Moynihan. South Bend, Ind.: St. Augustine's Press, 1998.

———. "Learning in War-Time." In *The Weight of Glory and Other Addresses*, edited by Walter Hooper. New York: Simon & Schuster, 1980.

———. *Letters of C. S. Lewis*, edited by Walter Hooper. Glasgow: HarperCollinsPublishers, 1993.

———. *Letters to Children.* Edited by Lyle W. Dorsett and Marjorie Lamp Mead. New York: Simon & Schuster, 1985.

———. *Letters to Malcolm: Chiefly on Prayer.* New York: Harcourt, 1992.

———. *The Lewis Papers.* Edited by Warren Lewis. Unpublished.

———. *The Lion, the Witch and the Wardrobe.* New York: Macmillan, 1950.

———. *The Magician's Nephew.* New York: Macmillan, 1955.

———. "Membership." In *Fern-Seed and Elephants and Other Essays on Christianity*, edited by Walter Hooper. Glasgow: William Collins Sons, 1975.

———. *Mere Christianity.* New York: HarperCollins, 1980, 2001.

———. "Modern Man and His Categories of Thought." In *Present Concerns*, edited by Walter Hooper. San Diego: Harcourt Brace Jovanovich, 1986.

———. "My First School." In *Present Concerns*, edited by Walter Hooper. San Diego: Harcourt Brace Jovanovich, 1986.

———. "Notes on the Way." In *Present Concerns* as "Democratic Education," edited by Walter Hooper. San Diego: Harcourt Brace Jovanovich, 1986.

———. "On the Reading of Old Books." In *God in the Dock*, edited by Walter Hooper. Grand Rapids: Eerdmans, 1970.

———. "On Stories." In *On Stories and Other Essays on Literature*, edited by Walter Hooper. New York: Harcourt Brace Jovanovich, 1982.

———. "On the Transmission of Christianity." In *God in the Dock*, edited by Walter Hooper. Eerdmans: Grand Rapids, 1970.

———. "Our English Syllabus." In *Rehabilitations.* London: Oxford University Press, 1939.

———. *Out of the Silent Planet*. New York: Macmillan, 1965.

———. "The Parthenon and the Optative." In *On Stories and Other Essays on Literature*, edited by Walter Hooper. New York: Harcourt Brace Jovanovich, 1982.

———. *Perelandra*. New York: Macmillan, 1944.

———. *The Pilgrim's Regress*. Grand Rapids: Eerdmans, 1958.

———. *Poems*. Edited by Walter Hooper. New York: Harcourt Brace Jovanovich, 1964, 1977.

———. "The Poison of Subjectivism." In *Christian Reflections*, edited by Walter Hooper. Grand Rapids: Eerdmans, 1967.

———. *A Preface to Paradise Lost*. New York: Oxford University Press, 1942.

———. *Prince Caspian*. New York: Macmillan, 1951.

———. "A Reply to Professor Haldane." In *Of Other Worlds*, edited by Walter Hooper. New York: Harcourt Brace & Company, 1966.

———. "Revival or Decay?" In *God in the Dock*, edited by Walter Hooper. Grand Rapids: Eerdmans, 1970.

———. *The Screwtape Letters with Screwtape Proposes a Toast*. New York: HarperCollins, 1996.

———. *The Silver Chair*. New York: Macmillan, 1953.

———. *Studies in Medieval and Renaissance Literature*. Cambridge: Cambridge University Press, 1966, 1998.

———. *Studies in Words*. 2d edition. Cambridge: Cambridge University Press, 1967.

———. *Surprised by Joy: The Shape of My Early Life*. New York: Harcourt Brace Jovanovich, 1955.

———. *That Hideous Strength*. New York: Macmillan, 1946.

———. *They Stand Together: The Letters of C. S. Lewis to Arthur Greeves, 1914–1963*, edited by Walter Hooper. New York: Macmillan, 1979.

———. *The Voyage of the 'Dawn Treader.'* New York: Macmillan, 1952.

———. "The Weight of Glory." In *The Weight of Glory and Other Addresses*, edited by Walter Hooper. New York: Simon & Schuster, 1980.

Lewis, Warren, ed. *The Lewis Papers*. Unpublished.

Leyerle, John. "No Glory, Please, I'm Cringing." *The Canadian C. S. Lewis Journal*, no. 3 (January 1979): 12.

Lindskoog, Kathryn. *C. S. Lewis: Mere Christian*. 4th ed. Chicago: Cornerstone, 1997. Especially Chapter 16, "Education."

————. *Journey into Narnia*. Pasadena, Calif.: Hope, 1998.

Long, E. John. "Oxford, Mother of Anglo-Saxon Learning." *The National Geographic Magazine* 56, no. 5 (November 1929): 563–96.

Luckett, Richard. Personal interview with the author at Magdalene College, Cambridge. January 10, 2003.

Magnus, Laurie. *Herbert Warren of Magdalen: President and Friend, 1853–1930.* London: John Murray, 1932.

Makin, John, ed. "Magdalene College Cambridge." Cambridge: Magdalene College, n.d.

Martin, Thomas L., ed. *Reading the Classics with C. S. Lewis*. Grand Rapids: Baker Academic, 2000.

Martindale, Wayne, and Jerry Root. *The Quotable Lewis*. Wheaton, Ill.: Tyndale, 1989.

Mason, Richard, ed. *Cambridge Minds*. Cambridge: Cambridge University Press, 1994.

Mathew, Gervase. "Orator." In *C. S. Lewis at the Breakfast Table and Other Reminiscences*, edited by James T. Como. San Diego: Harcourt Brace Jovanovich, 1992.

Mehta, Ved. "Personal History: A Lasting Impression." *New Yorker* (November 11, 1991): 83–110.

Meilaender, Gilbert. *The Taste for the Other*. Grand Rapids: Eerdmans, 1978.

Menuge, Angus J. L., ed. *C. S. Lewis, Lightbearer in the Shadowlands*. Wheaton, Ill.: Crossway, 1997.

Mitchell, Christopher W. "C. S. Lewis and the Oxford University Socratic Club." In *C. S. Lewis, Lightbearer in the Shadowlands*, edited by Angus J. L. Menuge. Wheaton, Ill.: Crossway, 1997.

Morris, Jan, ed. *The Oxford Book of Oxford*. Oxford: Oxford University Press, 1978.

Musacchio, George. *C. S. Lewis: Man and Writer*. Belton, Tex.: University of Mary Hardin-Baylor, 1994.

————. "Exorcising the Zeitgeist: Lewis as Evangelist to the Modernists." In *C. S. Lewis, Lightbearer in the Shadowlands*, edited by Angus J. L. Menuge. Wheaton, Ill.: Crossway, 1997.

Nicholls, C. S. *The Dictionary of National Biography, 1986–1990*. Oxford: Oxford University Press, 1996.

Norwood, Cyril, et al. *Curriculum and Examinations in Secondary Schools:*

Report of the Committee of the Secondary School Examinations Council Appointed by the President of the Board of Education in 1941. London: His Majesty's Stationery Office, 1943.

Oxford University Handbook being the Twenty-First Edition of the Students' Handbook Revised to September 1914 with Addenda December 1916. Oxford: Oxford University Press, 1917.

Patrick, James. *The Magdalen Metaphysicals: Idealism and Orthodoxy at Oxford, 1901–1945.* Macon, Ga.: Mercer University Press, 1985.

Perutz, M. F. "Molecular biology in Cambridge." In *Cambridge Minds*, edited by Richard Mason. Cambridge: Cambridge University Press, 1994.

Prothero, James. "Magdalene College, Cambridge University." In *The C. S. Lewis Readers' Encyclopedia*, edited by Jeffrey D. Schultz and John G. West Jr. Grand Rapids: Zondervan, 1998.

Reed, J. O. Unpublished diary. 2003. Used with permission.

Renfrew, Colin. "Three Cambridge Prehistorians." In *Cambridge Minds*, edited by Richard Mason. Cambridge: Cambridge University Press, 1994.

Rigby, Luke. "A Solid Man." In *C. S. Lewis at the Breakfast Table and Other Reminiscences*, edited by James T. Como. San Diego: Harcourt Brace Jovanovich, 1992.

Routley, Erik. "A Prophet." In *C. S. Lewis at the Breakfast Table and Other Reminiscences*, edited by James T. Como. San Diego: Harcourt Brace Jovanovich, 1992.

Rowse, A. L. *Oxford in the History of England*, New York: Putnam, 1975.

Sayer, George. *Jack: A Life of C. S. Lewis.* 2d ed. Wheaton, Ill.: Crossway, 1994.

Schofield, Stephen, ed. *In Search of C. S. Lewis.* South Plainfield, N.J.: Bridge Publishing, 1983.

Schultz, Jeffrey D. and John G. West Jr., eds. *The C. S. Lewis Readers' Encyclopedia.* Grand Rapids: Zondervan, 1998.

Stevens, John, and Raphael Lyne, eds. *Centenary Readings from C. S. Lewis.* Cambridge: Magdalene College, 2000.

Turner, F. M. "Religion." In *The Twentieth Century*, edited by Brian Harrison. Vol. 8 of *The History of the University of Oxford.* Oxford: Oxford University Press, 1994.

Vanauken, Sheldon. *A Severe Mercy.* San Francisco: Harper & Row, 1980.

Wain, John B., *Sprightly Running: Part of an Autobiography.* New York: St. Martin's Press, 1963.

————. "A Great Clerke." In *C. S. Lewis at the Breakfast Table and Other Reminiscences*, edited by James T. Como. San Diego: Harcourt Brace Jovanovich, 1992.

Watson, George. *Never Ones for Theory? England and the War of Ideas*. Cambridge: Lutterworth, 2000.

Webster, Charles. "Medicine." In *The Twentieth Century*, edited by Brian Harrison. Vol. 8 of *The History of the University of Oxford*. Oxford: Oxford University Press, 1994.

Williams, E.T., and C. S. Nicholls, eds. *The Dictionary of National Biography, 1961–1970*. Oxford: Oxford University Press, 1981.

Wordsworth, Dorothy. *Recollections of a Tour Made in Scotland*. New Haven: Yale University Press, 1997.